RON RANDALL'S

TREKKER ™

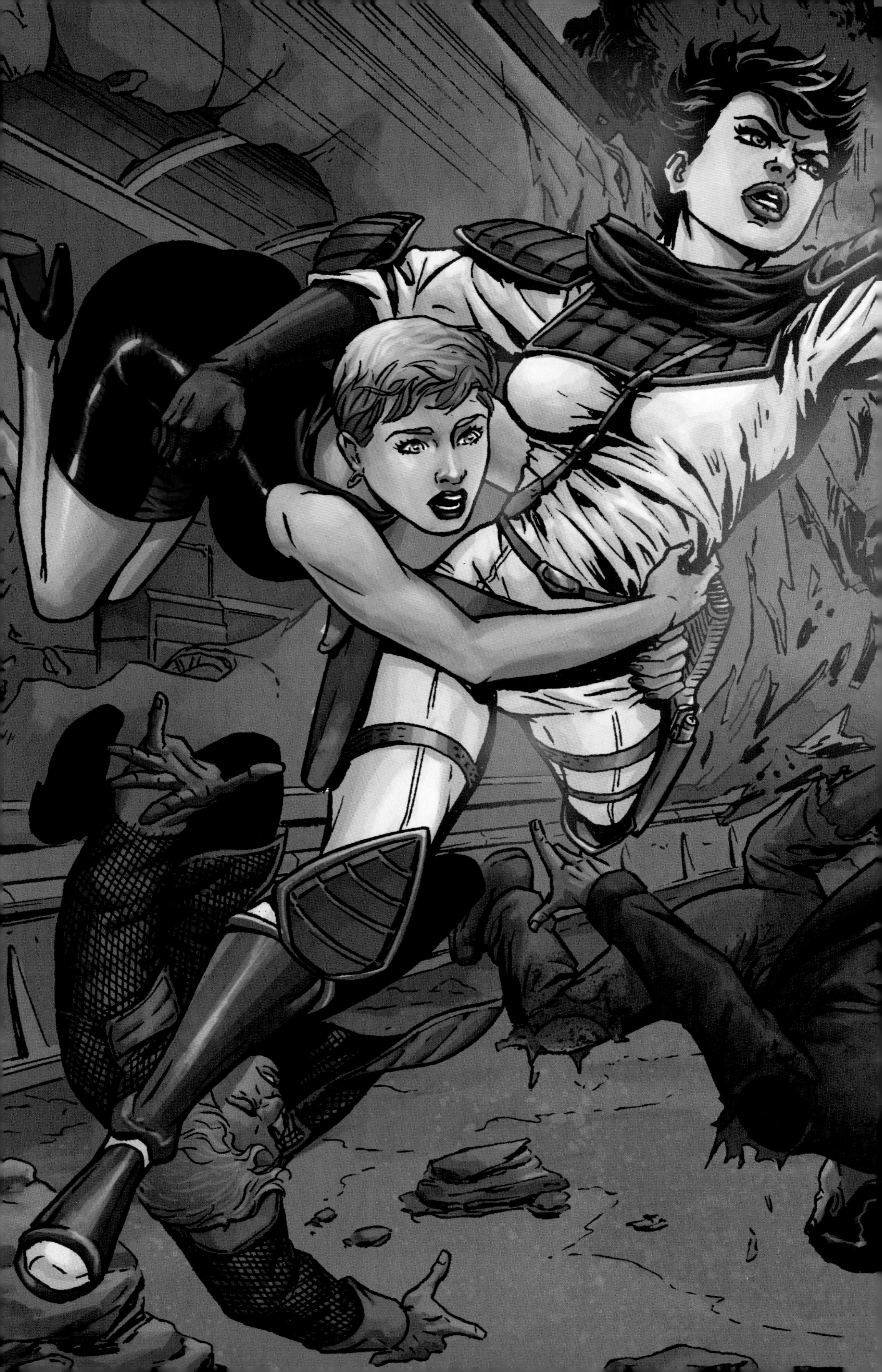

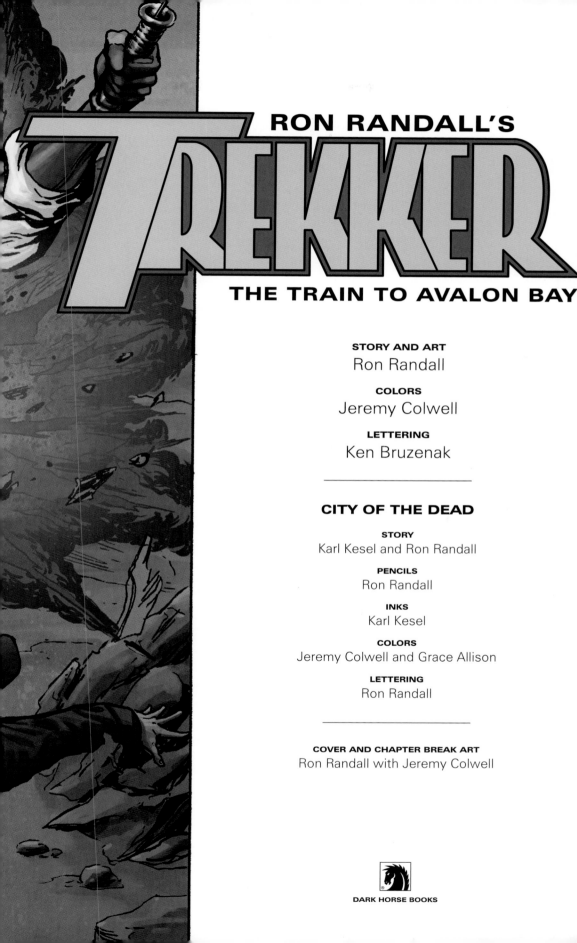

RON RANDALL'S

TREKKER™

THE TRAIN TO AVALON BAY

STORY AND ART
Ron Randall

COLORS
Jeremy Colwell

LETTERING
Ken Bruzenak

CITY OF THE DEAD

STORY
Karl Kesel and Ron Randall

PENCILS
Ron Randall

INKS
Karl Kesel

COLORS
Jeremy Colwell and Grace Allison

LETTERING
Ron Randall

COVER AND CHAPTER BREAK ART
Ron Randall with Jeremy Colwell

DARK HORSE BOOKS

PRESIDENT & PUBLISHER
Mike Richardson

EDITOR
Jim Gibbons

COLLECTION DESIGNER
Adam Grano

PRODUCTION
Allyson Willsey

Special thanks to the gang at Periscope Studio. Don't know how
Trekker would have made it into the twenty-first century without you.

Thanks always to Lyn. I am as lucky as a chap can be.

This one's for Lisa and Eric, who inspire me every day.

Neil Hankerson, Executive Vice President | Tom Weddle, Chief Financial Officer | Randy Stradley, Vice President of Publishing | Michael Martens, Vice President of Book Trade Sales | Anita Nelson, Vice President of Business Affairs | Scott Allie, Editor in Chief | Matt Parkinson, Vice President of Marketing | David Scroggy, Vice President of Product Development | Dale LaFountain, Vice President of Information Technology | Darlene Vogel, Senior Director of Print, Design, and Production | Ken Lizzi, General Counsel | Davey Estrada, Editorial Director | Chris Warner, Senior Books Editor | Diana Schutz, Executive Editor | Cary Grazzini, Director of Print and Development | Lia Ribacchi, Art Director | Cara Niece, Director of Scheduling | Tim Wiesch, Director of International Licensing | Mark Bernardi, Director of Digital Publishing

This volume collects Trekker: The Train to Avalon Bay *parts 1–6, originally published by Dark Horse Comics in* Dark Horse Presents *issues #24–#29, and "City of the Dead," originally published digitally on Thrillbent.com.*

Published by Dark Horse Books
A division of Dark Horse Comics, Inc.
10956 SE Main Street
Milwaukie, OR 97222

DarkHorse.com

International Licensing: (503) 905-2377
To find a comics shop in your area, call the Comic Shop Locator Service toll-free at (888) 266-4226.

First edition: April 2014
ISBN 978-1-61655-343-2

10 9 8 7 6 5 4 3 2 1
Printed in China

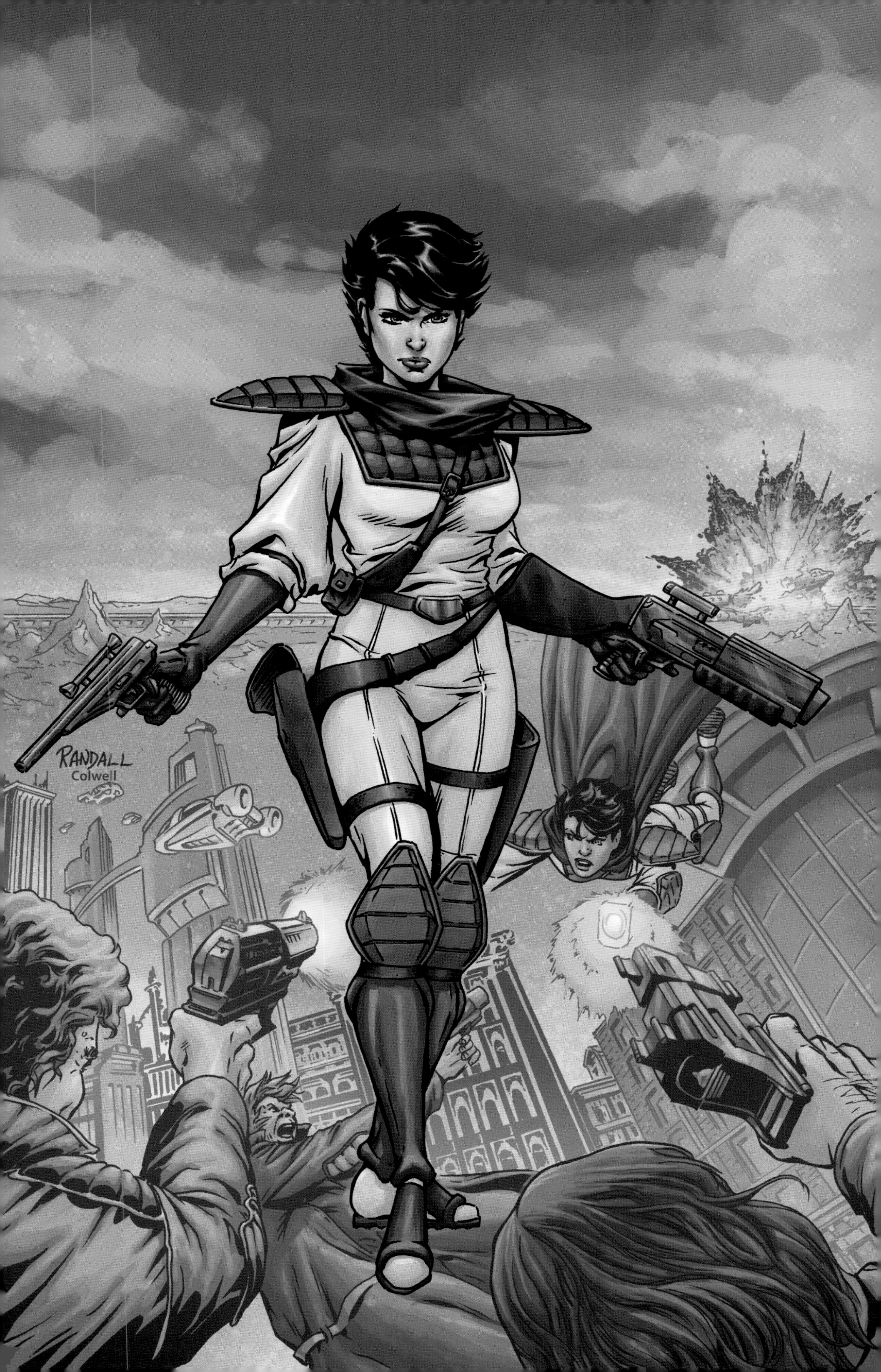
RANDALL
Colwell

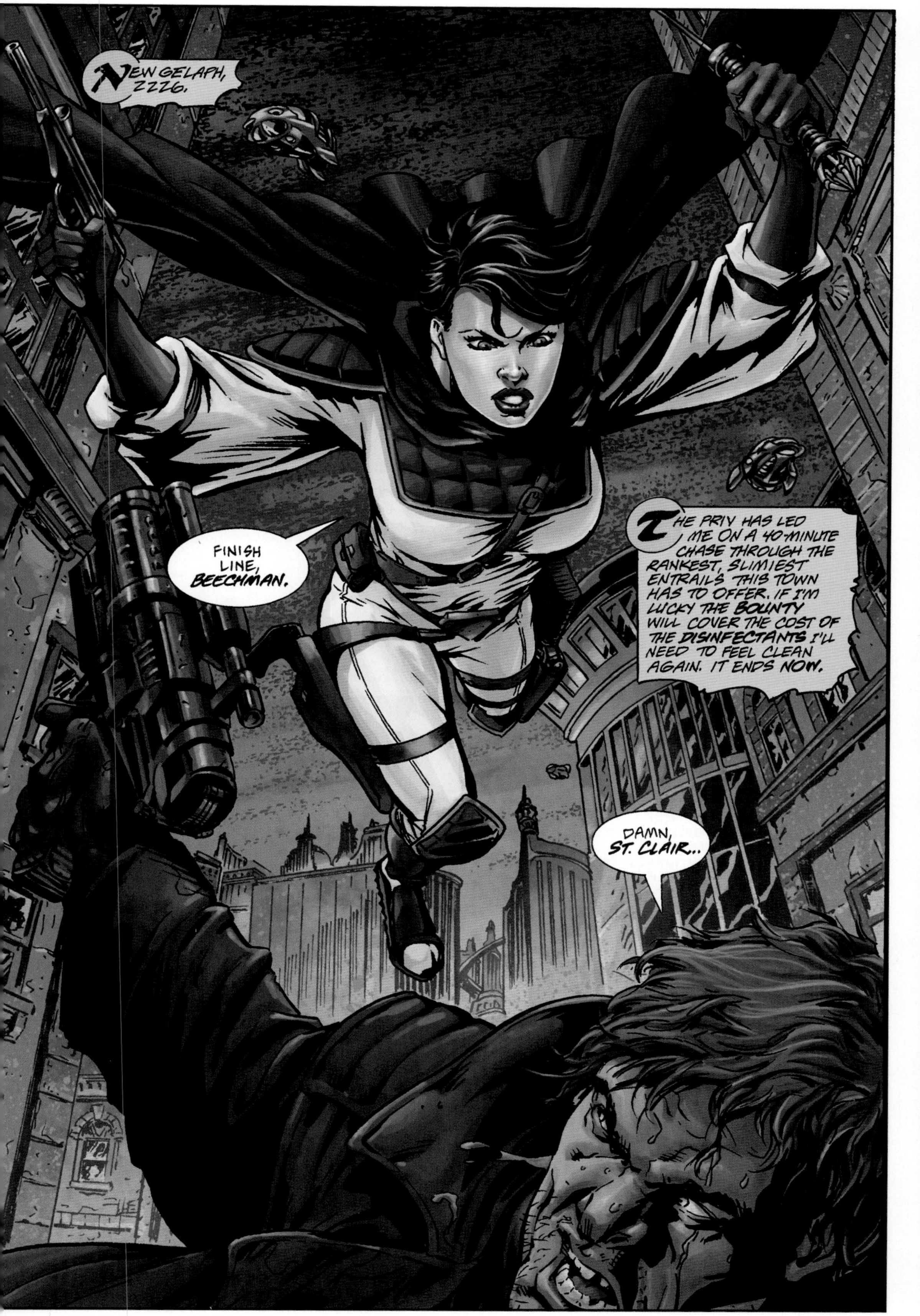
NEW GELAPH, 2226.
FINISH LINE, BEECHMAN.
THE PRIV HAS LED ME ON A 40-MINUTE CHASE THROUGH THE RANKEST, SLIMIEST ENTRAILS THIS TOWN HAS TO OFFER. IF I'M LUCKY THE BOUNTY WILL COVER THE COST OF THE DISINFECTANTS I'LL NEED TO FEEL CLEAN AGAIN. IT ENDS NOW.
DAMN, ST. CLAIR..

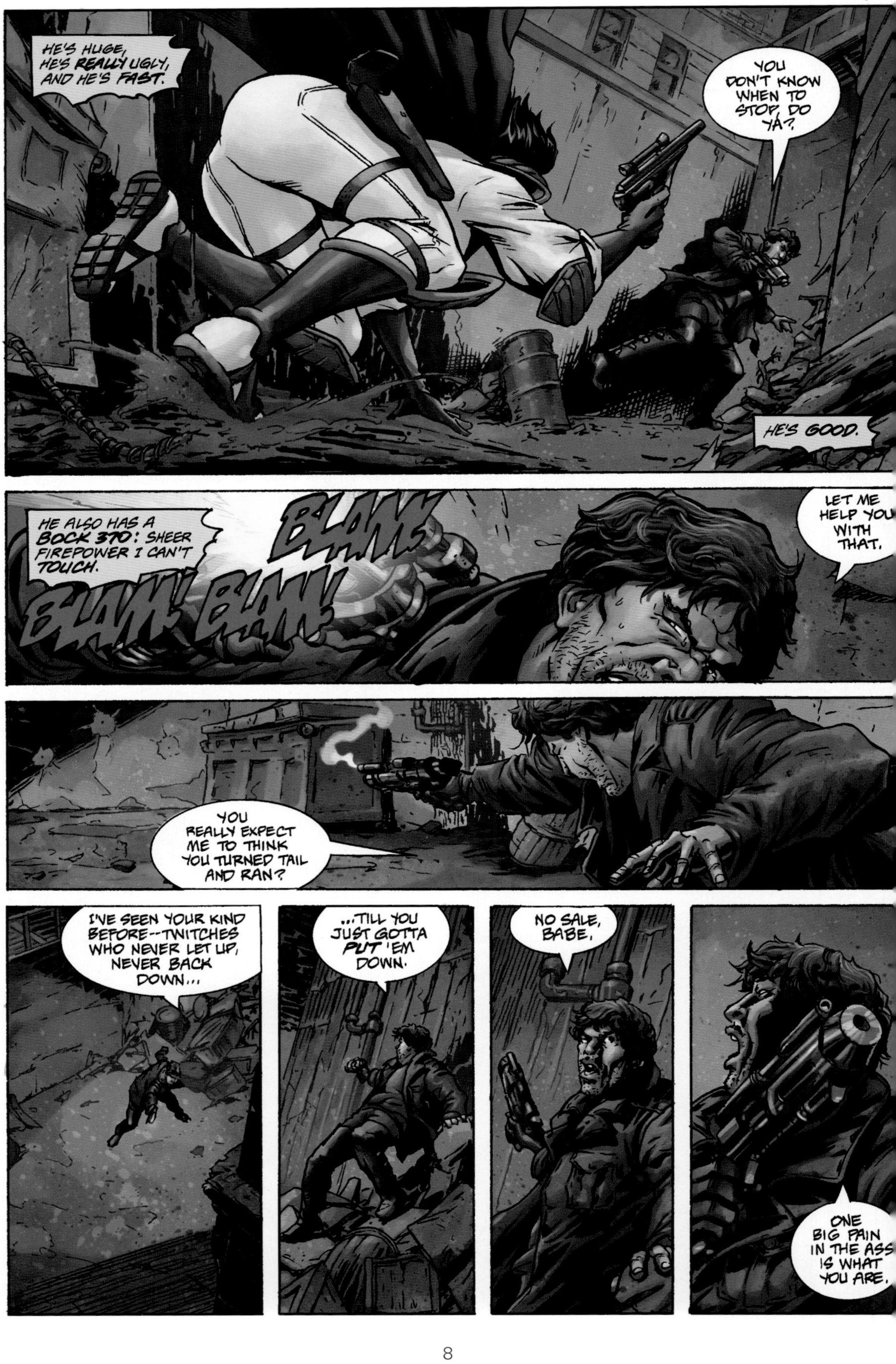

HE'S HUGE, HE'S REALLY UGLY, AND HE'S FAST.
YOU DON'T KNOW WHEN TO STOP, DO YA?
HE'S GOOD.
HE ALSO HAS A BOCK 370: SHEER FIREPOWER I CAN'T TOUCH.
BLAM!
BLAM! BLAM!
LET ME HELP YOU WITH THAT.
YOU REALLY EXPECT ME TO THINK YOU TURNED TAIL AND RAN?
I'VE SEEN YOUR KIND BEFORE--TWITCHES WHO NEVER LET UP, NEVER BACK DOWN...
...TILL YOU JUST GOTTA PUT 'EM DOWN.
NO SALE, BABE.
ONE BIG PAIN IN THE ASS IS WHAT YOU ARE.

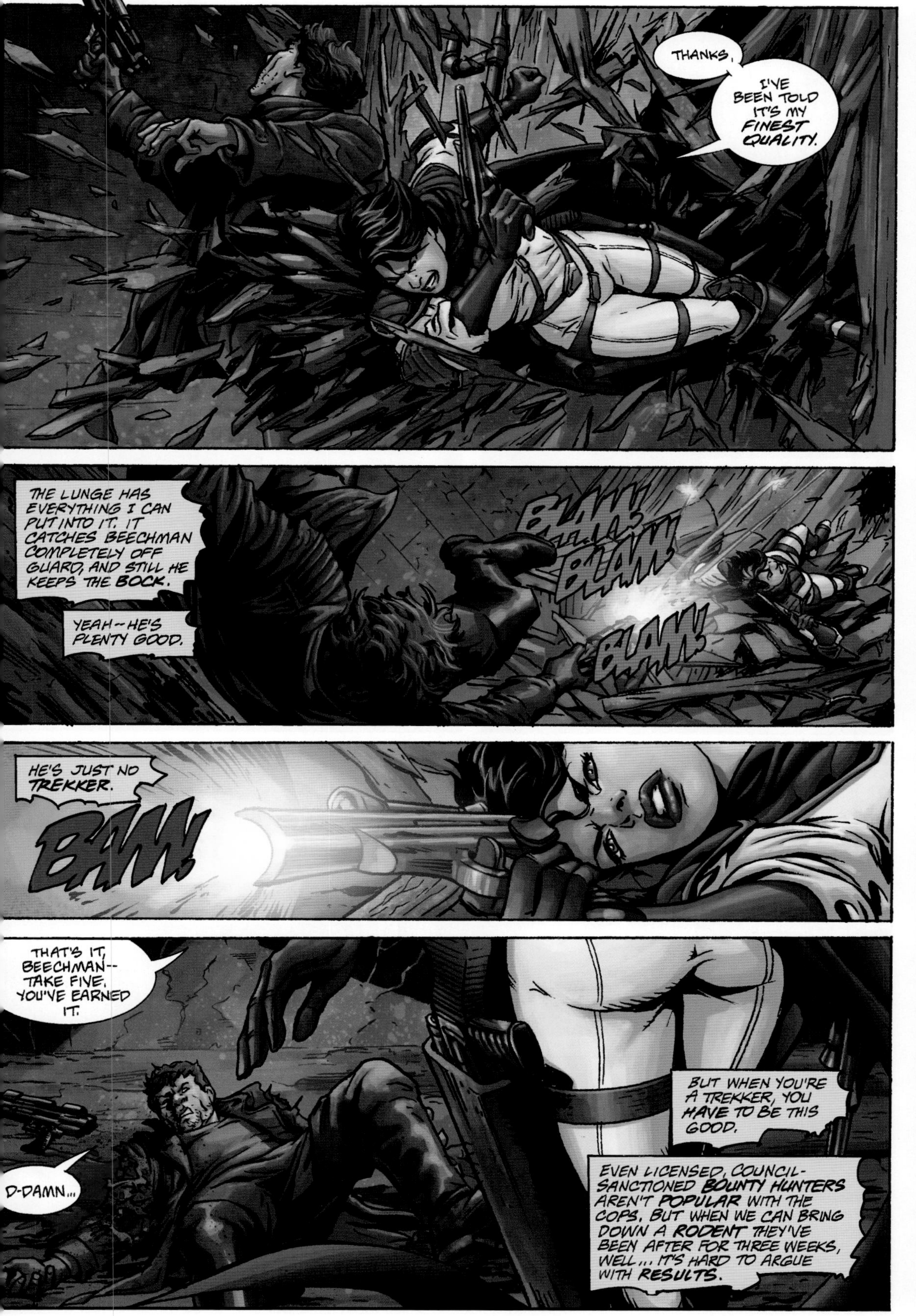
THANKS,
I'VE BEEN TOLD IT'S MY FINEST QUALITY.
THE LUNGE HAS EVERYTHING I CAN PUT INTO IT. IT CATCHES BEECHMAN COMPLETELY OFF GUARD, AND STILL HE KEEPS THE BOCK.
YEAH--HE'S PLENTY GOOD.
BLAM!
BLAM!
BLAM!
HE'S JUST NO TREKKER.
BLAM!
THAT'S IT, BEECHMAN-- TAKE FIVE. YOU'VE EARNED IT.
BUT WHEN YOU'RE A TREKKER, YOU HAVE TO BE THIS GOOD.
D-DAMN...
EVEN LICENSED, COUNCIL-SANCTIONED BOUNTY HUNTERS AREN'T POPULAR WITH THE COPS. BUT WHEN WE CAN BRING DOWN A RODENT THEY'VE BEEN AFTER FOR THREE WEEKS, WELL... IT'S HARD TO ARGUE WITH RESULTS.

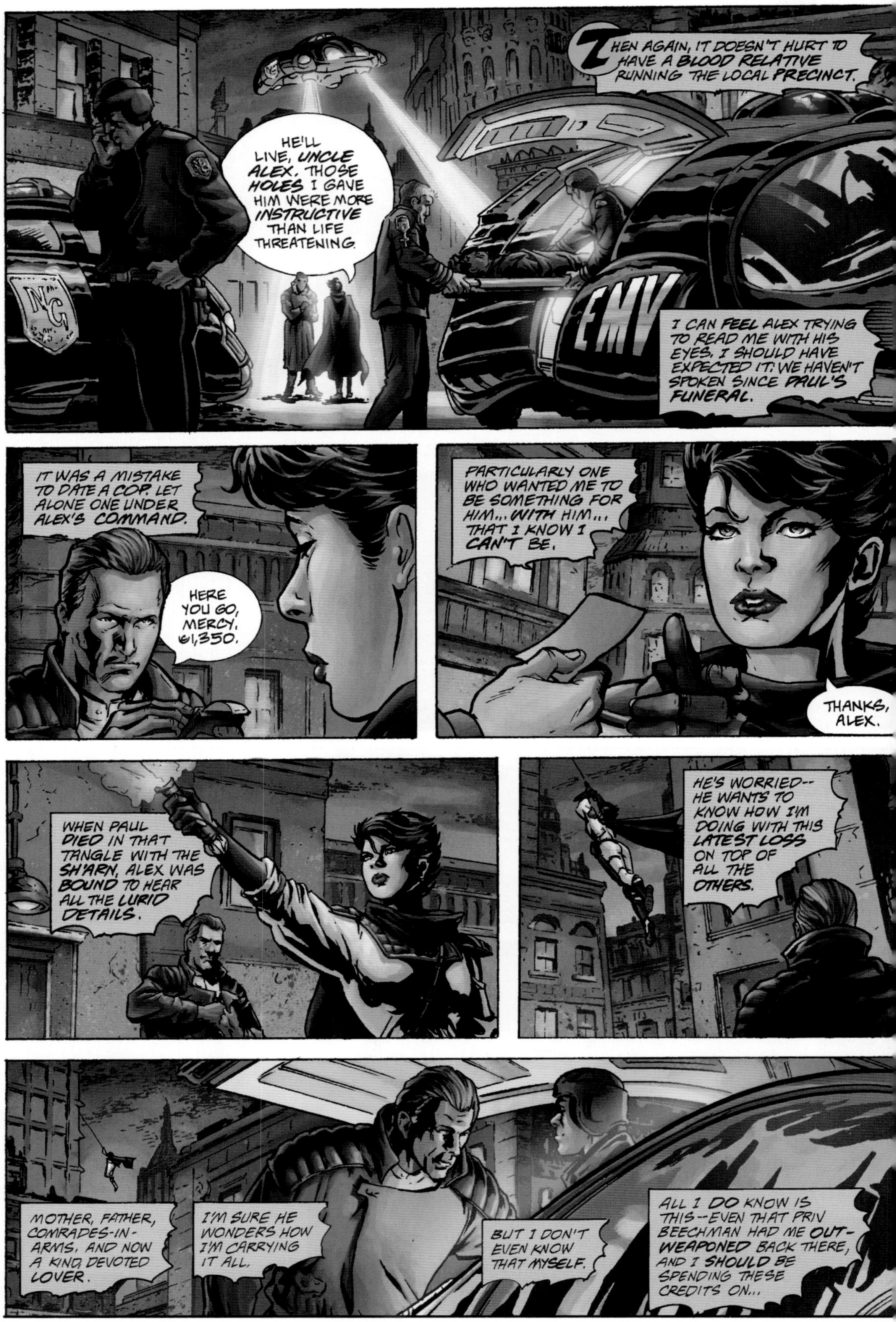
THEN AGAIN, IT DOESN'T HURT TO HAVE A BLOOD RELATIVE RUNNING THE LOCAL PRECINCT.
HE'LL LIVE, UNCLE ALEX. THOSE HOLES I GAVE HIM WERE MORE INSTRUCTIVE THAN LIFE THREATENING.
EMV
I CAN FEEL ALEX TRYING TO READ ME WITH HIS EYES. I SHOULD HAVE EXPECTED IT: WE HAVEN'T SPOKEN SINCE PAUL'S FUNERAL.
IT WAS A MISTAKE TO DATE A COP. LET ALONE ONE UNDER ALEX'S COMMAND.
HERE YOU GO, MERCY. ₢1,350.
PARTICULARLY ONE WHO WANTED ME TO BE SOMETHING FOR HIM... WITH HIM... THAT I KNOW I CAN'T BE.
THANKS, ALEX.
WHEN PAUL DIED IN THAT TANGLE WITH THE SH'ARN, ALEX WAS BOUND TO HEAR ALL THE LURID DETAILS.
HE'S WORRIED-- HE WANTS TO KNOW HOW I'M DOING WITH THIS LATEST LOSS ON TOP OF ALL THE OTHERS.
MOTHER, FATHER, COMRADES-IN-ARMS, AND NOW A KIND, DEVOTED LOVER.
I'M SURE HE WONDERS HOW I'M CARRYING IT ALL.
BUT I DON'T EVEN KNOW THAT MYSELF.
ALL I DO KNOW IS THIS--EVEN THAT PRIV BEECHMAN HAD ME OUT-WEAPONED BACK THERE, AND I SHOULD BE SPENDING THESE CREDITS ON...

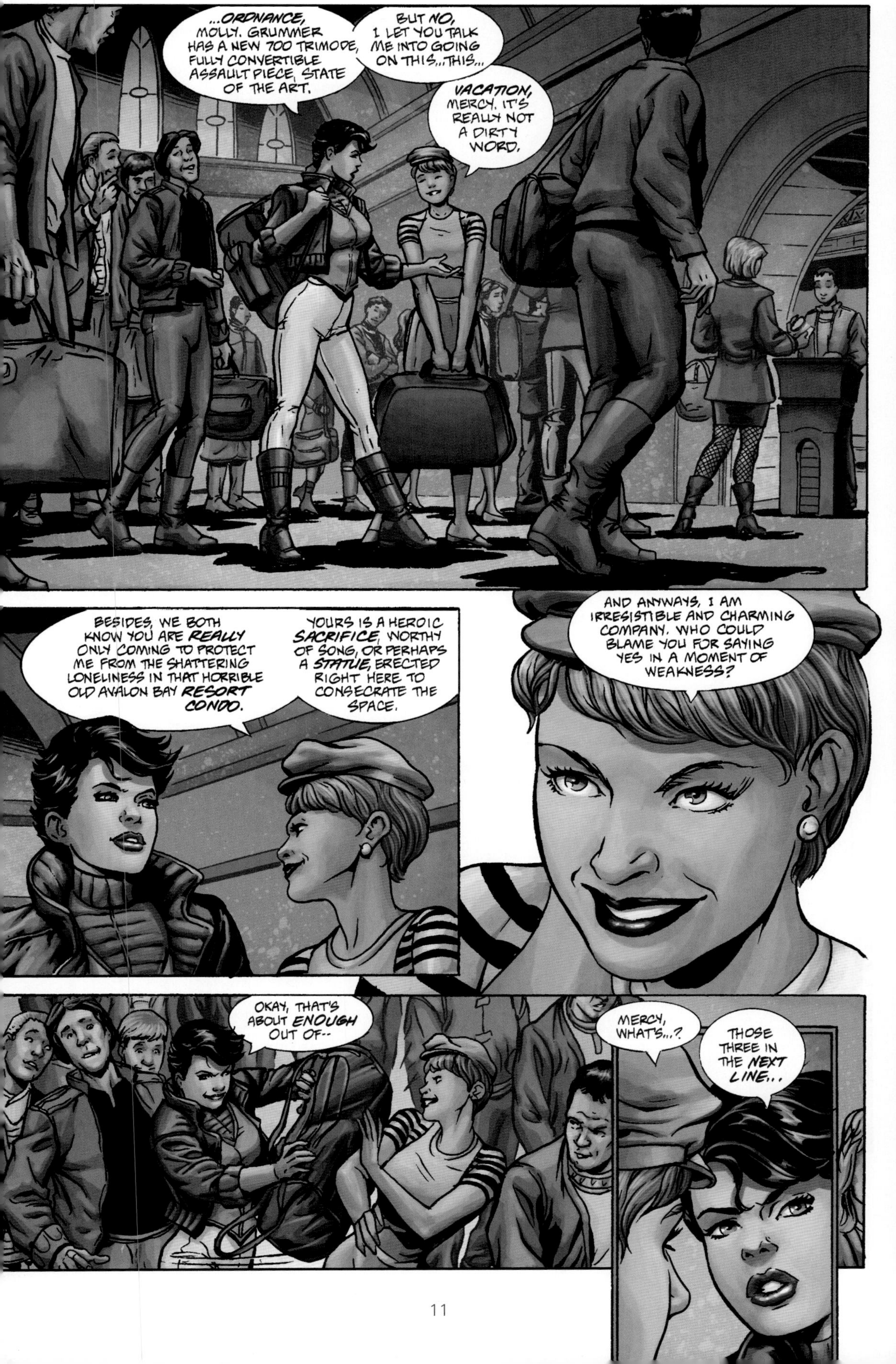
...ORDNANCE, MOLLY. GRUMMER HAS A NEW 700 TRIMODE, FULLY CONVERTIBLE ASSAULT PIECE, STATE OF THE ART.
BUT NO, I LET YOU TALK ME INTO GOING ON THIS... THIS...
VACATION, MERCY. IT'S REALLY NOT A DIRTY WORD.
BESIDES, WE BOTH KNOW YOU ARE REALLY ONLY COMING TO PROTECT ME FROM THE SHATTERING LONELINESS IN THAT HORRIBLE OLD AVALON BAY RESORT CONDO.
YOURS IS A HEROIC SACRIFICE, WORTHY OF SONG, OR PERHAPS A STATUE, ERECTED RIGHT HERE TO CONSECRATE THE SPACE.
AND ANYWAYS, I AM IRRESISTIBLE AND CHARMING COMPANY. WHO COULD BLAME YOU FOR SAYING YES IN A MOMENT OF WEAKNESS?
OKAY, THAT'S ABOUT ENOUGH OUT OF--
MERCY, WHAT'S...?
THOSE THREE IN THE NEXT LINE...

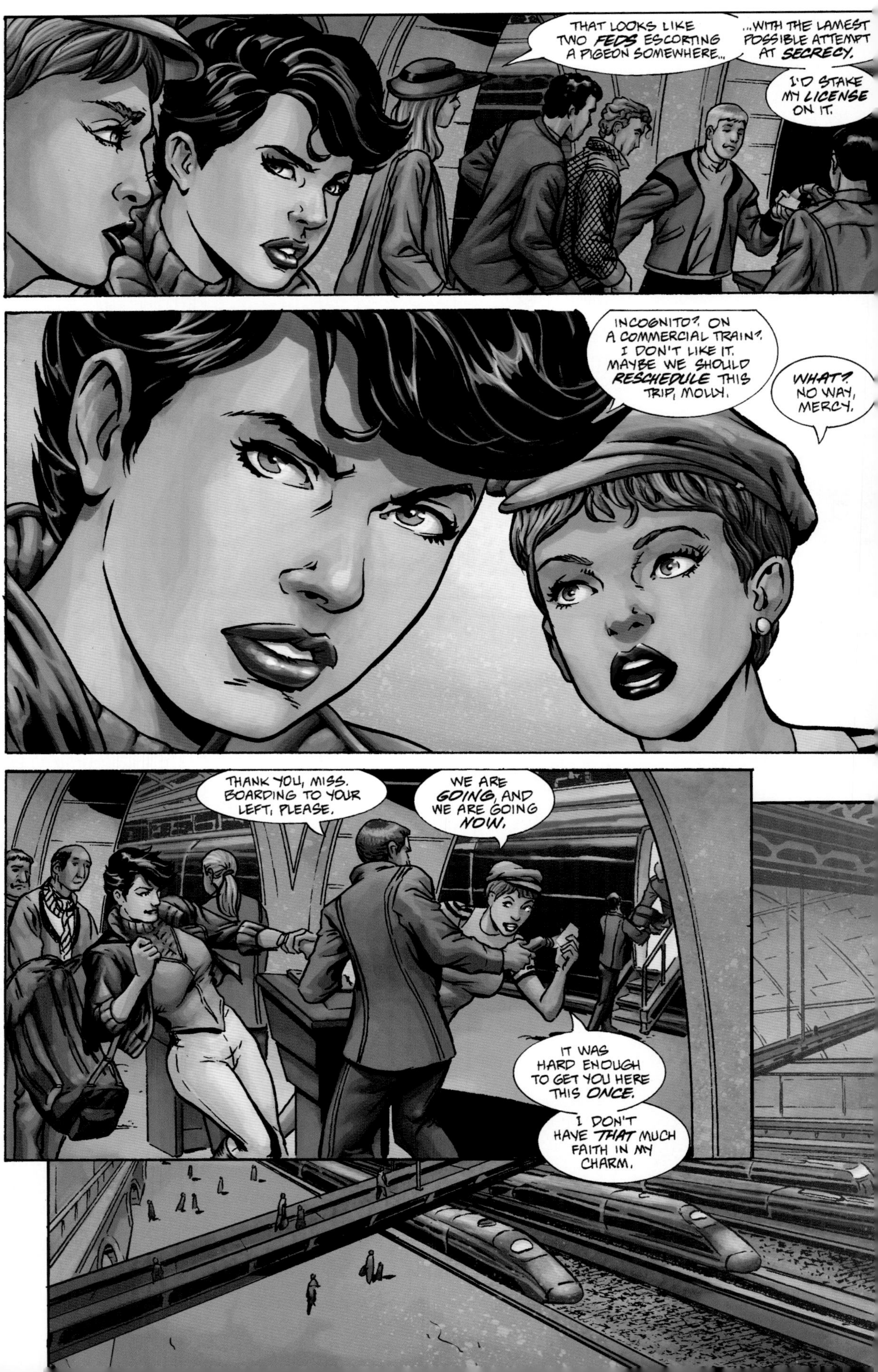
THAT LOOKS LIKE TWO FEDS ESCORTING A PIGEON SOMEWHERE...
...WITH THE LAMEST POSSIBLE ATTEMPT AT SECRECY.
I'D STAKE MY LICENSE ON IT.
INCOGNITO? ON A COMMERCIAL TRAIN? I DON'T LIKE IT. MAYBE WE SHOULD RESCHEDULE THIS TRIP, MOLLY.
WHAT? NO WAY, MERCY.
THANK YOU, MISS. BOARDING TO YOUR LEFT, PLEASE.
WE ARE GOING, AND WE ARE GOING NOW.
IT WAS HARD ENOUGH TO GET YOU HERE THIS ONCE.
I DON'T HAVE THAT MUCH FAITH IN MY CHARM.

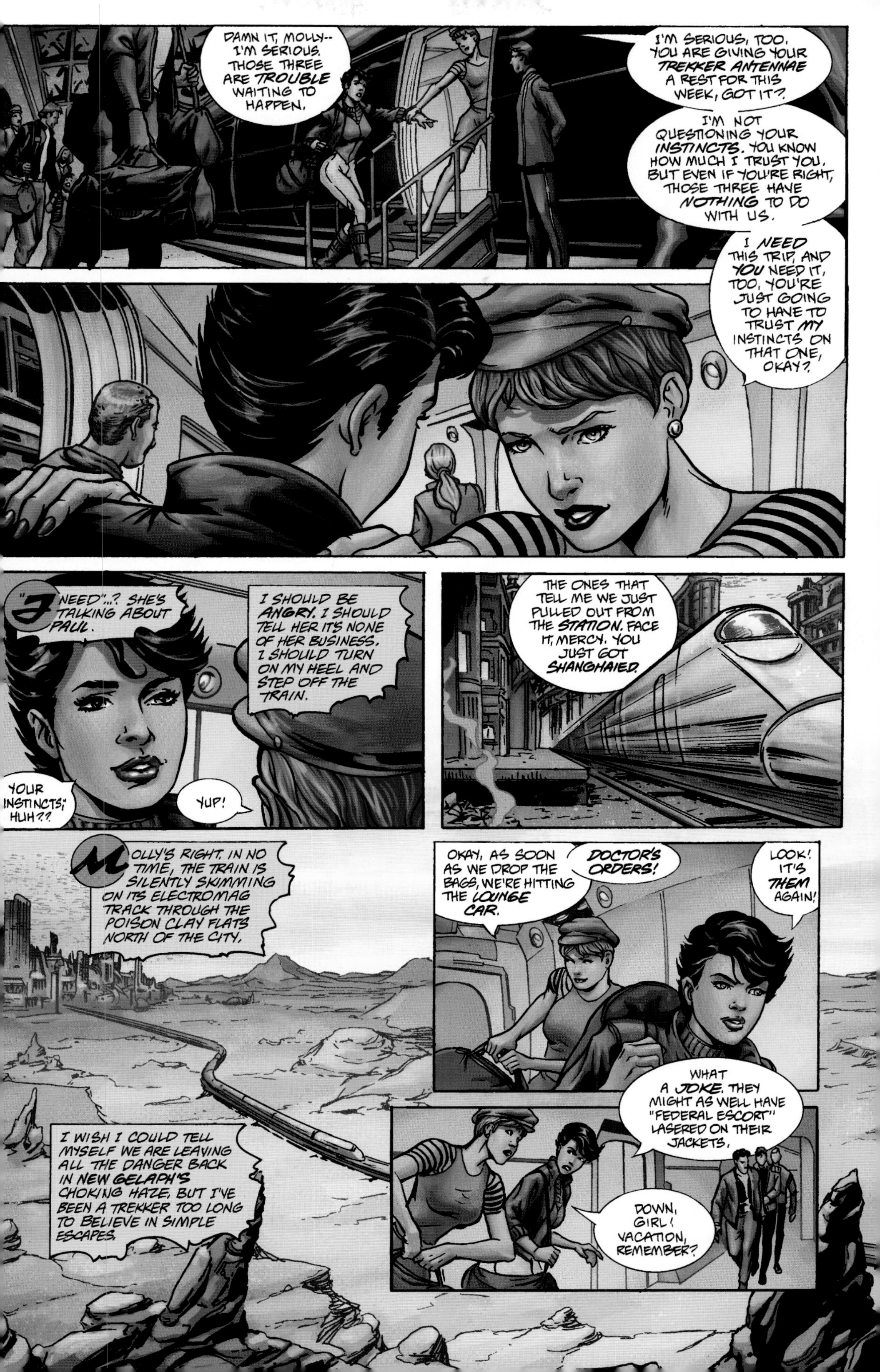
DAMN IT, MOLLY-- I'M SERIOUS. THOSE THREE ARE TROUBLE WAITING TO HAPPEN.
I'M SERIOUS, TOO. YOU ARE GIVING YOUR TREKKER ANTENNAE A REST FOR THIS WEEK, GOT IT?
I'M NOT QUESTIONING YOUR INSTINCTS. YOU KNOW HOW MUCH I TRUST YOU. BUT EVEN IF YOU'RE RIGHT, THOSE THREE HAVE NOTHING TO DO WITH US.
I NEED THIS TRIP, AND YOU NEED IT, TOO. YOU'RE JUST GOING TO HAVE TO TRUST MY INSTINCTS ON THAT ONE, OKAY?
"I NEED"...? SHE'S TALKING ABOUT PAUL.
I SHOULD BE ANGRY. I SHOULD TELL HER IT'S NONE OF HER BUSINESS. I SHOULD TURN ON MY HEEL AND STEP OFF THE TRAIN.
YOUR INSTINCTS, HUH??
YUP!
THE ONES THAT TELL ME WE JUST PULLED OUT FROM THE STATION. FACE IT, MERCY. YOU JUST GOT SHANGHAIED.
MOLLY'S RIGHT. IN NO TIME, THE TRAIN IS SILENTLY SKIMMING ON ITS ELECTROMAG TRACK THROUGH THE POISON CLAY FLATS NORTH OF THE CITY.
I WISH I COULD TELL MYSELF WE ARE LEAVING ALL THE DANGER BACK IN NEW GELAPH'S CHOKING HAZE, BUT I'VE BEEN A TREKKER TOO LONG TO BELIEVE IN SIMPLE ESCAPES.
OKAY, AS SOON AS WE DROP THE BAGS, WE'RE HITTING THE LOUNGE CAR.
DOCTOR'S ORDERS!
LOOK! IT'S THEM AGAIN!
WHAT A JOKE. THEY MIGHT AS WELL HAVE "FEDERAL ESCORT" LASERED ON THEIR JACKETS.
DOWN, GIRL! VACATION, REMEMBER?

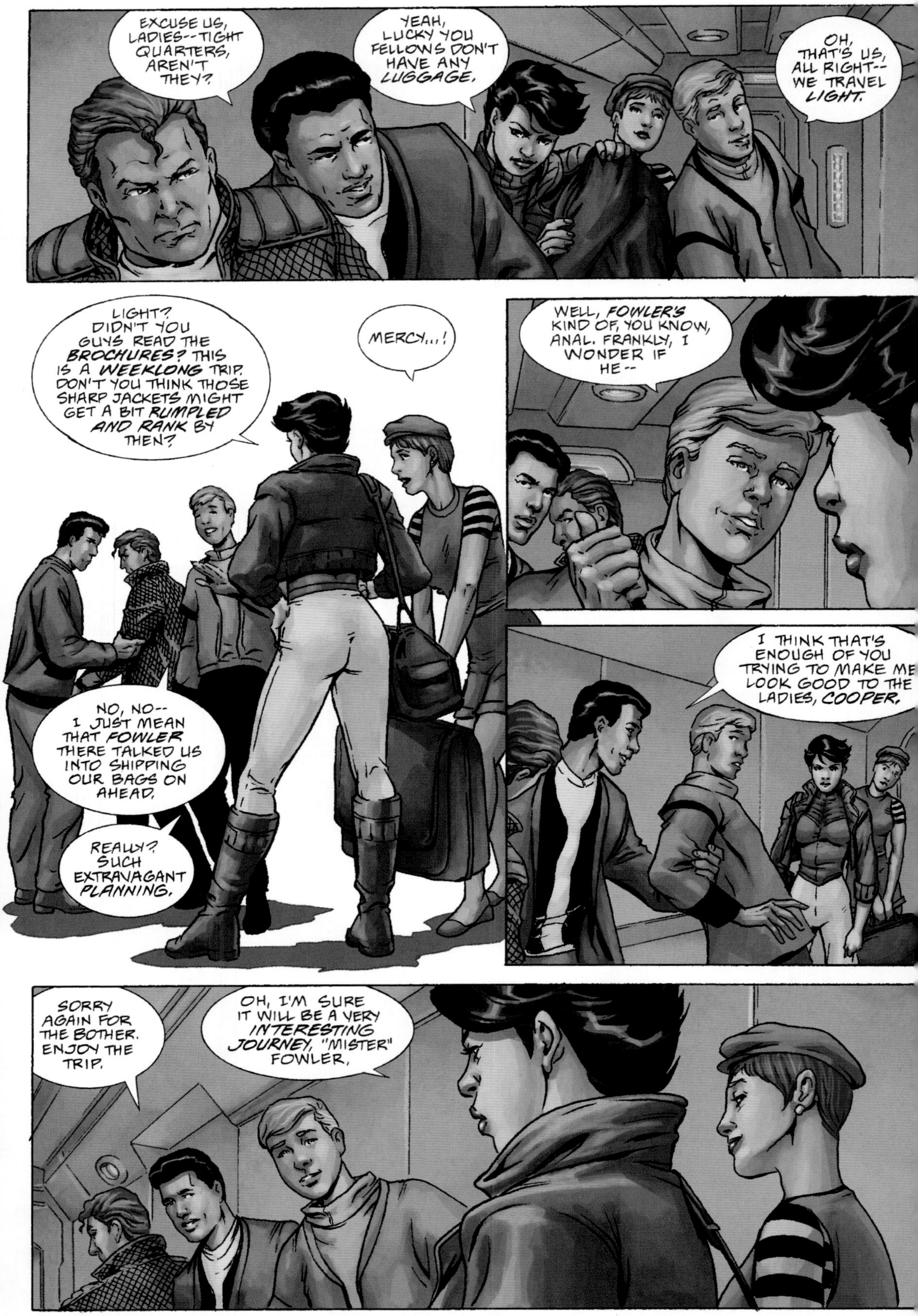
EXCUSE US, LADIES--TIGHT QUARTERS, AREN'T THEY?
YEAH, LUCKY YOU FELLOWS DON'T HAVE ANY LUGGAGE.
OH, THAT'S US, ALL RIGHT--WE TRAVEL LIGHT.
LIGHT? DIDN'T YOU GUYS READ THE BROCHURES? THIS IS A WEEKLONG TRIP. DON'T YOU THINK THOSE SHARP JACKETS MIGHT GET A BIT RUMPLED AND RANK BY THEN?
MERCY...!
NO, NO--I JUST MEAN THAT FOWLER THERE TALKED US INTO SHIPPING OUR BAGS ON AHEAD.
REALLY? SUCH EXTRAVAGANT PLANNING.
WELL, FOWLER'S KIND OF, YOU KNOW, ANAL. FRANKLY, I WONDER IF HE--
I THINK THAT'S ENOUGH OF YOU TRYING TO MAKE ME LOOK GOOD TO THE LADIES, COOPER.
SORRY AGAIN FOR THE BOTHER. ENJOY THE TRIP.
OH, I'M SURE IT WILL BE A VERY INTERESTING JOURNEY, "MISTER" FOWLER.

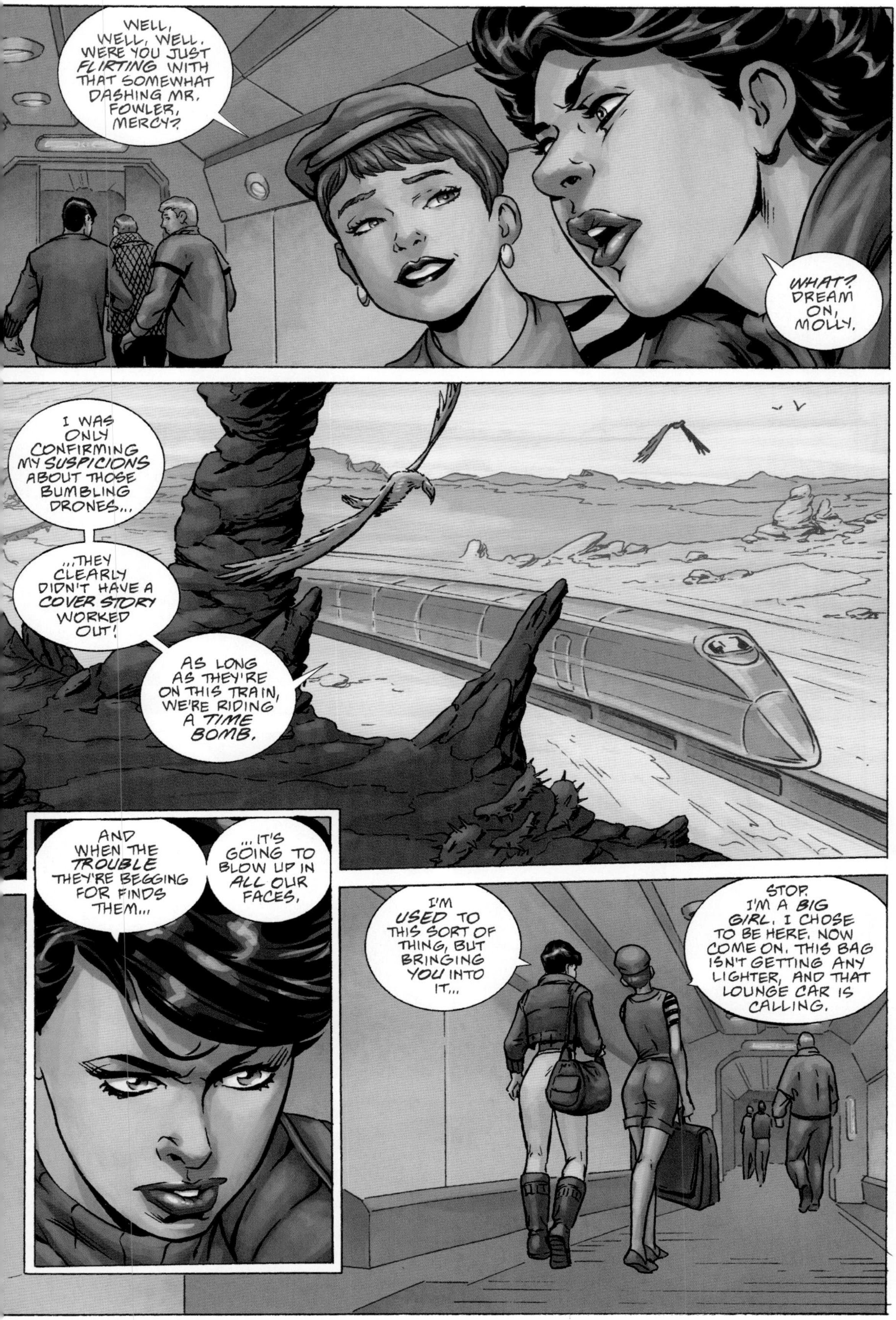
WELL, WELL, WELL. WERE YOU JUST FLIRTING WITH THAT SOMEWHAT DASHING MR. FOWLER, MERCY?
WHAT? DREAM ON, MOLLY.
I WAS ONLY CONFIRMING MY SUSPICIONS ABOUT THOSE BUMBLING DRONES...
...THEY CLEARLY DIDN'T HAVE A COVER STORY WORKED OUT!
AS LONG AS THEY'RE ON THIS TRAIN, WE'RE RIDING A TIME BOMB.
AND WHEN THE TROUBLE THEY'RE BEGGING FOR FINDS THEM...
...IT'S GOING TO BLOW UP IN ALL OUR FACES.
I'M USED TO THIS SORT OF THING, BUT BRINGING YOU INTO IT...
STOP. I'M A BIG GIRL. I CHOSE TO BE HERE. NOW COME ON. THIS BAG ISN'T GETTING ANY LIGHTER, AND THAT LOUNGE CAR IS CALLING.

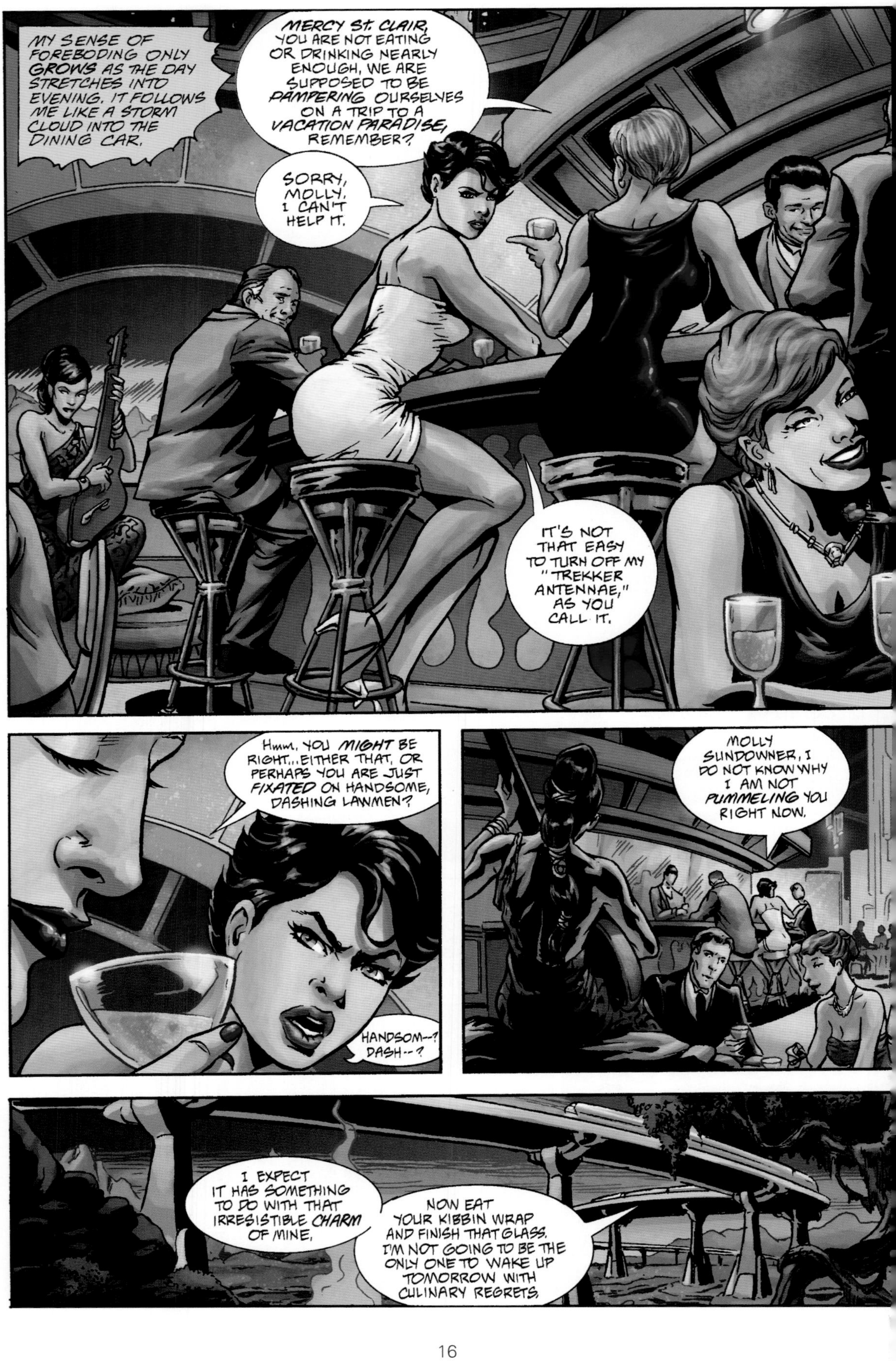
MY SENSE OF FOREBODING ONLY GROWS AS THE DAY STRETCHES INTO EVENING. IT FOLLOWS ME LIKE A STORM CLOUD INTO THE DINING CAR.
MERCY ST. CLAIR, YOU ARE NOT EATING OR DRINKING NEARLY ENOUGH. WE ARE SUPPOSED TO BE PAMPERING OURSELVES ON A TRIP TO A VACATION PARADISE, REMEMBER?
SORRY, MOLLY. I CAN'T HELP IT.
IT'S NOT THAT EASY TO TURN OFF MY "TREKKER ANTENNAE," AS YOU CALL IT.
Hmm. YOU MIGHT BE RIGHT... EITHER THAT, OR PERHAPS YOU ARE JUST FIXATED ON HANDSOME, DASHING LAWMEN?
HANDSOM--? DASH--?
MOLLY SUNDOWNER, I DO NOT KNOW WHY I AM NOT PUMMELING YOU RIGHT NOW.
I EXPECT IT HAS SOMETHING TO DO WITH THAT IRRESISTIBLE CHARM OF MINE.
NOW EAT YOUR KIBBIN WRAP AND FINISH THAT GLASS. I'M NOT GOING TO BE THE ONLY ONE TO WAKE UP TOMORROW WITH CULINARY REGRETS.

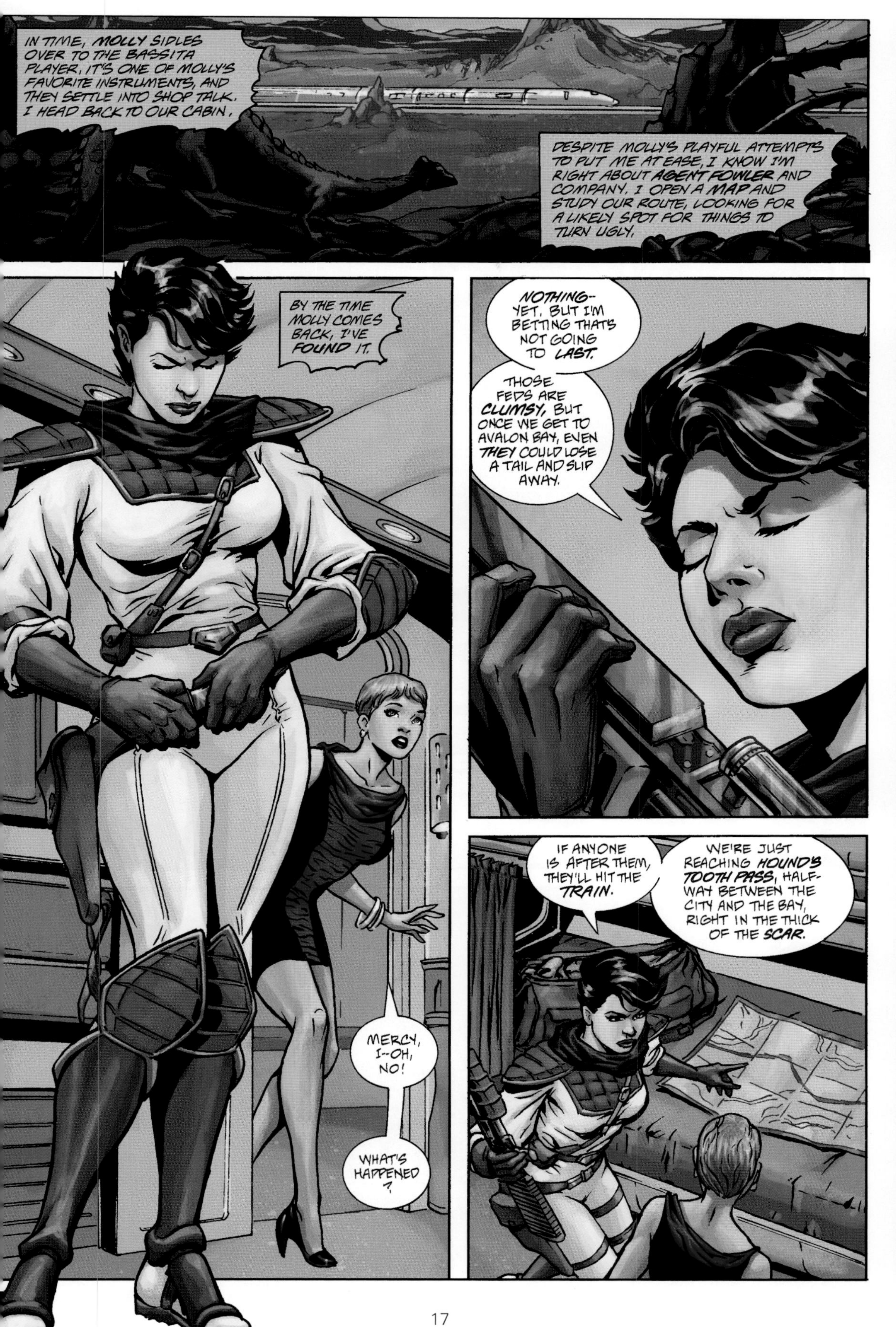
IN TIME, MOLLY SIDLES OVER TO THE BASSITA PLAYER. IT'S ONE OF MOLLY'S FAVORITE INSTRUMENTS, AND THEY SETTLE INTO SHOP TALK. I HEAD BACK TO OUR CABIN.
DESPITE MOLLY'S PLAYFUL ATTEMPTS TO PUT ME AT EASE, I KNOW I'M RIGHT ABOUT AGENT FOWLER AND COMPANY. I OPEN A MAP AND STUDY OUR ROUTE, LOOKING FOR A LIKELY SPOT FOR THINGS TO TURN UGLY.
BY THE TIME MOLLY COMES BACK, I'VE FOUND IT.
MERCY, I--OH, NO!
WHAT'S HAPPENED?
NOTHING-- YET, BUT I'M BETTING THAT'S NOT GOING TO LAST.
THOSE FEDS ARE CLUMSY, BUT ONCE WE GET TO AVALON BAY, EVEN THEY COULD LOSE A TAIL AND SLIP AWAY.
IF ANYONE IS AFTER THEM, THEY'LL HIT THE TRAIN.
WE'RE JUST REACHING HOUND'S TOOTH PASS, HALF-WAY BETWEEN THE CITY AND THE BAY, RIGHT IN THE THICK OF THE SCAR.

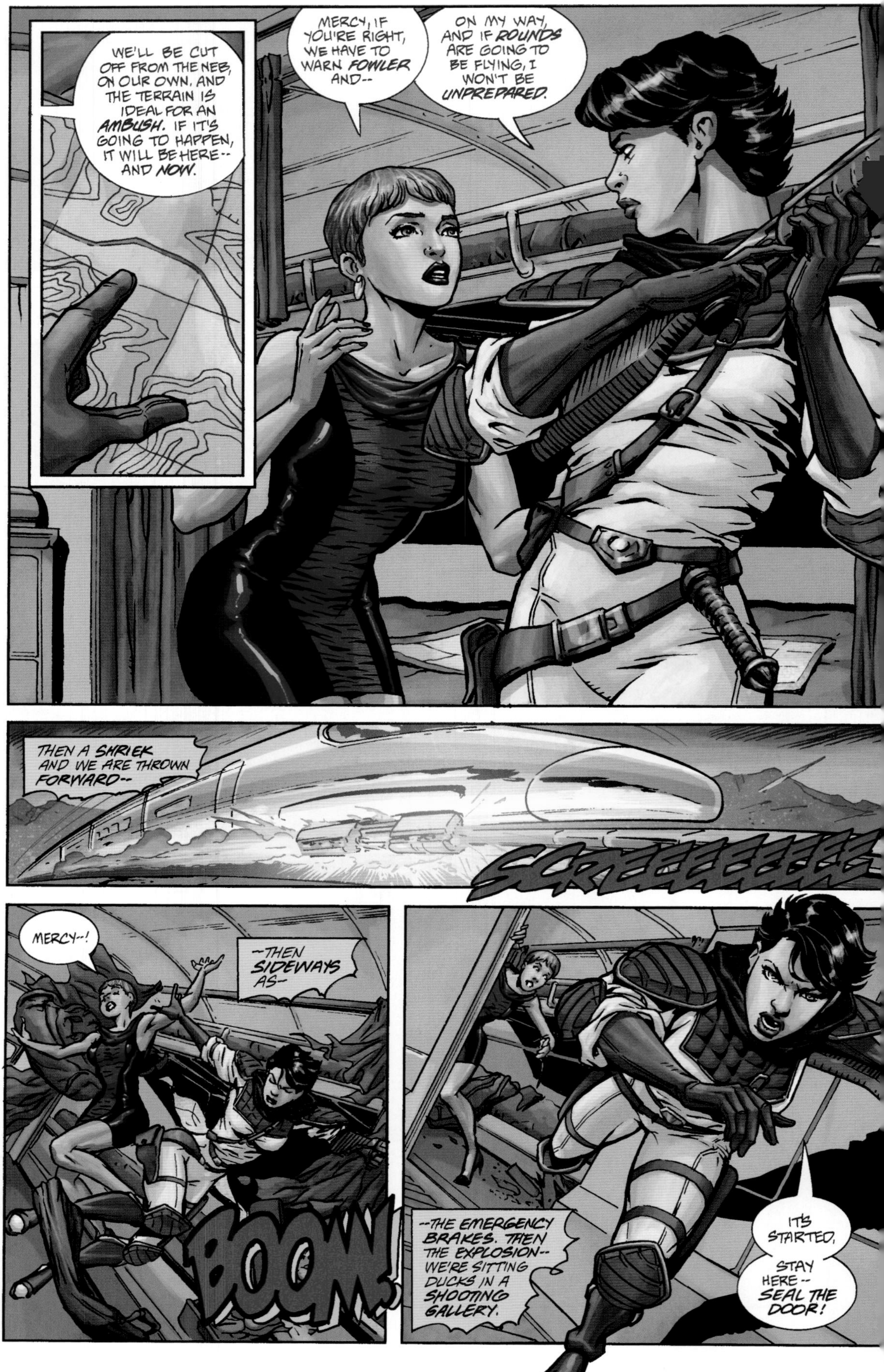
WE'LL BE CUT OFF FROM THE NEB, ON OUR OWN, AND THE TERRAIN IS IDEAL FOR AN AMBUSH. IF IT'S GOING TO HAPPEN, IT WILL BE HERE-- AND NOW.
MERCY, IF YOU'RE RIGHT, WE HAVE TO WARN FOWLER AND--
ON MY WAY, AND IF ROUNDS ARE GOING TO BE FLYING, I WON'T BE UNPREPARED.
THEN A SHRIEK AND WE ARE THROWN FORWARD--
SCREEEEEEEE
MERCY--!
--THEN SIDEWAYS AS--
BOOM!
--THE EMERGENCY BRAKES. THEN THE EXPLOSION-- WE'RE SITTING DUCKS IN A SHOOTING GALLERY.
IT'S STARTED.
STAY HERE-- SEAL THE DOOR!

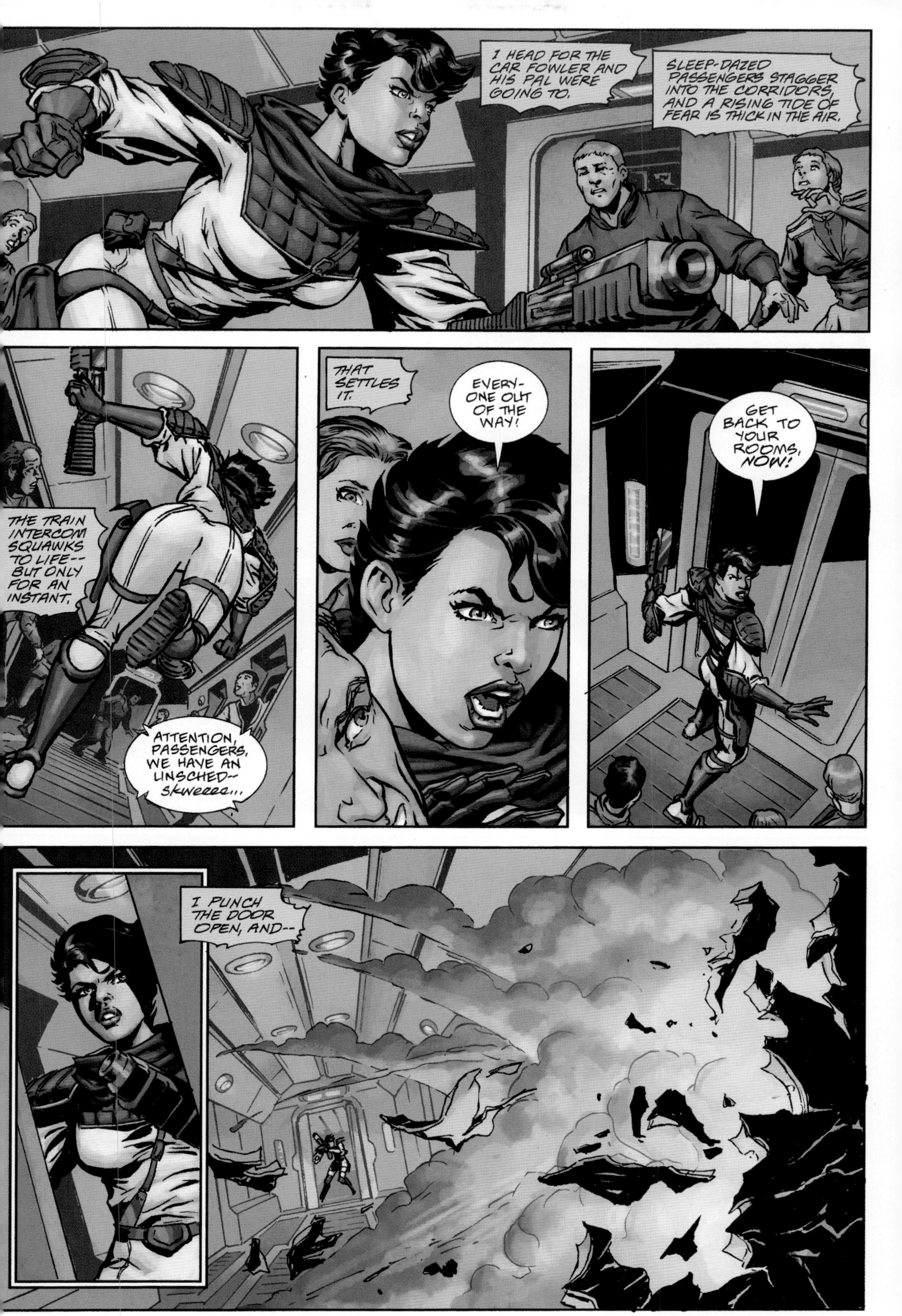
I HEAD FOR THE CAR FOWLER AND HIS PAL WERE GOING TO.
SLEEP-DAZED PASSENGERS STAGGER INTO THE CORRIDORS, AND A RISING TIDE OF FEAR IS THICK IN THE AIR.
THE TRAIN INTERCOM SQUAWKS TO LIFE-- BUT ONLY FOR AN INSTANT.
ATTENTION, PASSENGERS, WE HAVE AN UNSCHED-- skweeee...
THAT SETTLES IT.
EVERY-ONE OUT OF THE WAY!
GET BACK TO YOUR ROOMS, NOW!
I PUNCH THE DOOR OPEN, AND--

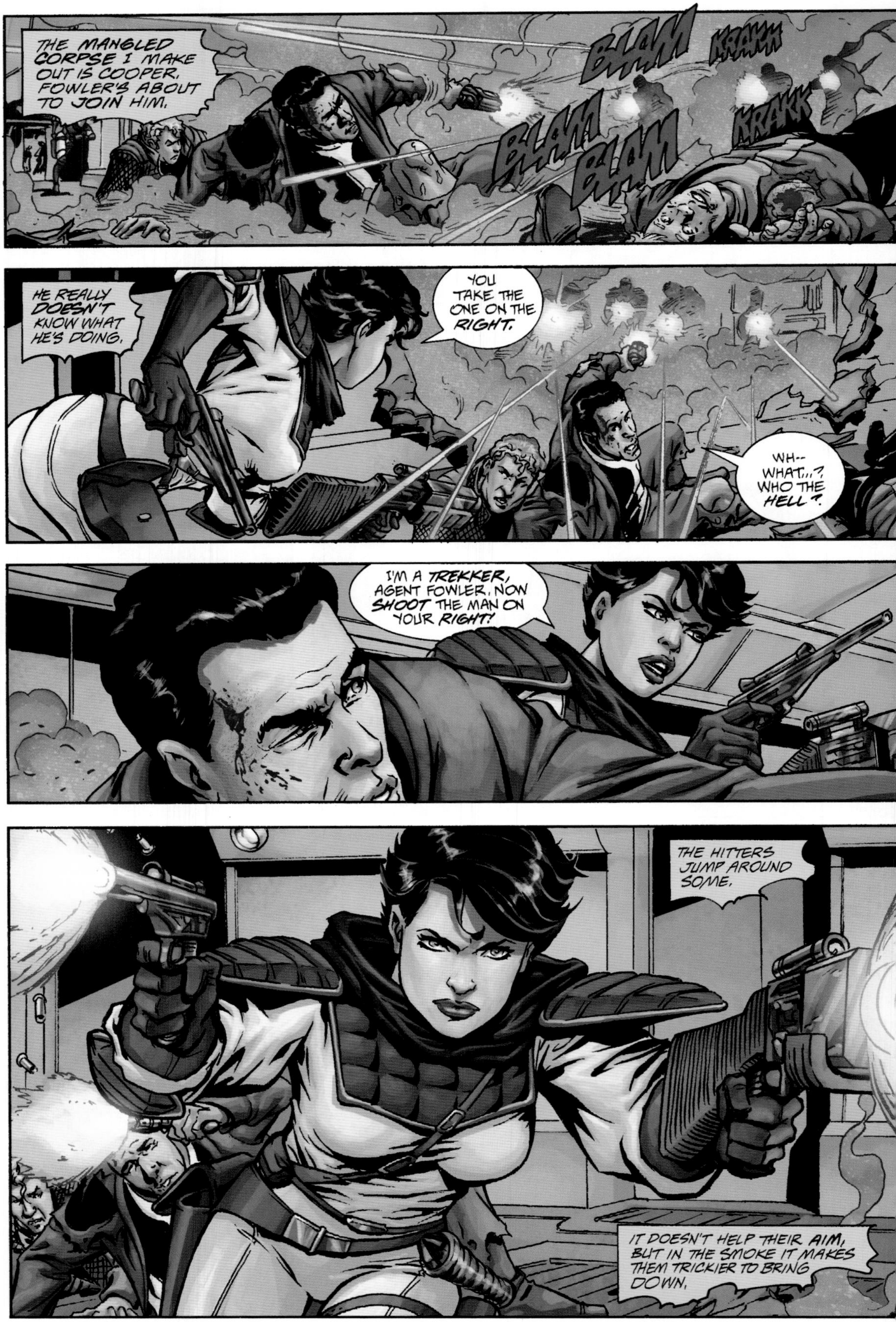
THE MANGLED CORPSE I MAKE OUT IS COOPER. FOWLER'S ABOUT TO JOIN HIM.
BLAM
KRAKK
BLAM
BLAM
KRAKK
HE REALLY DOESN'T KNOW WHAT HE'S DOING.
YOU TAKE THE ONE ON THE RIGHT.
WH-- WHAT...? WHO THE HELL?
I'M A TREKKER, AGENT FOWLER. NOW SHOOT THE MAN ON YOUR RIGHT!
THE HITTERS JUMP AROUND SOME.
IT DOESN'T HELP THEIR AIM, BUT IN THE SMOKE IT MAKES THEM TRICKIER TO BRING DOWN.

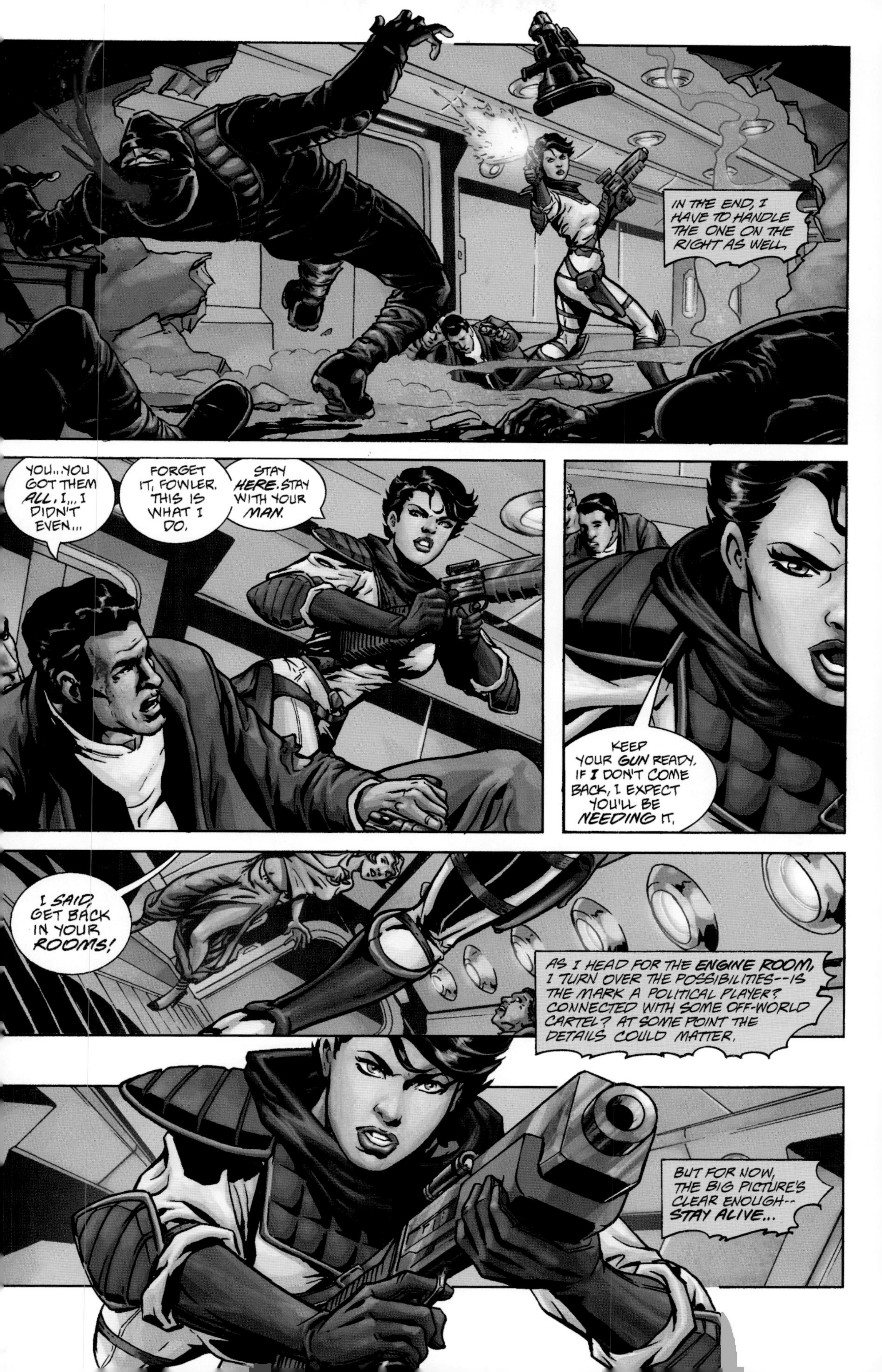
IN THE END, I HAVE TO HANDLE THE ONE ON THE RIGHT AS WELL.
YOU... YOU GOT THEM ALL. I... I DIDN'T EVEN...
FORGET IT, FOWLER. THIS IS WHAT I DO.
STAY HERE. STAY WITH YOUR MAN.
KEEP YOUR GUN READY. IF I DON'T COME BACK, I EXPECT YOU'LL BE NEEDING IT.
I SAID, GET BACK IN YOUR ROOMS!
AS I HEAD FOR THE ENGINE ROOM, I TURN OVER THE POSSIBILITIES--IS THE MARK A POLITICAL PLAYER? CONNECTED WITH SOME OFF-WORLD CARTEL? AT SOME POINT THE DETAILS COULD MATTER.
BUT FOR NOW, THE BIG PICTURE'S CLEAR ENOUGH-- STAY ALIVE...

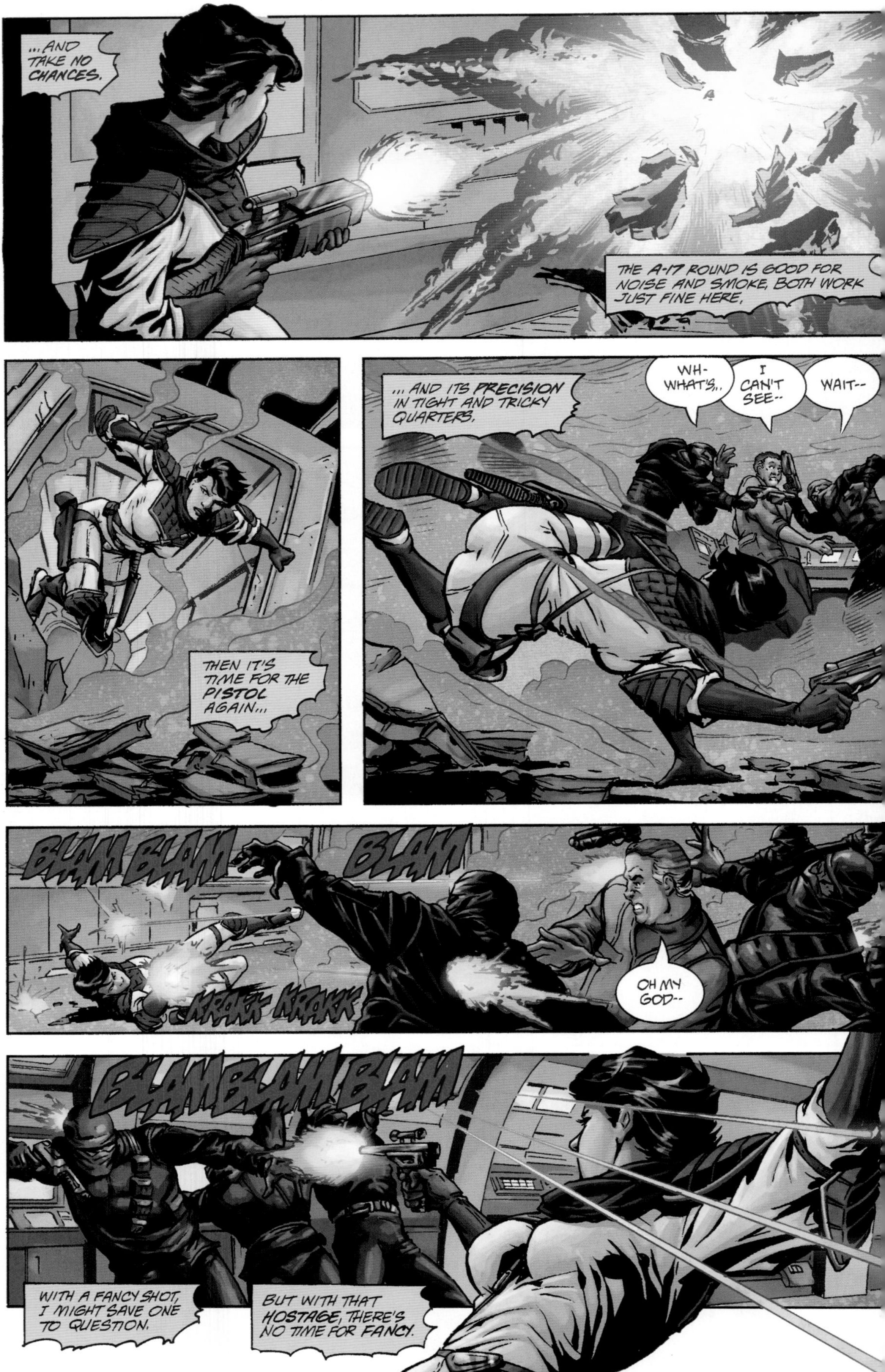
...AND TAKE NO CHANCES.
THE A-17 ROUND IS GOOD FOR NOISE AND SMOKE, BOTH WORK JUST FINE HERE.
THEN IT'S TIME FOR THE PISTOL AGAIN...
... AND ITS PRECISION IN TIGHT AND TRICKY QUARTERS.
WH- WHAT'S...
I CAN'T SEE--
WAIT--
BLAM BLAM BLAM
KRAKK KRAKK
OH MY GOD--
BLAMBLAM BLAM
WITH A FANCY SHOT, I MIGHT SAVE ONE TO QUESTION.
BUT WITH THAT HOSTAGE, THERE'S NO TIME FOR FANCY.

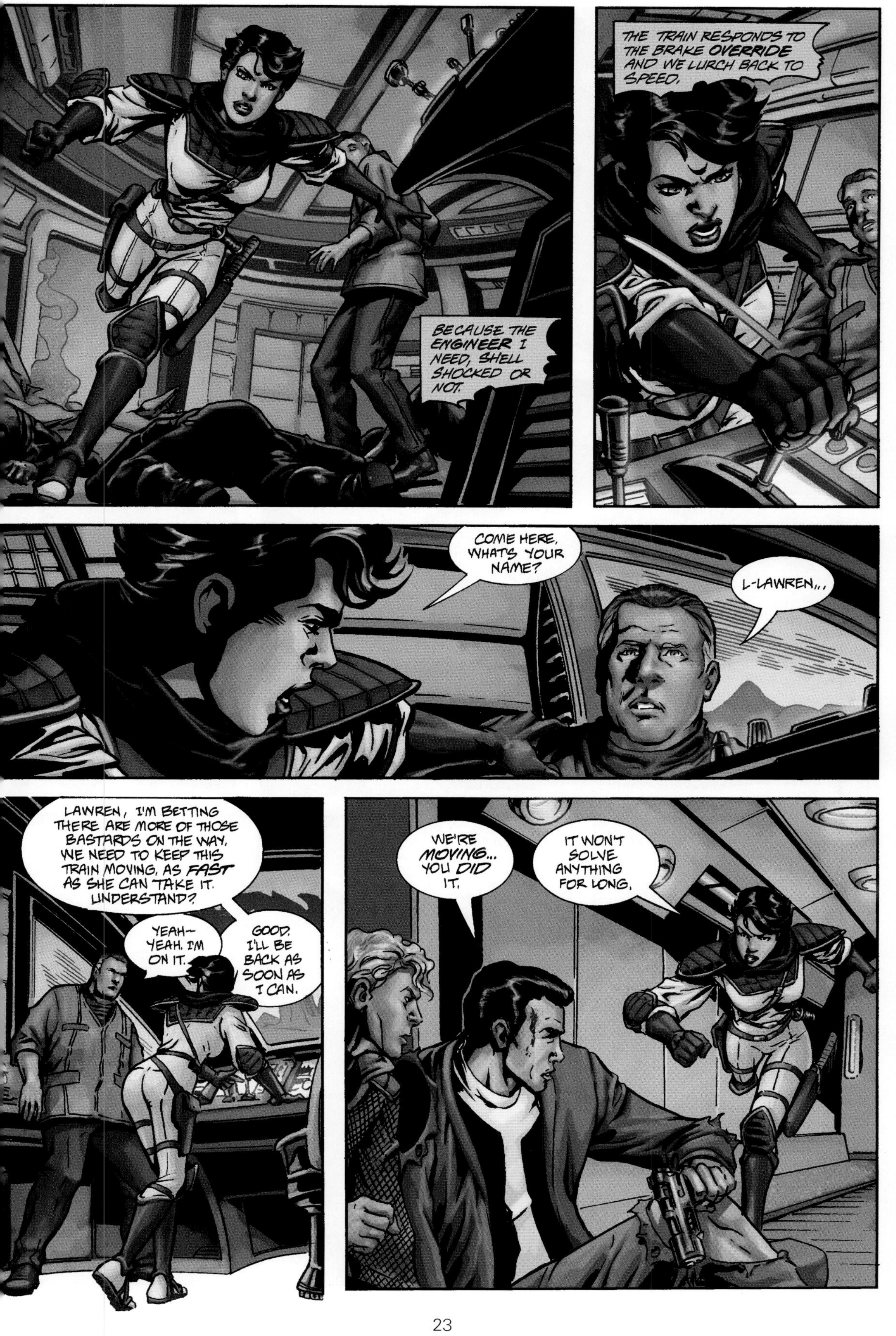
BECAUSE THE ENGINEER I NEED, SHELL SHOCKED OR NOT.
THE TRAIN RESPONDS TO THE BRAKE OVERRIDE AND WE LURCH BACK TO SPEED.
COME HERE. WHAT'S YOUR NAME?
L-LAWREN...
LAWREN, I'M BETTING THERE ARE MORE OF THOSE BASTARDS ON THE WAY. WE NEED TO KEEP THIS TRAIN MOVING, AS FAST AS SHE CAN TAKE IT. UNDERSTAND?
YEAH-- YEAH. I'M ON IT.
GOOD. I'LL BE BACK AS SOON AS I CAN.
WE'RE MOVING... YOU DID IT.
IT WON'T SOLVE ANYTHING FOR LONG.

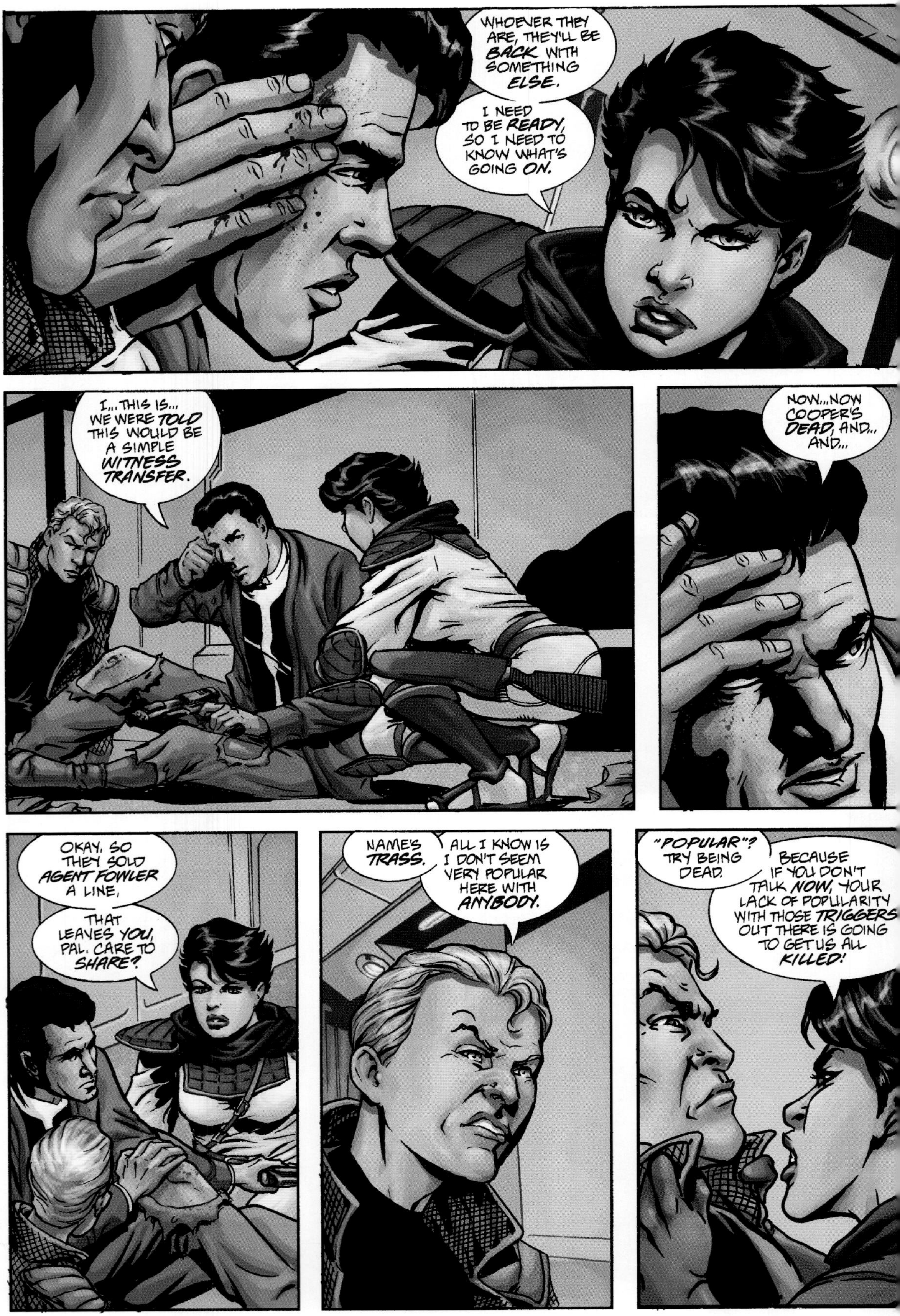
WHOEVER THEY ARE, THEY'LL BE BACK WITH SOMETHING ELSE.
I NEED TO BE READY, SO I NEED TO KNOW WHAT'S GOING ON.
I... THIS IS... WE WERE TOLD THIS WOULD BE A SIMPLE WITNESS TRANSFER.
NOW... NOW COOPER'S DEAD, AND... AND...
OKAY, SO THEY SOLD AGENT FOWLER A LINE,
THAT LEAVES YOU, PAL. CARE TO SHARE?
NAME'S TRASS.
ALL I KNOW IS I DON'T SEEM VERY POPULAR HERE WITH ANYBODY.
"POPULAR"? TRY BEING DEAD.
BECAUSE IF YOU DON'T TALK NOW, YOUR LACK OF POPULARITY WITH THOSE TRIGGERS OUT THERE IS GOING TO GET US ALL KILLED!

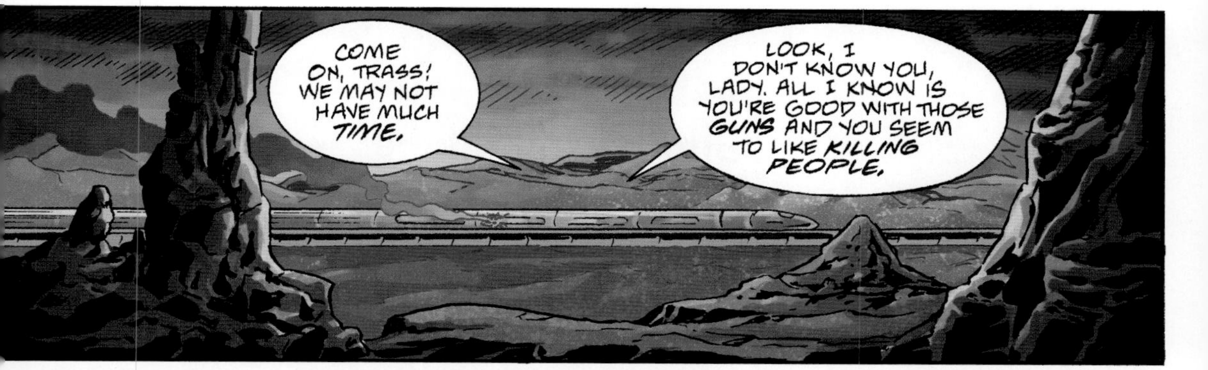
COME ON, TRASS! WE MAY NOT HAVE MUCH TIME.
LOOK, I DON'T KNOW YOU, LADY. ALL I KNOW IS YOU'RE GOOD WITH THOSE GUNS AND YOU SEEM TO LIKE KILLING PEOPLE.

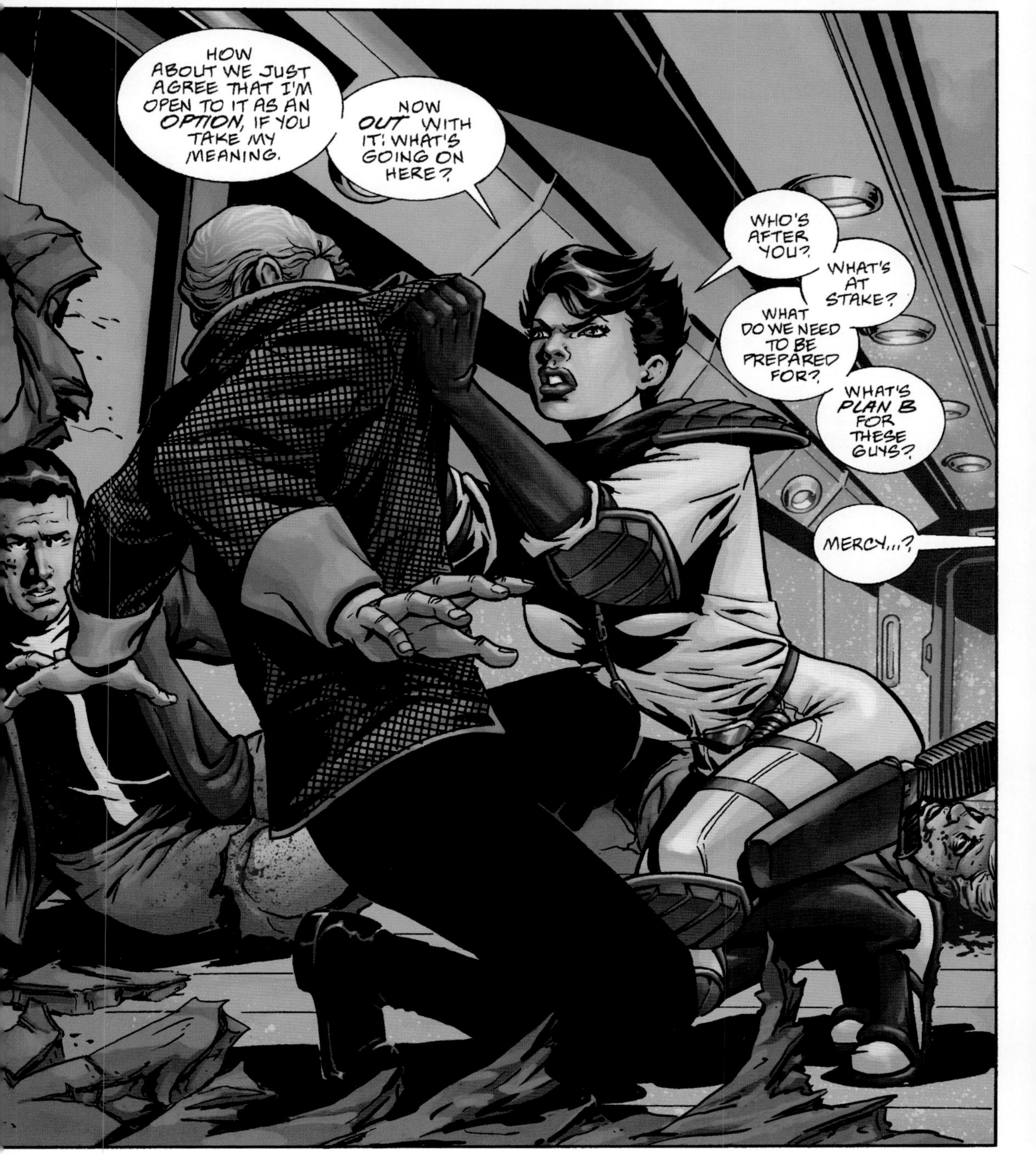
HOW ABOUT WE JUST AGREE THAT I'M OPEN TO IT AS AN OPTION, IF YOU TAKE MY MEANING.
NOW OUT WITH IT: WHAT'S GOING ON HERE?
WHO'S AFTER YOU?
WHAT'S AT STAKE?
WHAT DO WE NEED TO BE PREPARED FOR?
WHAT'S PLAN B FOR THESE GUYS?
MERCY...?

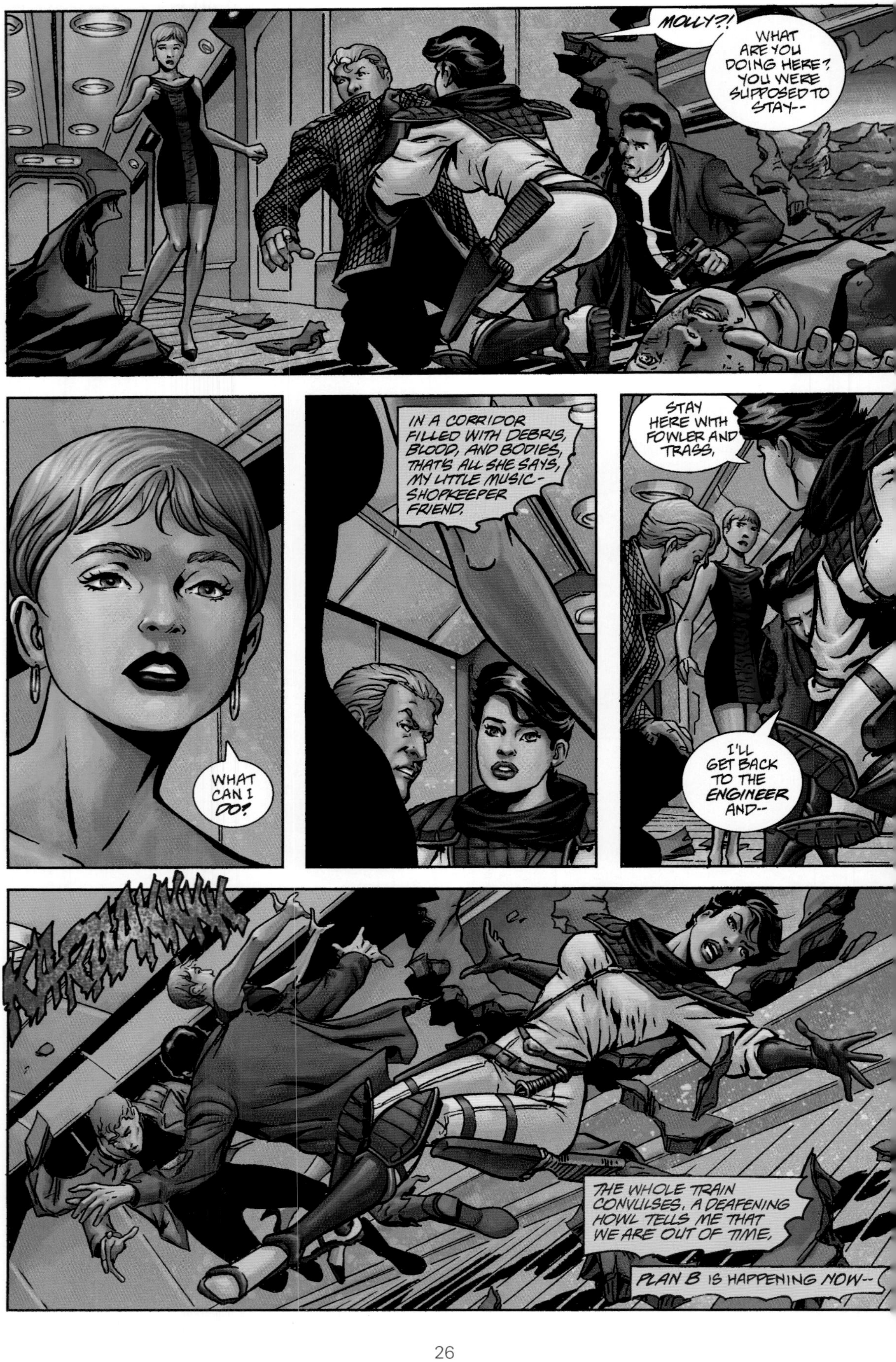
MOLLY?!
WHAT ARE YOU DOING HERE? YOU WERE SUPPOSED TO STAY--
WHAT CAN I DO?
IN A CORRIDOR FILLED WITH DEBRIS, BLOOD, AND BODIES, THAT'S ALL SHE SAYS, MY LITTLE MUSIC-SHOPKEEPER FRIEND.
STAY HERE WITH FOWLER AND TRASS,
I'LL GET BACK TO THE ENGINEER AND--
KAROOMMMM
THE WHOLE TRAIN CONVULSES. A DEAFENING HOWL TELLS ME THAT WE ARE OUT OF TIME.
PLAN B IS HAPPENING NOW--

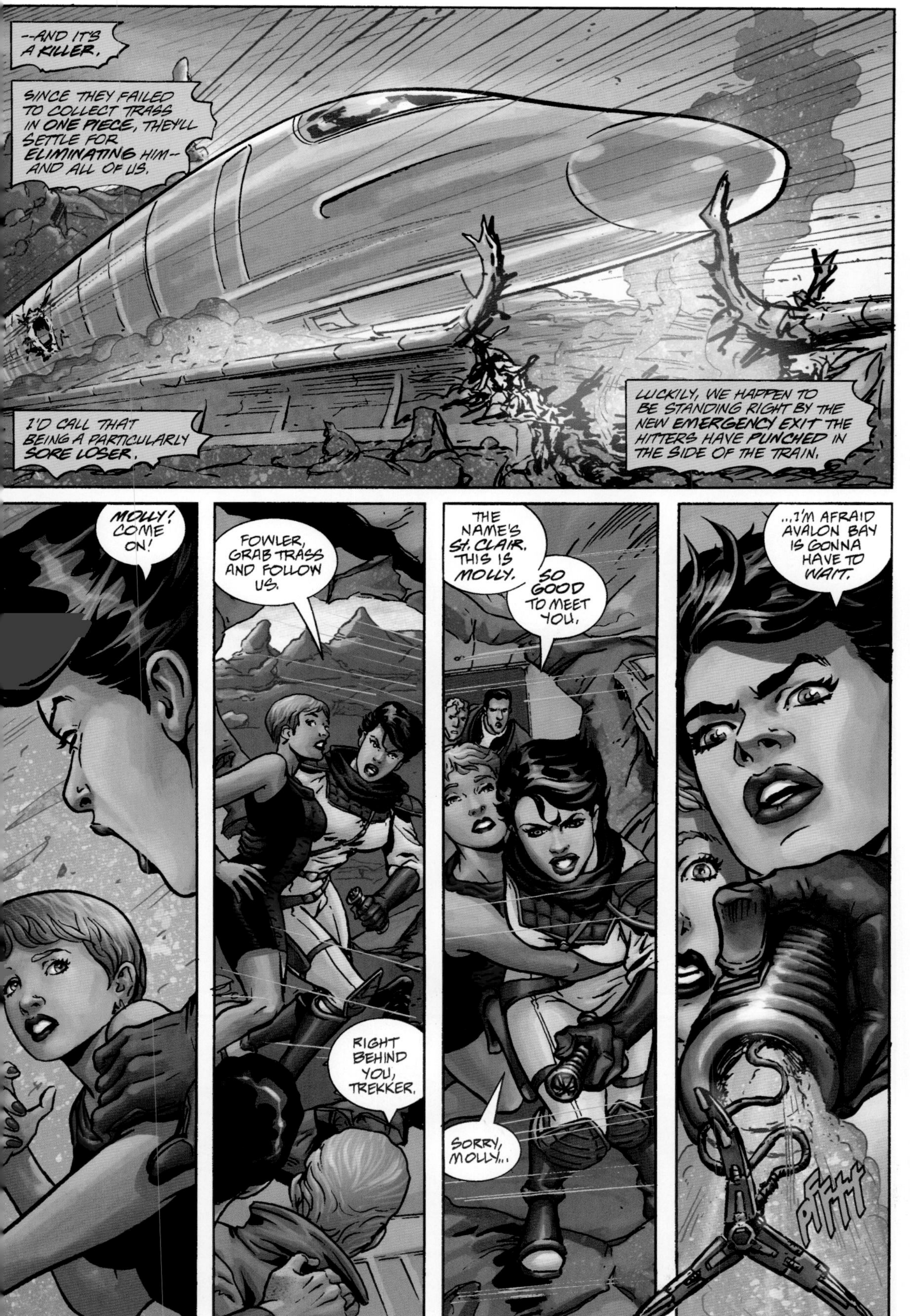
--AND IT'S A KILLER.
SINCE THEY FAILED TO COLLECT TRASS IN ONE PIECE, THEY'LL SETTLE FOR ELIMINATING HIM-- AND ALL OF US.
I'D CALL THAT BEING A PARTICULARLY SORE LOSER.
LUCKILY, WE HAPPEN TO BE STANDING RIGHT BY THE NEW EMERGENCY EXIT THE HITTERS HAVE PUNCHED IN THE SIDE OF THE TRAIN.
MOLLY! COME ON!
FOWLER, GRAB TRASS AND FOLLOW US.
RIGHT BEHIND YOU, TREKKER.
THE NAME'S ST. CLAIR. THIS IS MOLLY.
SO GOOD TO MEET YOU.
SORRY, MOLLY...
...I'M AFRAID AVALON BAY IS GONNA HAVE TO WAIT.
FSSSS PTTTT

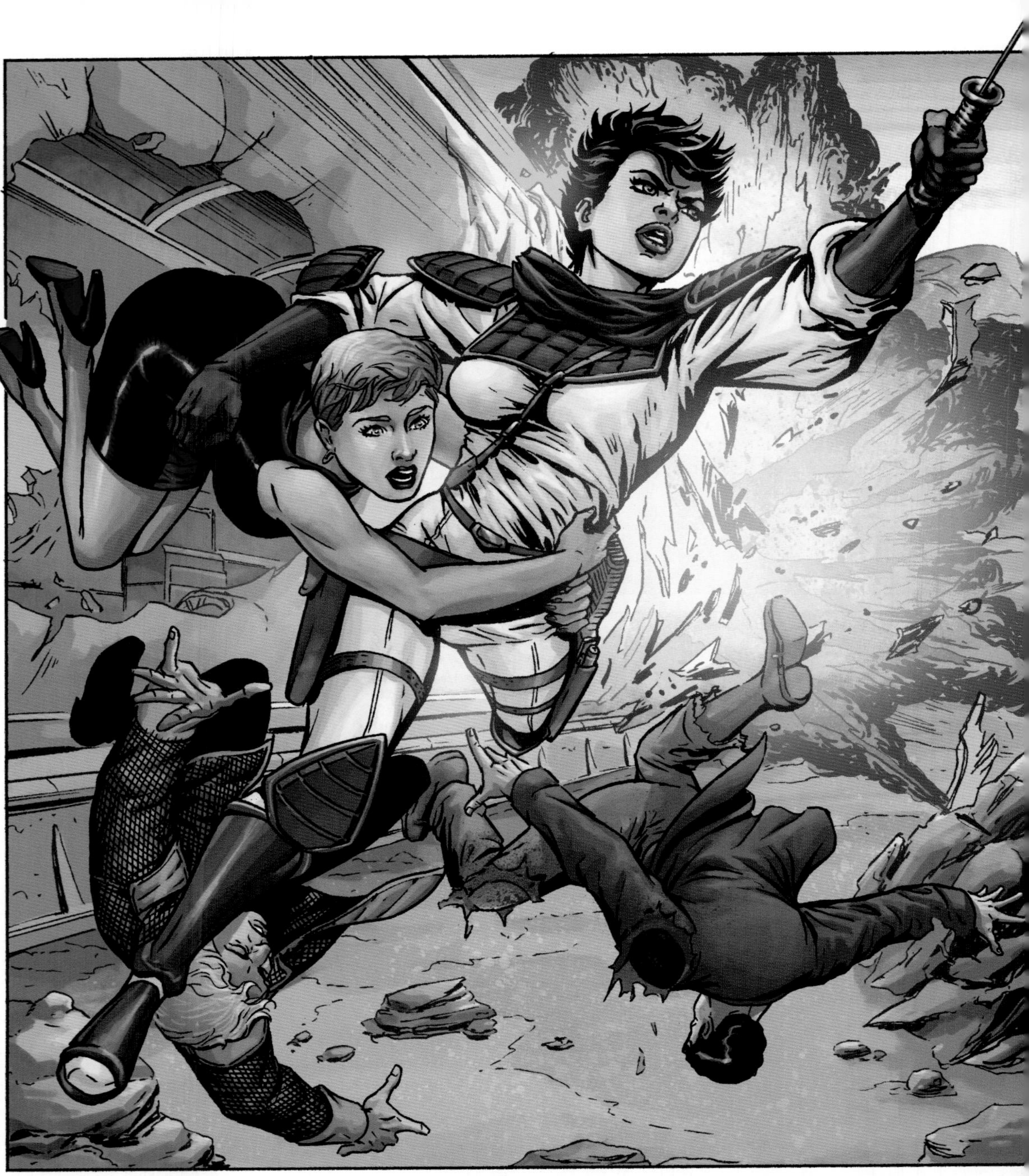

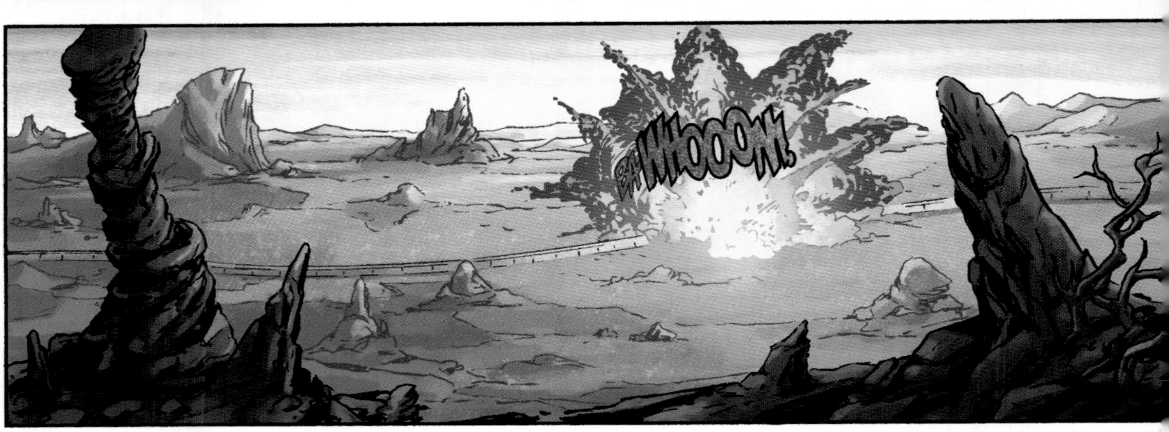
BAWHOOOM!

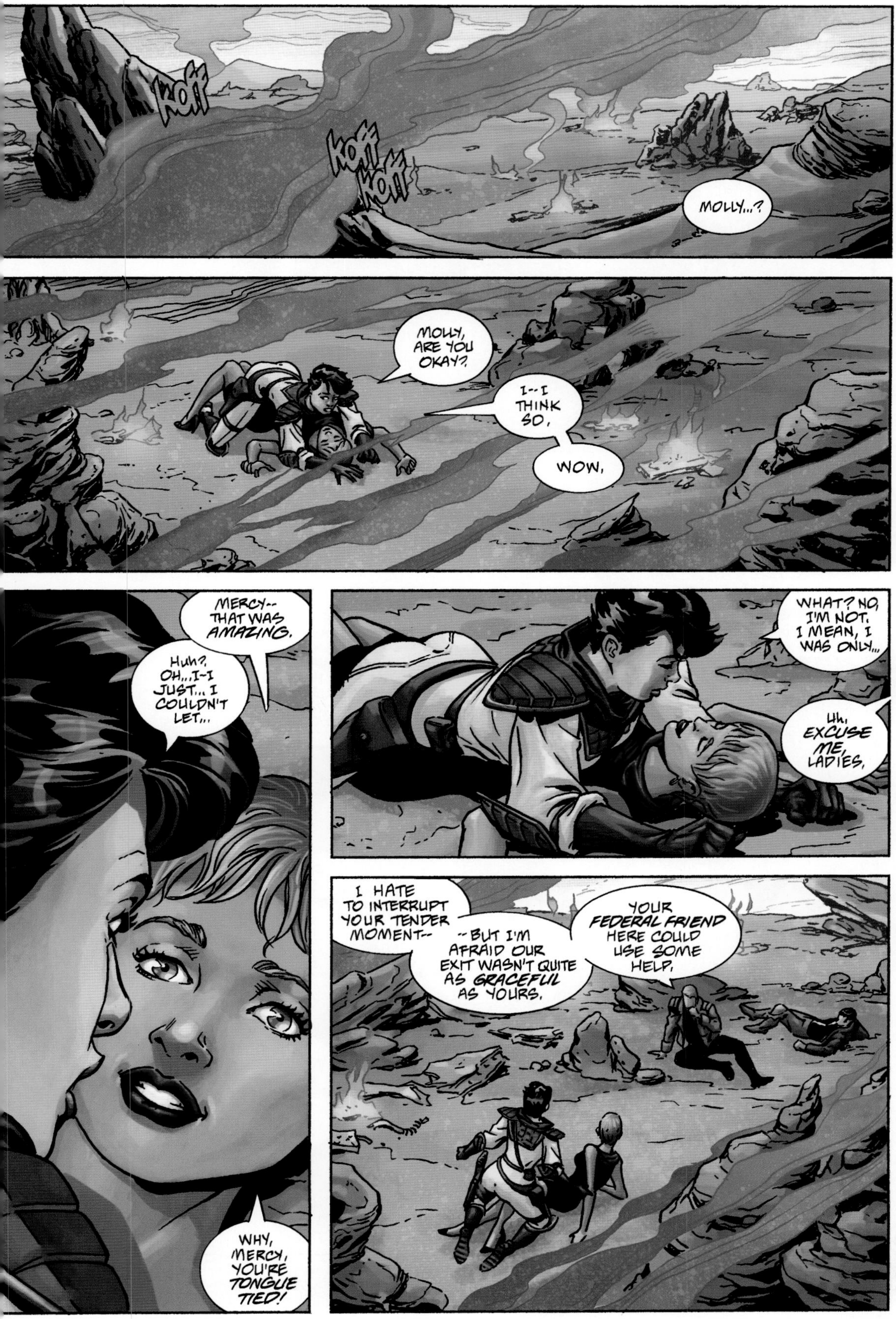

KOFF
KOFF KOFF
MOLLY...?
MOLLY, ARE YOU OKAY?
I--I THINK SO.
WOW.
MERCY-- THAT WAS AMAZING.
Huh? OH...I--I JUST... I COULDN'T LET...
WHY, MERCY, YOU'RE TONGUE TIED!
WHAT? NO, I'M NOT. I MEAN, I WAS ONLY...
Uh, EXCUSE ME, LADIES.
I HATE TO INTERRUPT YOUR TENDER MOMENT--
--BUT I'M AFRAID OUR EXIT WASN'T QUITE AS GRACEFUL AS YOURS.
YOUR FEDERAL FRIEND HERE COULD USE SOME HELP.

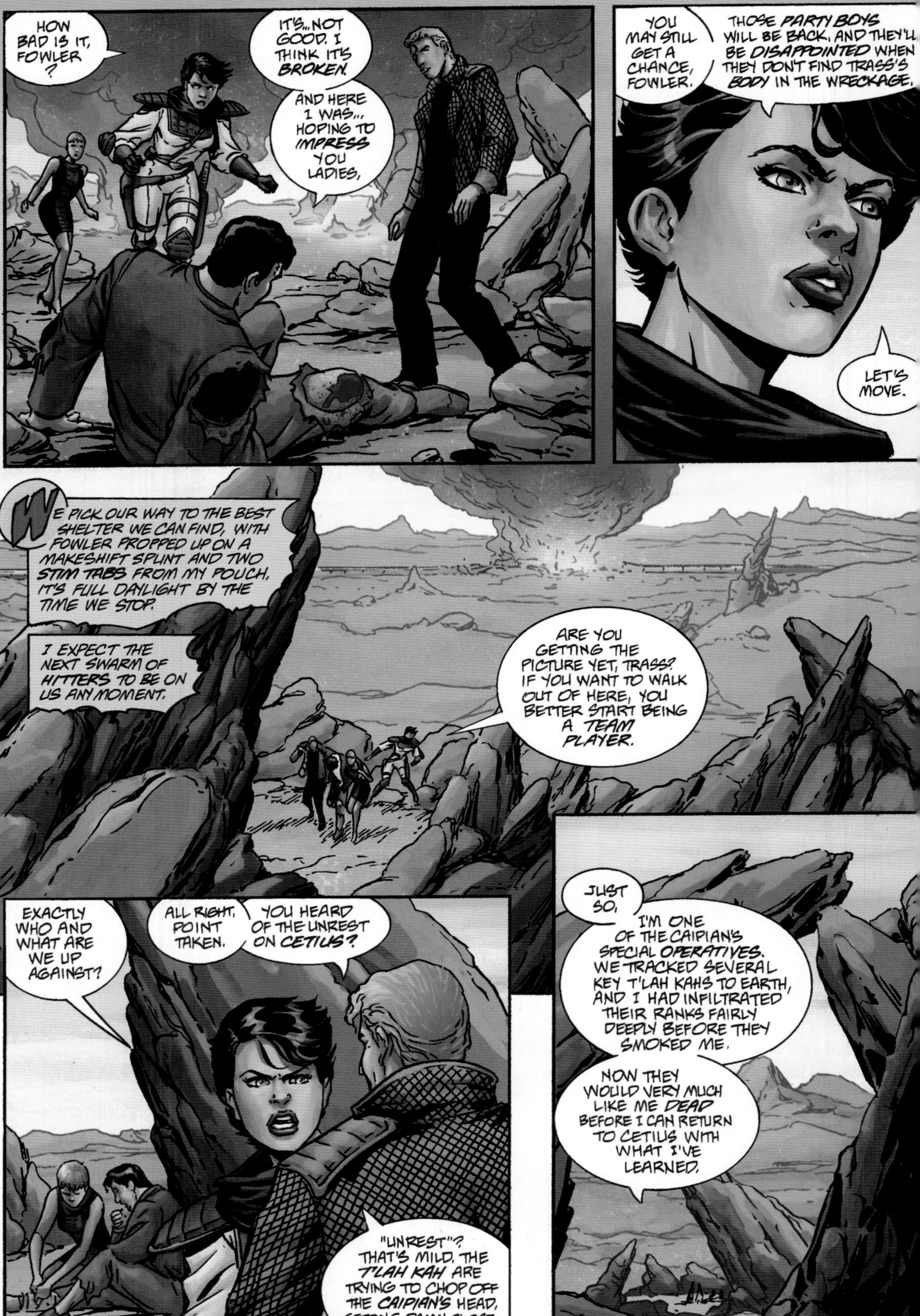
HOW BAD IS IT, FOWLER?
IT'S... NOT GOOD. I THINK IT'S BROKEN.
AND HERE I WAS... HOPING TO IMPRESS YOU LADIES.
YOU MAY STILL GET A CHANCE, FOWLER.
THOSE PARTY BOYS WILL BE BACK, AND THEY'LL BE DISAPPOINTED WHEN THEY DON'T FIND TRASS'S BODY IN THE WRECKAGE.
LET'S MOVE.
WE PICK OUR WAY TO THE BEST SHELTER WE CAN FIND, WITH FOWLER PROPPED UP ON A MAKESHIFT SPLINT AND TWO STIM TABS FROM MY POUCH. IT'S FULL DAYLIGHT BY THE TIME WE STOP.
I EXPECT THE NEXT SWARM OF HITTERS TO BE ON US ANY MOMENT.
ARE YOU GETTING THE PICTURE YET, TRASS? IF YOU WANT TO WALK OUT OF HERE, YOU BETTER START BEING A TEAM PLAYER.
EXACTLY WHO AND WHAT ARE WE UP AGAINST?
ALL RIGHT, POINT TAKEN.
YOU HEARD OF THE UNREST ON CETIUS?
"UNREST"? THAT'S MILD. THE T'LAH KAH ARE TRYING TO CHOP OFF THE CAIPIAN'S HEAD, GETTING DAMN CLOSE TO IT, TOO.
JUST SO.
I'M ONE OF THE CAIPIAN'S SPECIAL OPERATIVES. WE TRACKED SEVERAL KEY T'LAH KAHS TO EARTH, AND I HAD INFILTRATED THEIR RANKS FAIRLY DEEPLY BEFORE THEY SMOKED ME.
NOW THEY WOULD VERY MUCH LIKE ME DEAD BEFORE I CAN RETURN TO CETIUS WITH WHAT I'VE LEARNED.

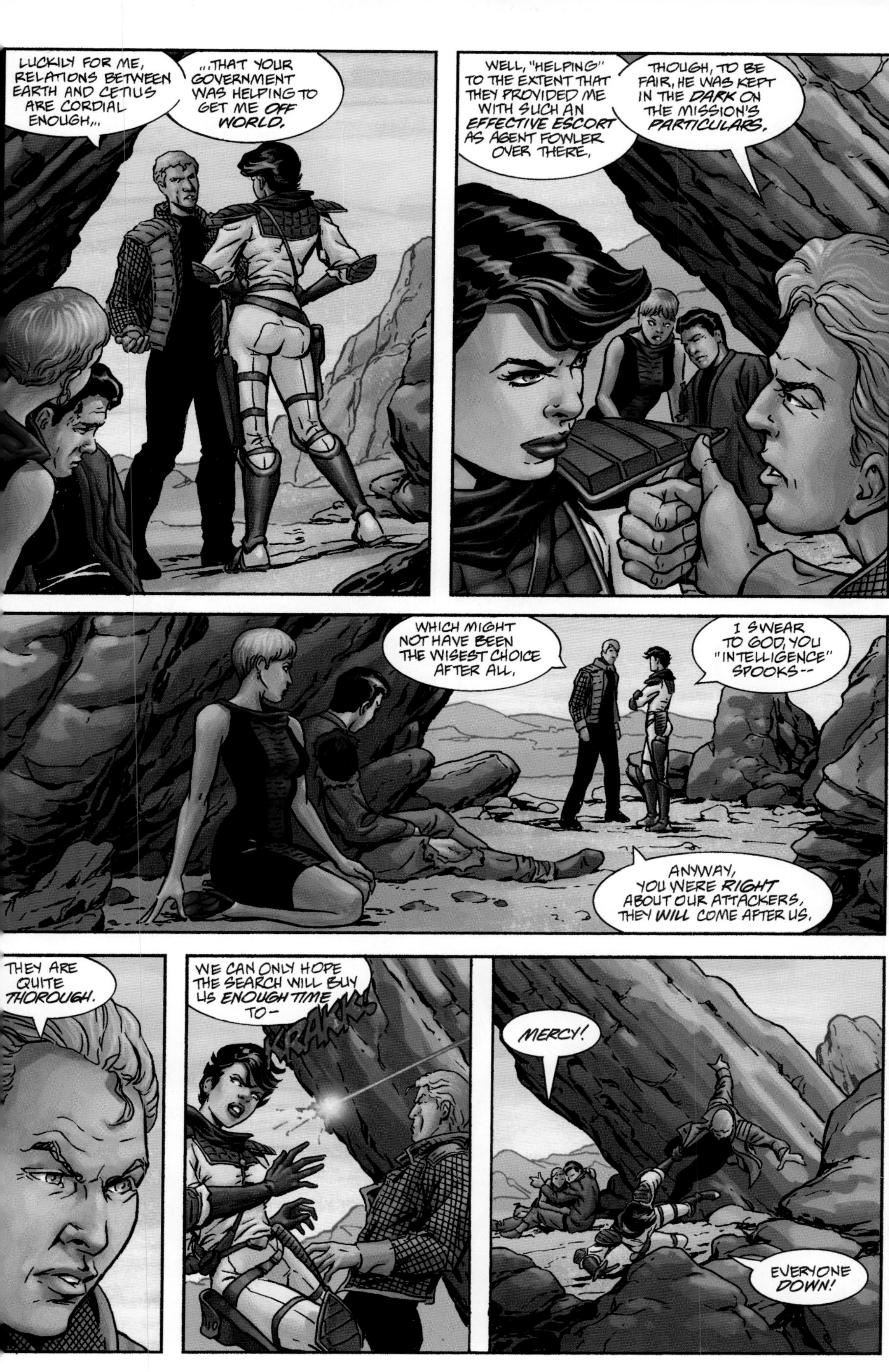
LUCKILY FOR ME, RELATIONS BETWEEN EARTH AND CETIUS ARE CORDIAL ENOUGH...
...THAT YOUR GOVERNMENT WAS HELPING TO GET ME OFF WORLD.
WELL, "HELPING" TO THE EXTENT THAT THEY PROVIDED ME WITH SUCH AN EFFECTIVE ESCORT AS AGENT FOWLER OVER THERE.
THOUGH, TO BE FAIR, HE WAS KEPT IN THE DARK ON THE MISSION'S PARTICULARS.
WHICH MIGHT NOT HAVE BEEN THE WISEST CHOICE AFTER ALL.
I SWEAR TO GOD, YOU "INTELLIGENCE" SPOOKS--
ANYWAY, YOU WERE RIGHT ABOUT OUR ATTACKERS. THEY WILL COME AFTER US.
THEY ARE QUITE THOROUGH.
WE CAN ONLY HOPE THE SEARCH WILL BUY US ENOUGH TIME TO-
KRAKKS
MERCY!
EVERYONE DOWN!

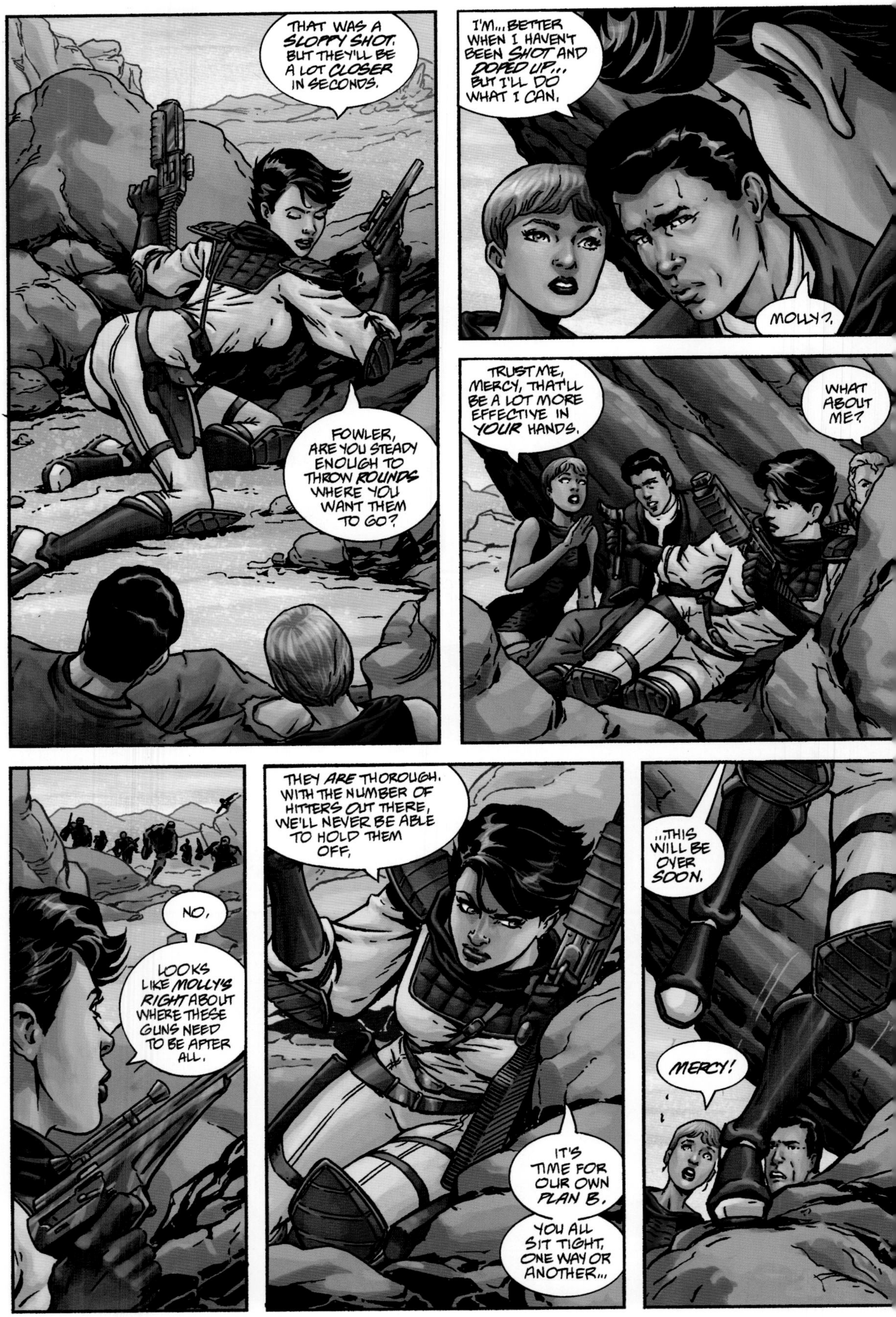
THAT WAS A SLOPPY SHOT. BUT THEY'LL BE A LOT CLOSER IN SECONDS.
FOWLER, ARE YOU STEADY ENOUGH TO THROW ROUNDS WHERE YOU WANT THEM TO GO?
I'M... BETTER WHEN I HAVEN'T BEEN SHOT AND DOPED UP... BUT I'LL DO WHAT I CAN.
MOLLY?
TRUST ME, MERCY, THAT'LL BE A LOT MORE EFFECTIVE IN YOUR HANDS.
WHAT ABOUT ME?
NO.
LOOKS LIKE MOLLY'S RIGHT ABOUT WHERE THESE GUNS NEED TO BE AFTER ALL.
THEY ARE THOROUGH. WITH THE NUMBER OF HITTERS OUT THERE, WE'LL NEVER BE ABLE TO HOLD THEM OFF.
IT'S TIME FOR OUR OWN PLAN B.
YOU ALL SIT TIGHT. ONE WAY OR ANOTHER...
...THIS WILL BE OVER SOON.
MERCY!

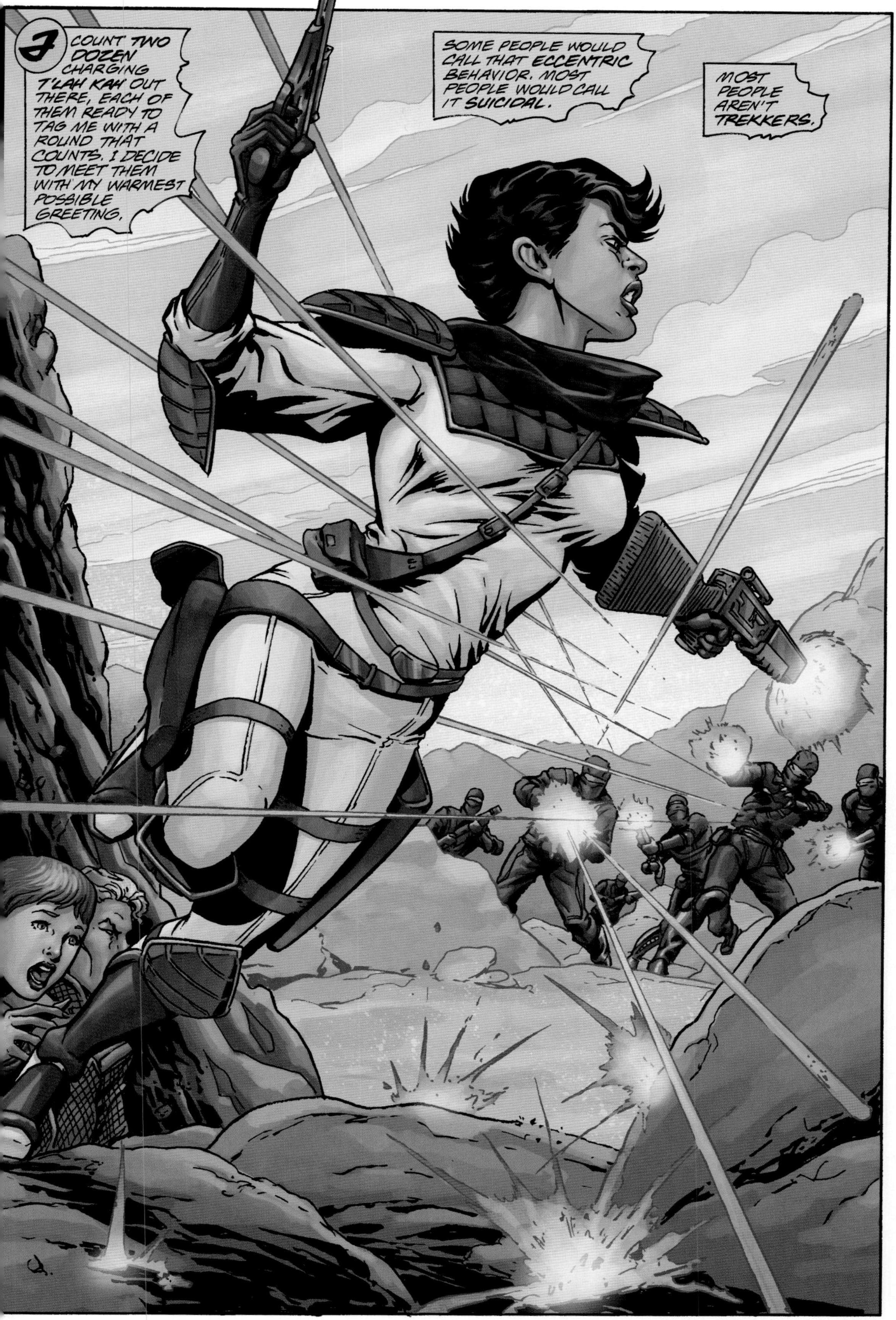
COUNT TWO DOZEN CHARGING T'LAH KAH OUT THERE, EACH OF THEM READY TO TAG ME WITH A ROUND THAT COUNTS. I DECIDE TO MEET THEM WITH MY WARMEST POSSIBLE GREETING.
SOME PEOPLE WOULD CALL THAT ECCENTRIC BEHAVIOR. MOST PEOPLE WOULD CALL IT SUICIDAL.
MOST PEOPLE AREN'T TREKKERS.

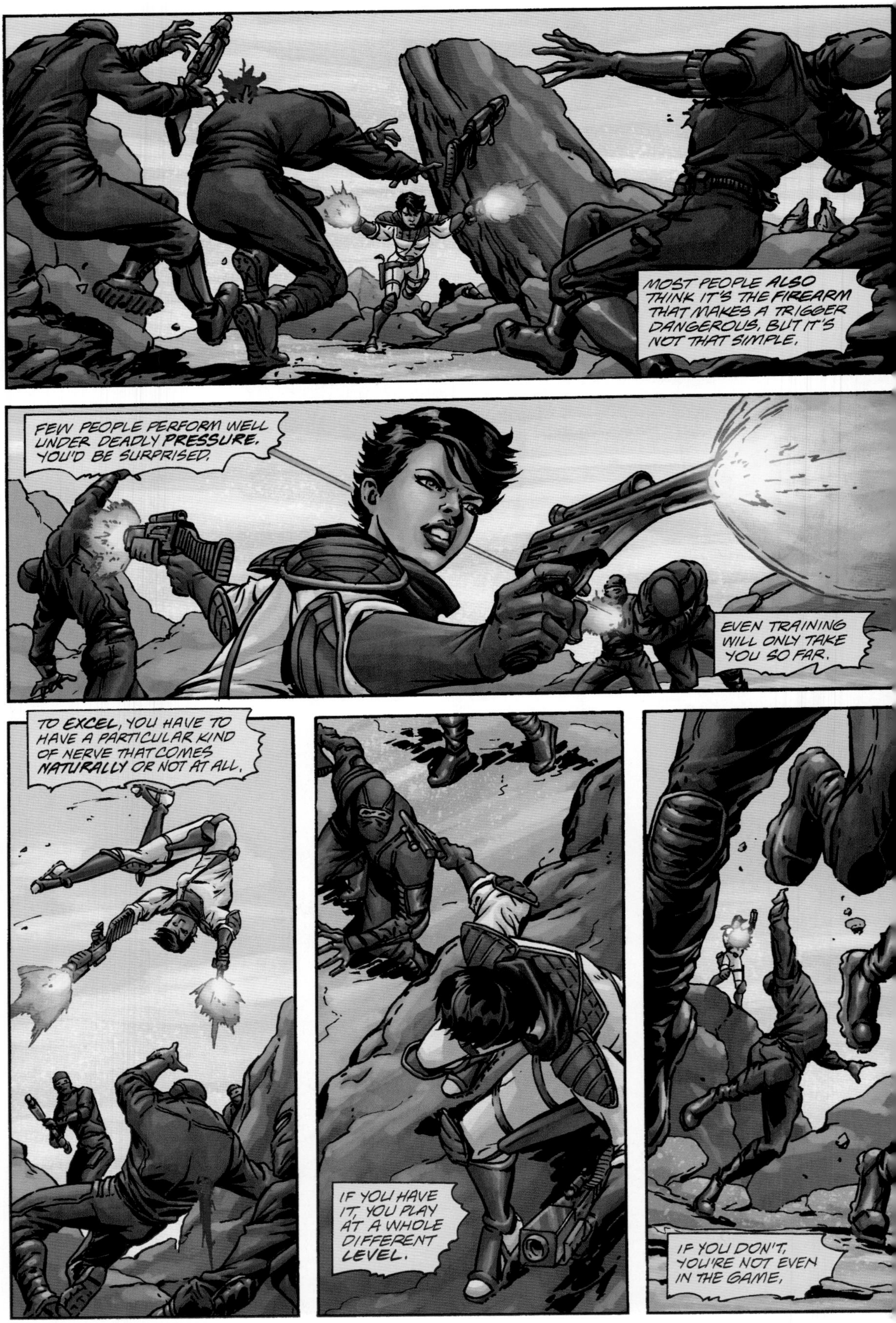
MOST PEOPLE ALSO THINK IT'S THE FIREARM THAT MAKES A TRIGGER DANGEROUS. BUT IT'S NOT THAT SIMPLE.
FEW PEOPLE PERFORM WELL UNDER DEADLY PRESSURE. YOU'D BE SURPRISED.
EVEN TRAINING WILL ONLY TAKE YOU SO FAR.
TO EXCEL, YOU HAVE TO HAVE A PARTICULAR KIND OF NERVE THAT COMES NATURALLY OR NOT AT ALL.
IF YOU HAVE IT, YOU PLAY AT A WHOLE DIFFERENT LEVEL.
IF YOU DON'T, YOU'RE NOT EVEN IN THE GAME.

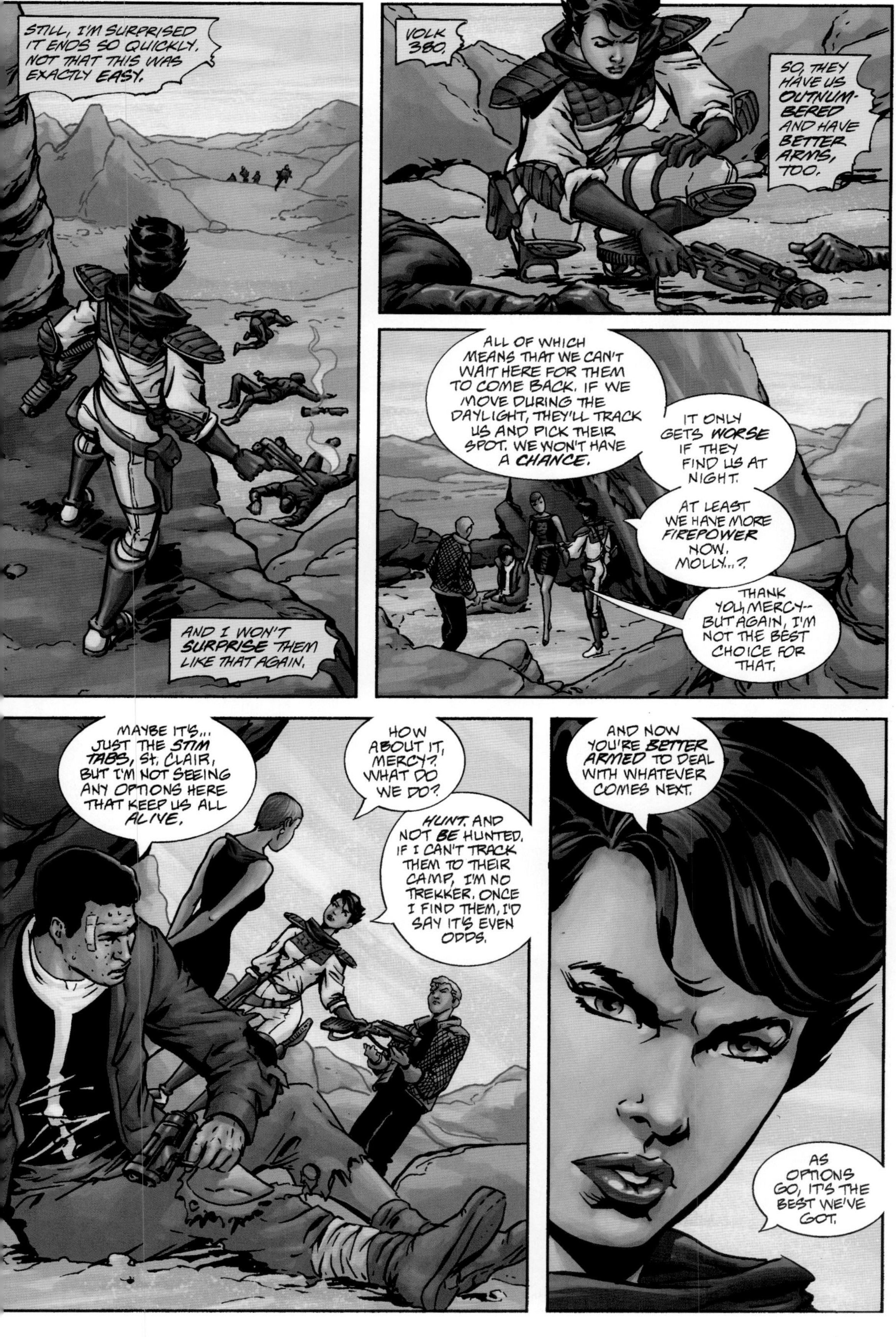
STILL, I'M SURPRISED IT ENDS SO QUICKLY. NOT THAT THIS WAS EXACTLY EASY.
AND I WON'T SURPRISE THEM LIKE THAT AGAIN.
VOLK 380.
SO, THEY HAVE US OUTNUMBERED AND HAVE BETTER ARMS, TOO.
ALL OF WHICH MEANS THAT WE CAN'T WAIT HERE FOR THEM TO COME BACK. IF WE MOVE DURING THE DAYLIGHT, THEY'LL TRACK US AND PICK THEIR SPOT. WE WON'T HAVE A CHANCE.
IT ONLY GETS WORSE IF THEY FIND US AT NIGHT.
AT LEAST WE HAVE MORE FIREPOWER NOW. MOLLY...?
THANK YOU, MERCY-- BUT AGAIN, I'M NOT THE BEST CHOICE FOR THAT.
MAYBE IT'S... JUST THE STIM TABS, St. CLAIR, BUT I'M NOT SEEING ANY OPTIONS HERE THAT KEEP US ALL ALIVE.
HOW ABOUT IT, MERCY? WHAT DO WE DO?
HUNT. AND NOT BE HUNTED. IF I CAN'T TRACK THEM TO THEIR CAMP, I'M NO TREKKER. ONCE I FIND THEM, I'D SAY IT'S EVEN ODDS.
AND NOW YOU'RE BETTER ARMED TO DEAL WITH WHATEVER COMES NEXT.
AS OPTIONS GO, IT'S THE BEST WE'VE GOT.

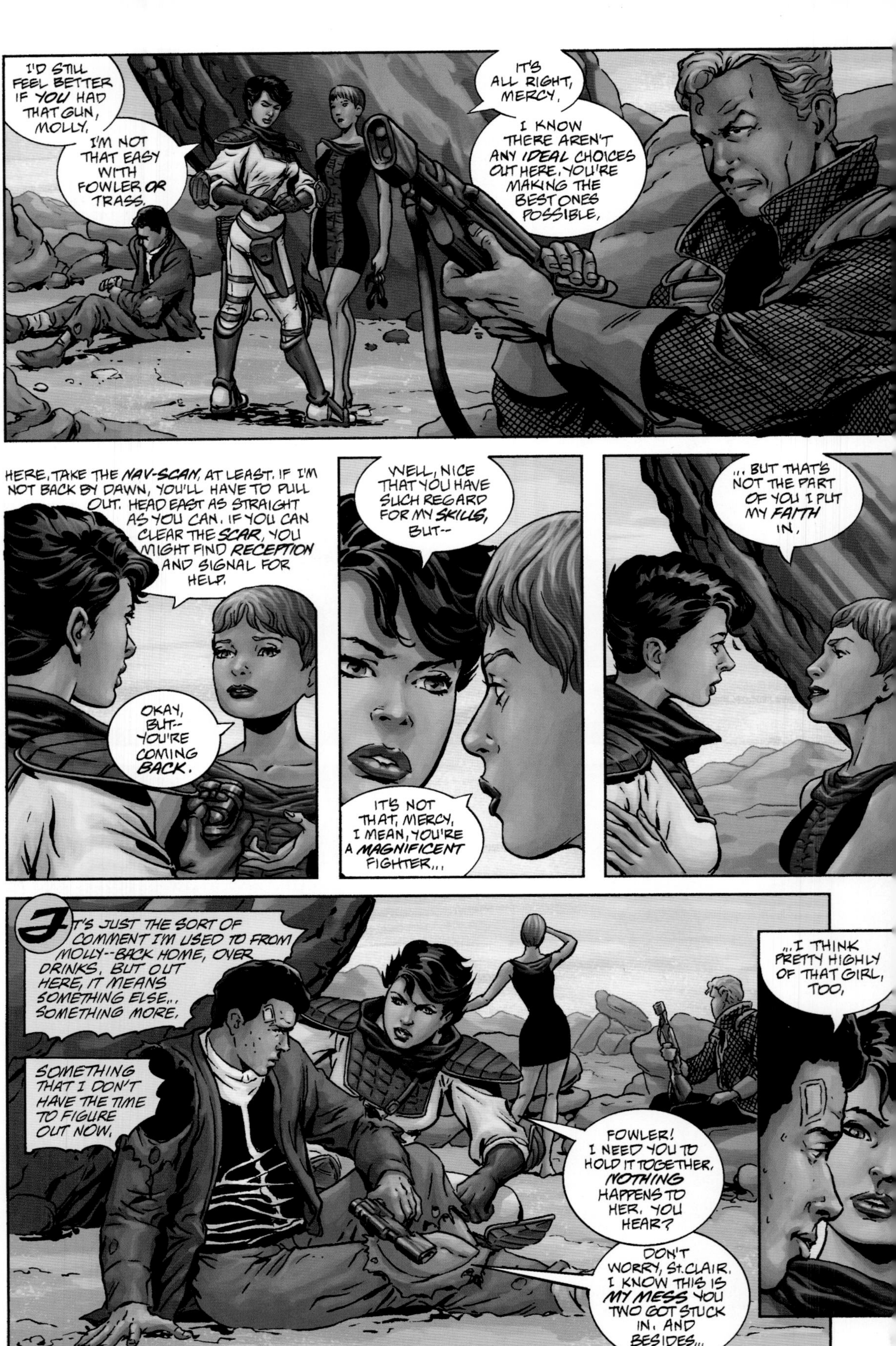
I'D STILL FEEL BETTER IF YOU HAD THAT GUN, MOLLY.
I'M NOT THAT EASY WITH FOWLER OR TRASS.
IT'S ALL RIGHT, MERCY.
I KNOW THERE AREN'T ANY IDEAL CHOICES OUT HERE. YOU'RE MAKING THE BEST ONES POSSIBLE.
HERE. TAKE THE NAV-SCAN, AT LEAST. IF I'M NOT BACK BY DAWN, YOU'LL HAVE TO PULL OUT. HEAD EAST AS STRAIGHT AS YOU CAN. IF YOU CAN CLEAR THE SCAR, YOU MIGHT FIND RECEPTION AND SIGNAL FOR HELP.
OKAY, BUT-- YOU'RE COMING BACK.
WELL, NICE THAT YOU HAVE SUCH REGARD FOR MY SKILLS, BUT--
IT'S NOT THAT, MERCY. I MEAN, YOU'RE A MAGNIFICENT FIGHTER...
... BUT THAT'S NOT THE PART OF YOU I PUT MY FAITH IN.
IT'S JUST THE SORT OF COMMENT I'M USED TO FROM MOLLY--BACK HOME, OVER DRINKS. BUT OUT HERE, IT MEANS SOMETHING ELSE... SOMETHING MORE.
SOMETHING THAT I DON'T HAVE THE TIME TO FIGURE OUT NOW.
FOWLER! I NEED YOU TO HOLD IT TOGETHER. NOTHING HAPPENS TO HER. YOU HEAR?
DON'T WORRY, St.CLAIR. I KNOW THIS IS MY MESS YOU TWO GOT STUCK IN. AND BESIDES...
...I THINK PRETTY HIGHLY OF THAT GIRL, TOO.

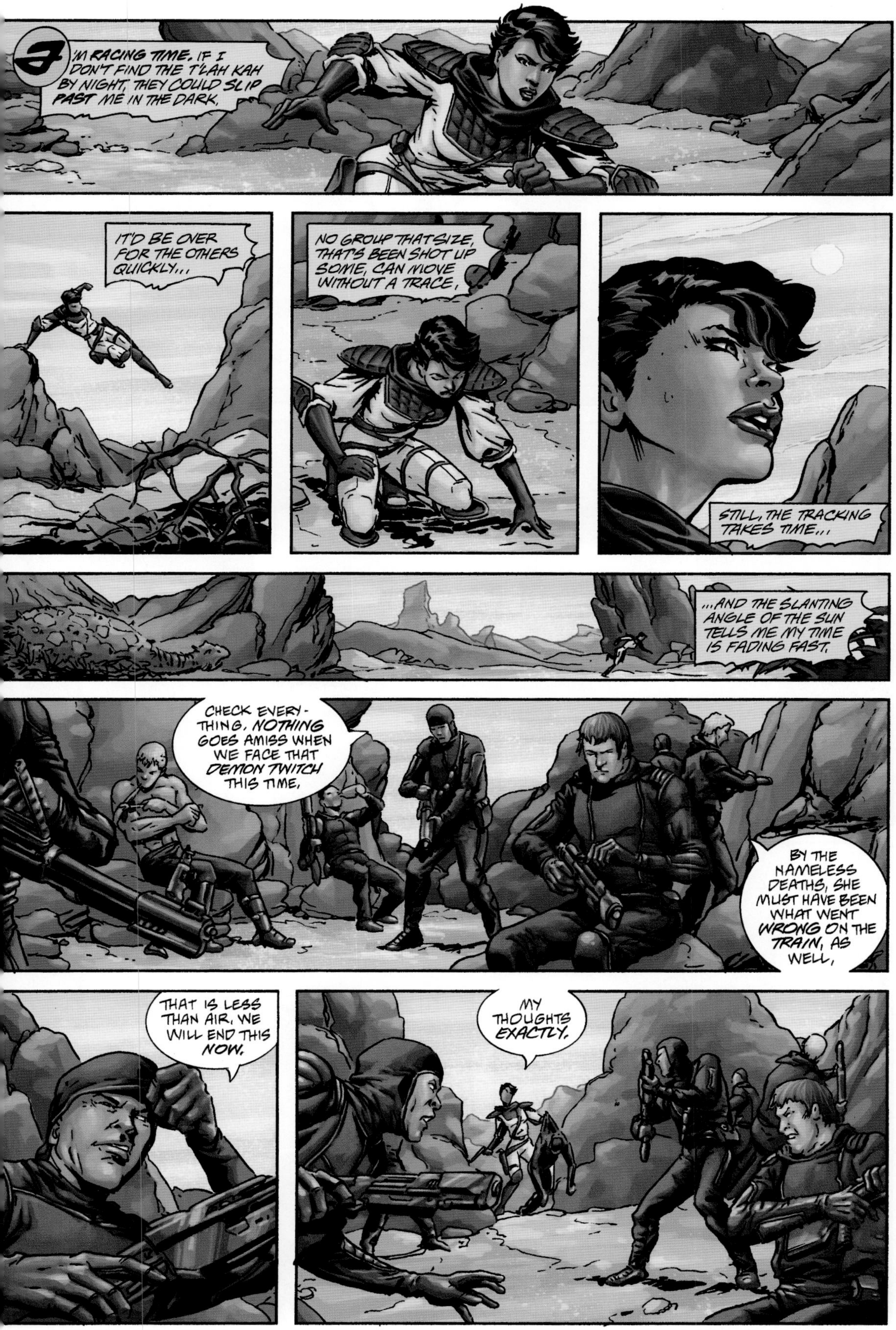
I'M RACING TIME. IF I DON'T FIND THE T'LAH KAH BY NIGHT, THEY COULD SLIP PAST ME IN THE DARK.
IT'D BE OVER FOR THE OTHERS QUICKLY...
NO GROUP THAT SIZE, THAT'S BEEN SHOT UP SOME, CAN MOVE WITHOUT A TRACE.
STILL, THE TRACKING TAKES TIME...
...AND THE SLANTING ANGLE OF THE SUN TELLS ME MY TIME IS FADING FAST.
CHECK EVERY-THING. NOTHING GOES AMISS WHEN WE FACE THAT DEMON TWITCH THIS TIME.
BY THE NAMELESS DEATHS, SHE MUST HAVE BEEN WHAT WENT WRONG ON THE TRAIN, AS WELL.
THAT IS LESS THAN AIR. WE WILL END THIS NOW.
MY THOUGHTS EXACTLY.

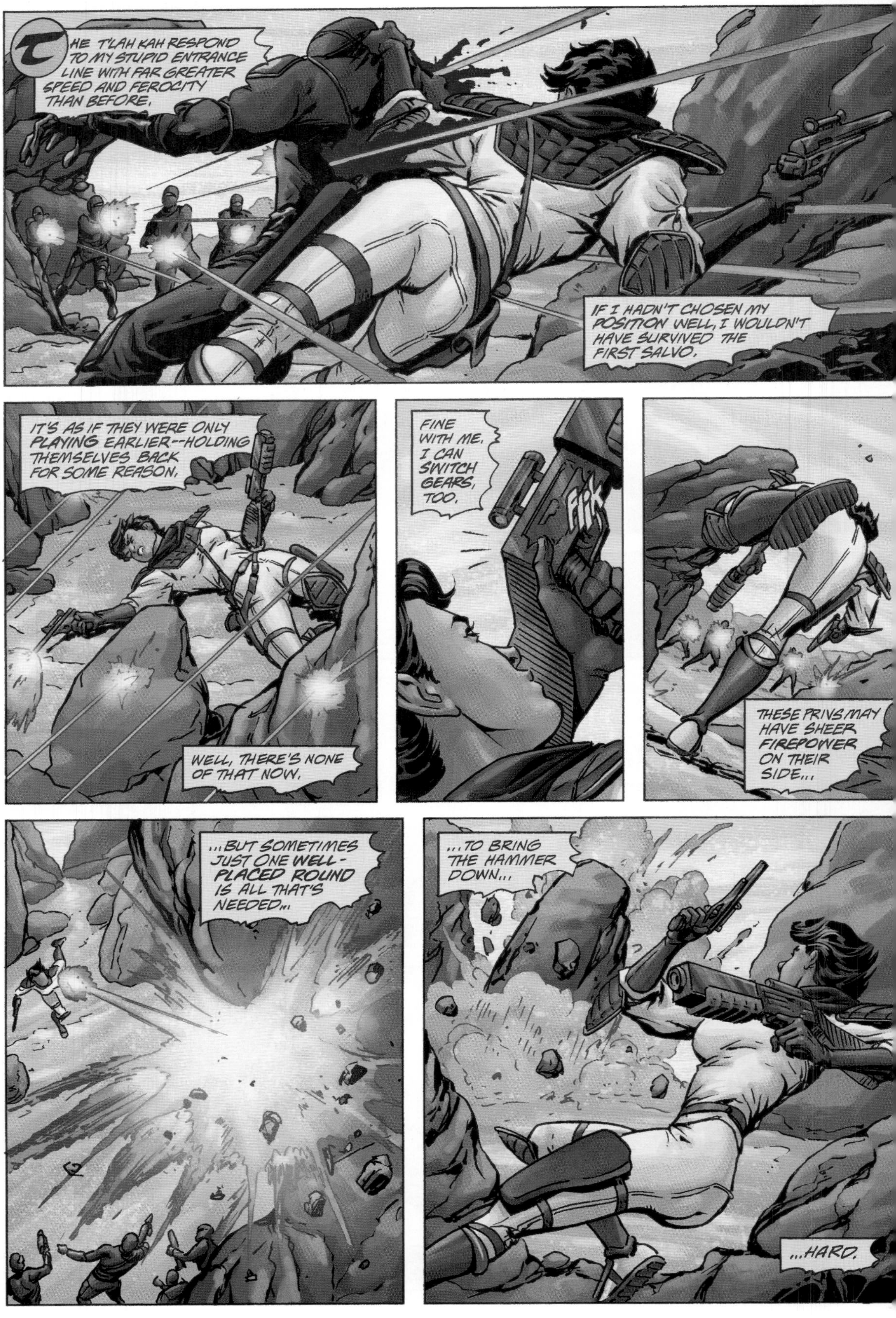
THE T'LAH KAH RESPOND TO MY STUPID ENTRANCE LINE WITH FAR GREATER SPEED AND FEROCITY THAN BEFORE.
IF I HADN'T CHOSEN MY POSITION WELL, I WOULDN'T HAVE SURVIVED THE FIRST SALVO.
IT'S AS IF THEY WERE ONLY PLAYING EARLIER--HOLDING THEMSELVES BACK FOR SOME REASON.
WELL, THERE'S NONE OF THAT NOW.
FINE WITH ME. I CAN SWITCH GEARS, TOO.
FLIK
THESE PRIVS MAY HAVE SHEER FIREPOWER ON THEIR SIDE...
...BUT SOMETIMES JUST ONE WELL-PLACED ROUND IS ALL THAT'S NEEDED...
...TO BRING THE HAMMER DOWN...
...HARD.

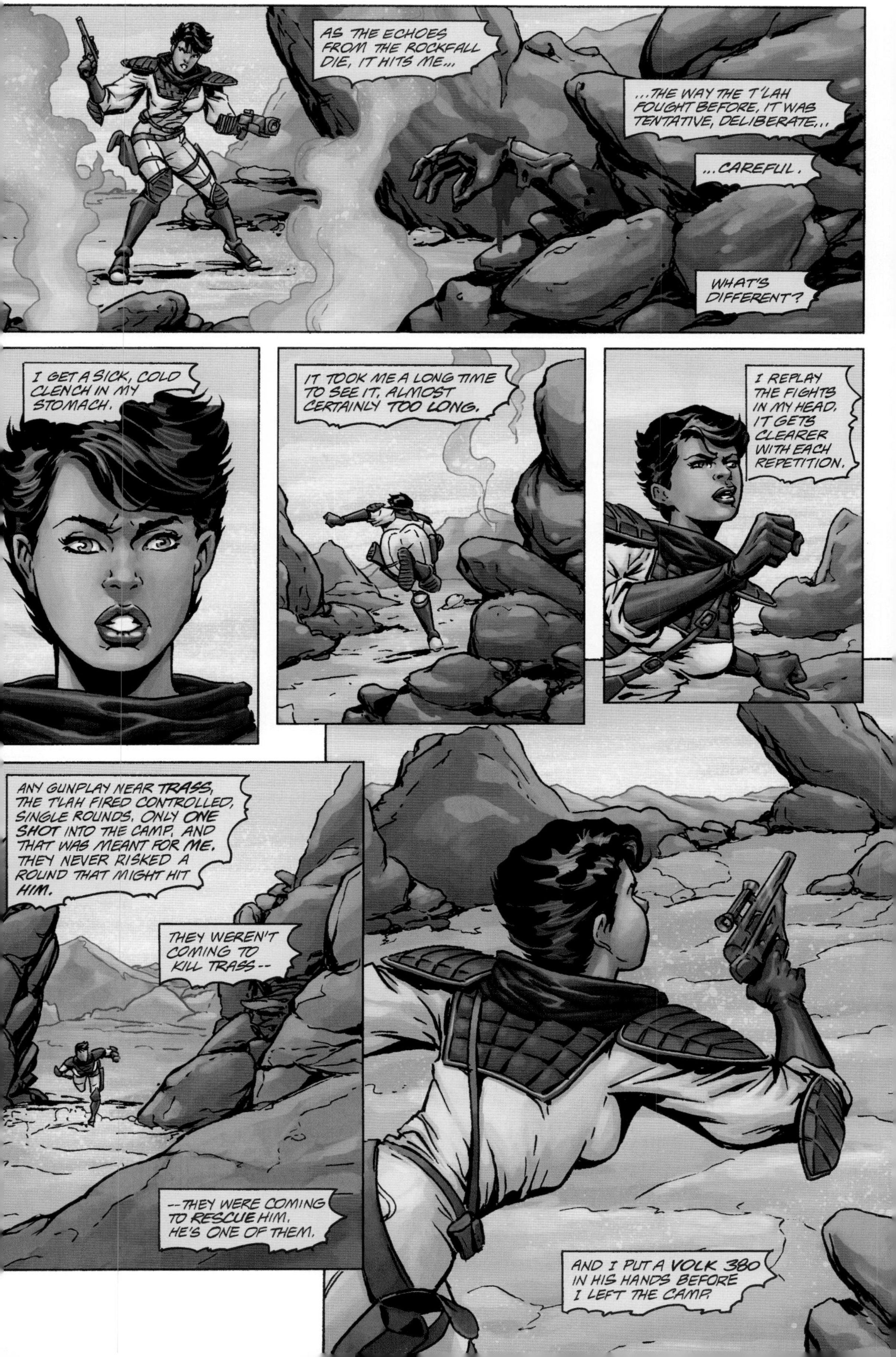
AS THE ECHOES FROM THE ROCKFALL DIE, IT HITS ME...
...THE WAY THE T'LAH FOUGHT BEFORE, IT WAS TENTATIVE, DELIBERATE...
...CAREFUL.
WHAT'S DIFFERENT?
I GET A SICK, COLD CLENCH IN MY STOMACH.
IT TOOK ME A LONG TIME TO SEE IT, ALMOST CERTAINLY TOO LONG.
I REPLAY THE FIGHTS IN MY HEAD. IT GETS CLEARER WITH EACH REPETITION.
ANY GUNPLAY NEAR TRASS, THE T'LAH FIRED CONTROLLED, SINGLE ROUNDS. ONLY ONE SHOT INTO THE CAMP, AND THAT WAS MEANT FOR ME. THEY NEVER RISKED A ROUND THAT MIGHT HIT HIM.
THEY WEREN'T COMING TO KILL TRASS--
--THEY WERE COMING TO RESCUE HIM. HE'S ONE OF THEM.
AND I PUT A VOLK 380 IN HIS HANDS BEFORE I LEFT THE CAMP.

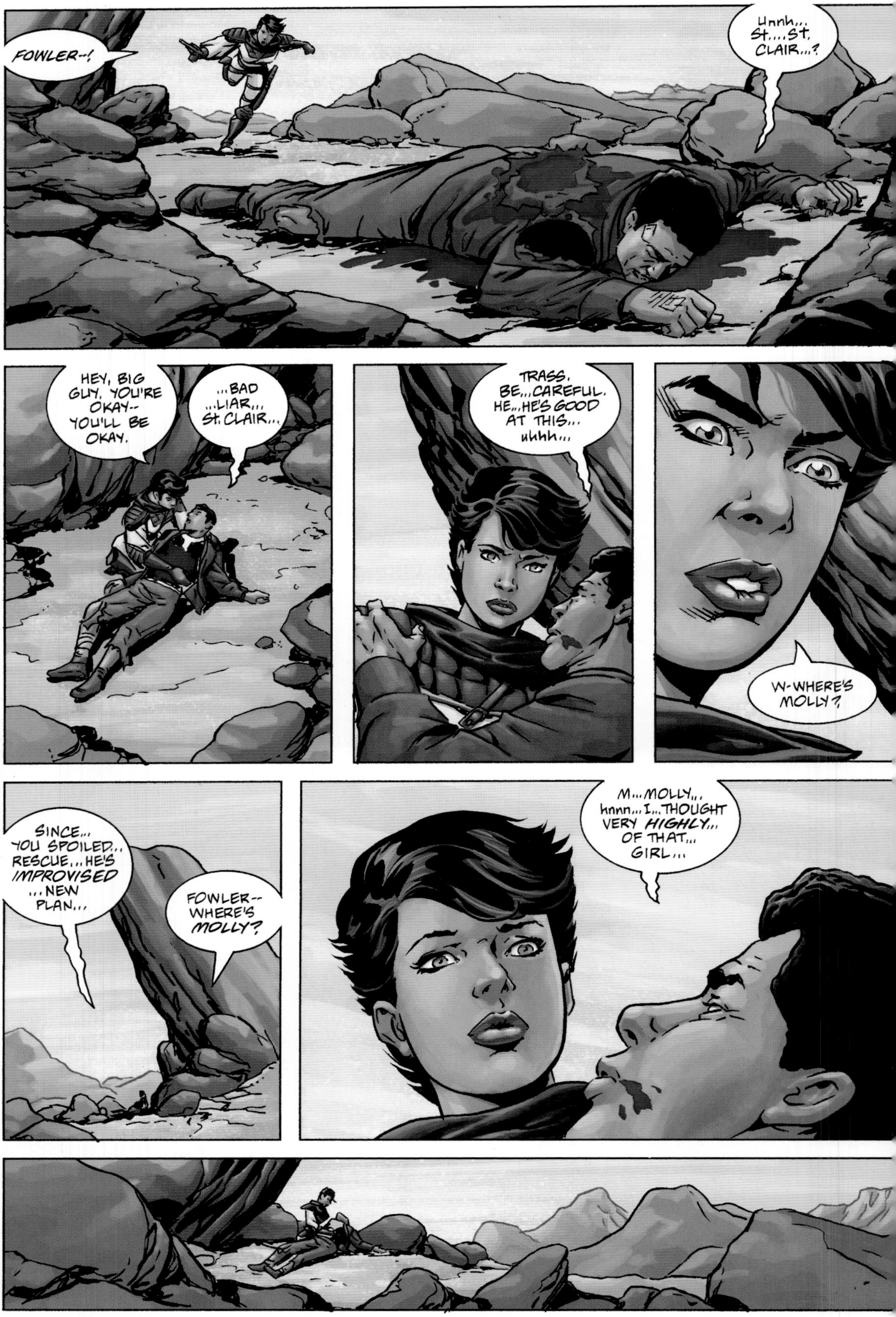
FOWLER--!
Unnh... St....St, CLAIR...?
HEY, BIG GUY, YOU'RE OKAY-- YOU'LL BE OKAY.
...BAD ...LIAR... St. CLAIR...
TRASS. BE...CAREFUL. HE...HE'S GOOD AT THIS... uhhh...
W-WHERE'S MOLLY?
SINCE... YOU SPOILED... RESCUE... HE'S IMPROVISED ...NEW PLAN...
FOWLER-- WHERE'S MOLLY?
M...MOLLY... hnnn... I...THOUGHT VERY HIGHLY... OF THAT... GIRL...

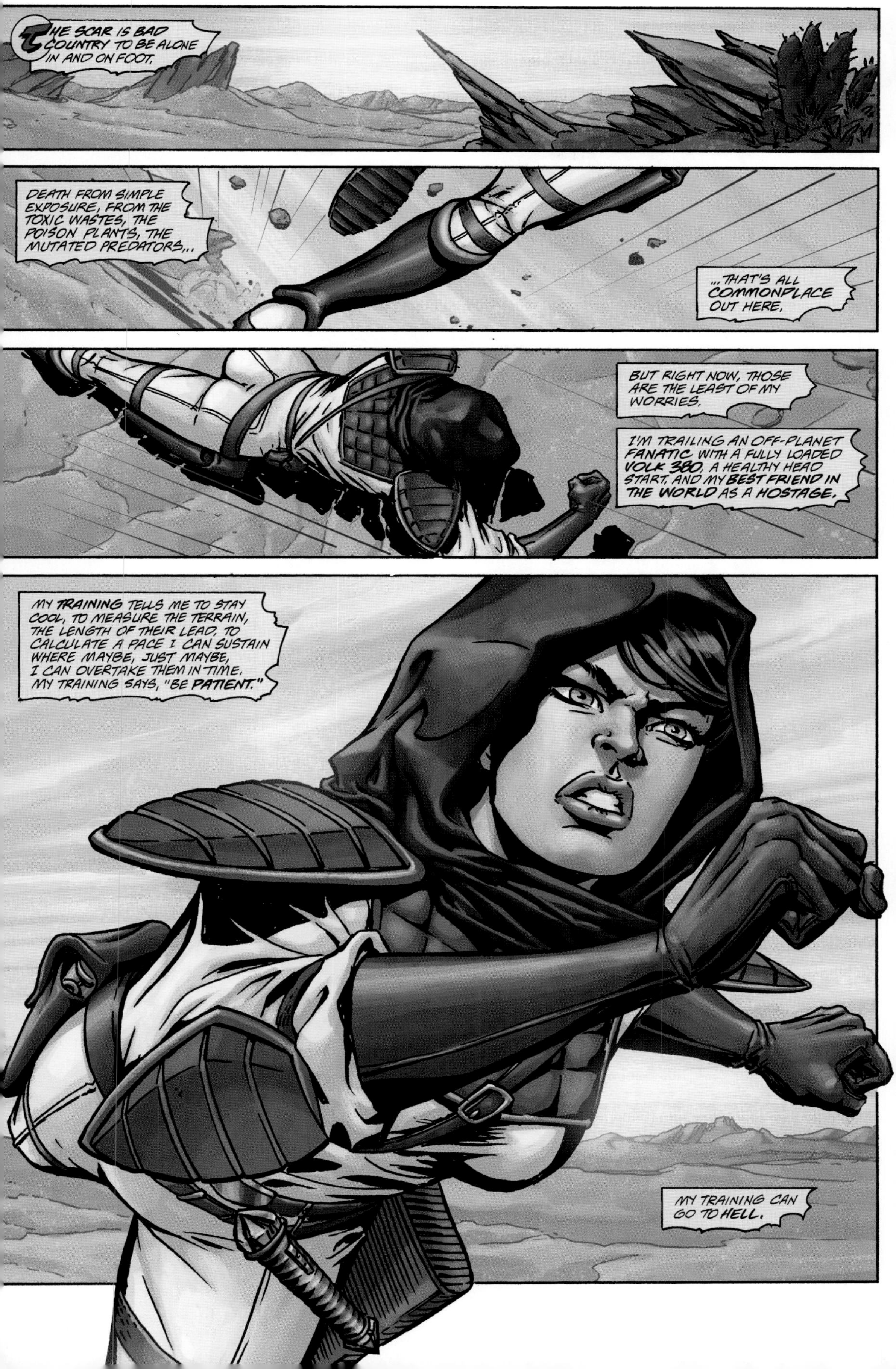
THE SCAR IS BAD COUNTRY TO BE ALONE IN AND ON FOOT.
DEATH FROM SIMPLE EXPOSURE, FROM THE TOXIC WASTES, THE POISON PLANTS, THE MUTATED PREDATORS...
...THAT'S ALL COMMONPLACE OUT HERE.
BUT RIGHT NOW, THOSE ARE THE LEAST OF MY WORRIES.
I'M TRAILING AN OFF-PLANET FANATIC WITH A FULLY LOADED VOLK 380, A HEALTHY HEAD START, AND MY BEST FRIEND IN THE WORLD AS A HOSTAGE.
MY TRAINING TELLS ME TO STAY COOL, TO MEASURE THE TERRAIN, THE LENGTH OF THEIR LEAD, TO CALCULATE A PACE I CAN SUSTAIN WHERE MAYBE, JUST MAYBE, I CAN OVERTAKE THEM IN TIME. MY TRAINING SAYS, "BE PATIENT."
MY TRAINING CAN GO TO HELL.

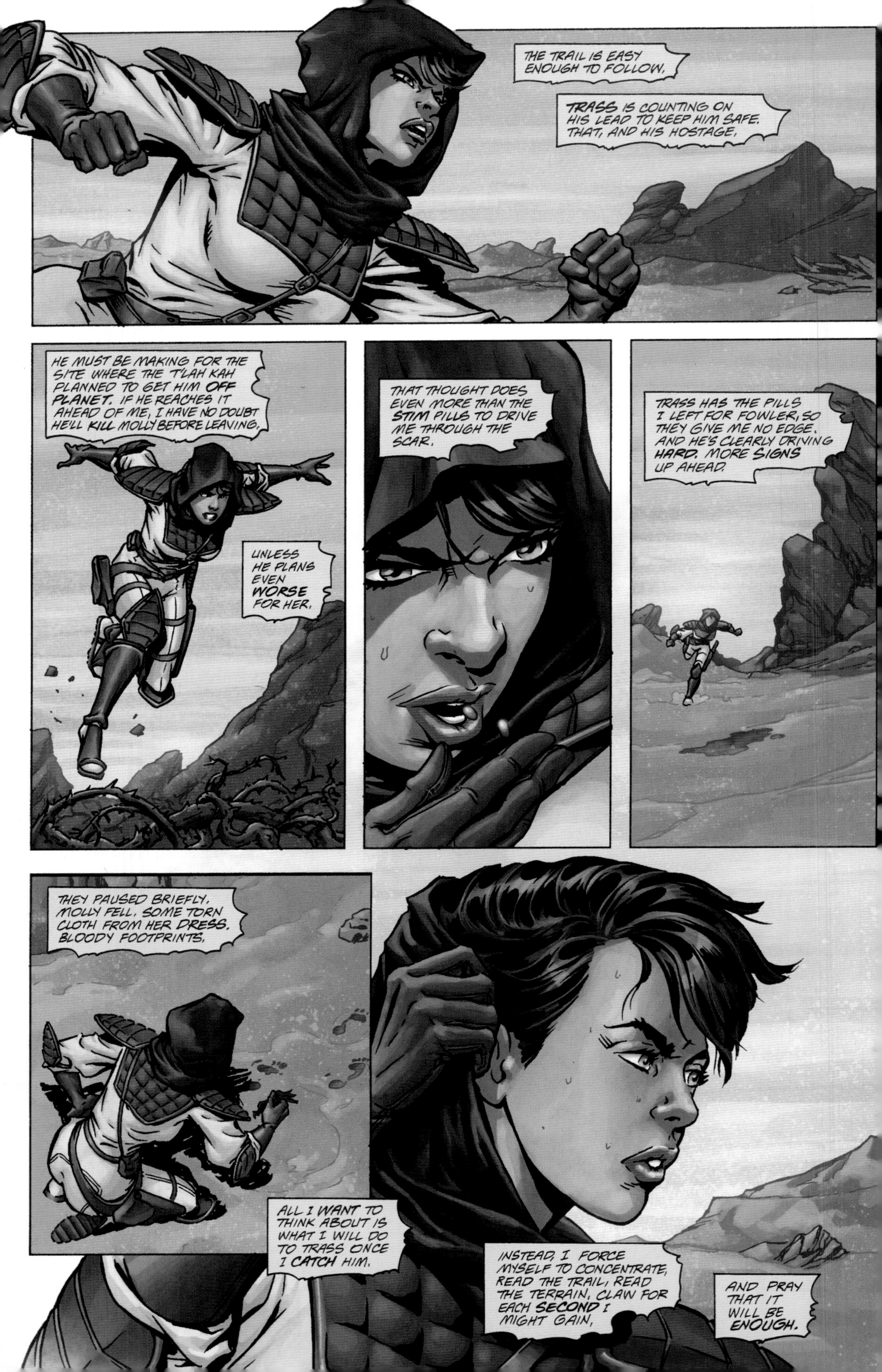
THE TRAIL IS EASY ENOUGH TO FOLLOW.
TRASS IS COUNTING ON HIS LEAD TO KEEP HIM SAFE. THAT, AND HIS HOSTAGE.
HE MUST BE MAKING FOR THE SITE WHERE THE T'LAH KAH PLANNED TO GET HIM OFF PLANET. IF HE REACHES IT AHEAD OF ME, I HAVE NO DOUBT HE'LL KILL MOLLY BEFORE LEAVING.
UNLESS HE PLANS EVEN WORSE FOR HER.
THAT THOUGHT DOES EVEN MORE THAN THE STIM PILLS TO DRIVE ME THROUGH THE SCAR.
TRASS HAS THE PILLS I LEFT FOR FOWLER, SO THEY GIVE ME NO EDGE. AND HE'S CLEARLY DRIVING HARD. MORE SIGNS UP AHEAD.
THEY PAUSED BRIEFLY. MOLLY FELL. SOME TORN CLOTH FROM HER DRESS. BLOODY FOOTPRINTS.
ALL I WANT TO THINK ABOUT IS WHAT I WILL DO TO TRASS ONCE I CATCH HIM.
INSTEAD, I FORCE MYSELF TO CONCENTRATE, READ THE TRAIL, READ THE TERRAIN, CLAW FOR EACH SECOND I MIGHT GAIN,
AND PRAY THAT IT WILL BE ENOUGH.

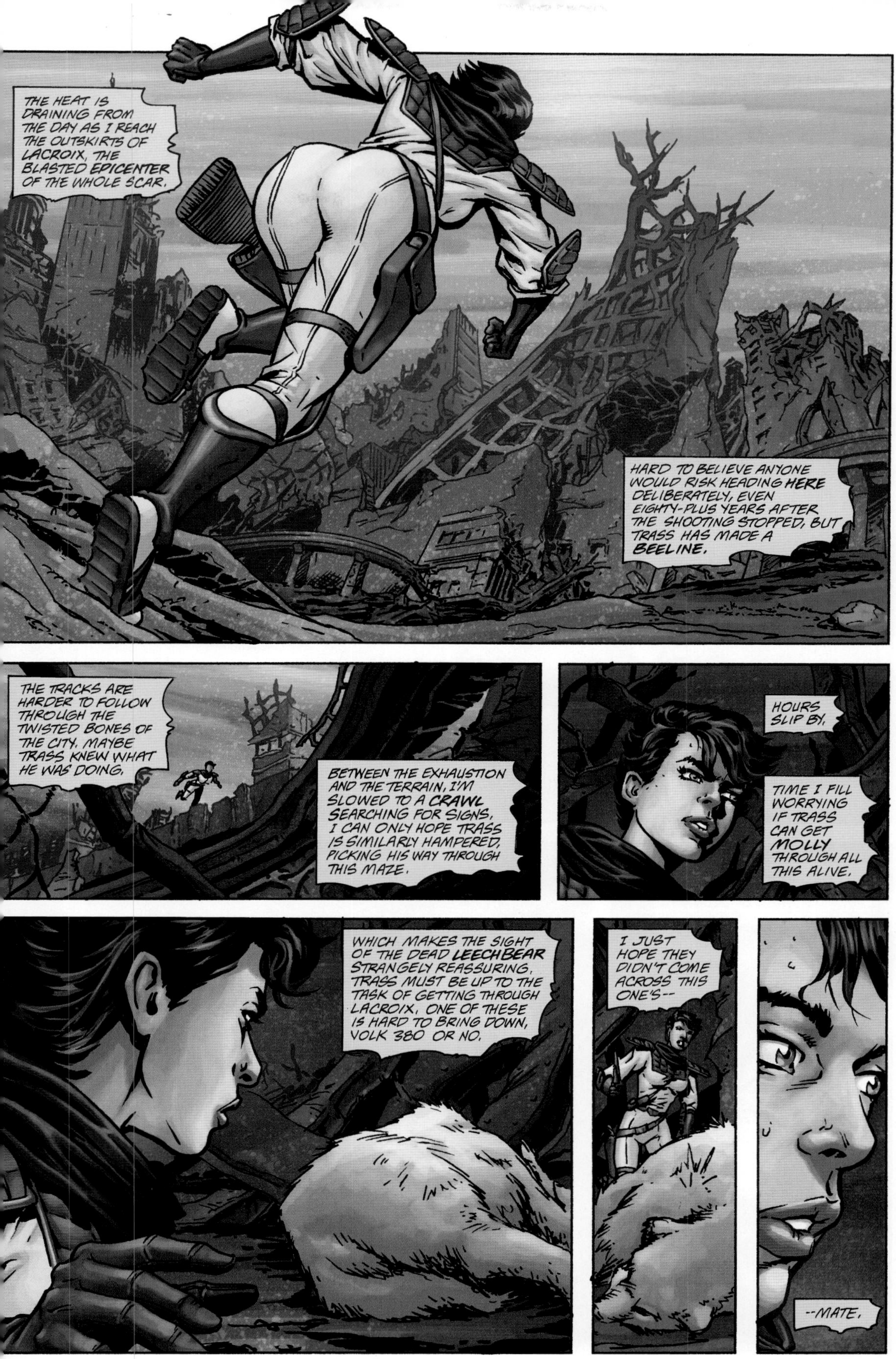
THE HEAT IS DRAINING FROM THE DAY AS I REACH THE OUTSKIRTS OF LACROIX, THE BLASTED EPICENTER OF THE WHOLE SCAR.
HARD TO BELIEVE ANYONE WOULD RISK HEADING HERE DELIBERATELY, EVEN EIGHTY-PLUS YEARS AFTER THE SHOOTING STOPPED, BUT TRASS HAS MADE A BEELINE.
THE TRACKS ARE HARDER TO FOLLOW THROUGH THE TWISTED BONES OF THE CITY. MAYBE TRASS KNEW WHAT HE WAS DOING.
BETWEEN THE EXHAUSTION AND THE TERRAIN, I'M SLOWED TO A CRAWL SEARCHING FOR SIGNS. I CAN ONLY HOPE TRASS IS SIMILARLY HAMPERED, PICKING HIS WAY THROUGH THIS MAZE.
HOURS SLIP BY.
TIME I FILL WORRYING IF TRASS CAN GET MOLLY THROUGH ALL THIS ALIVE.
WHICH MAKES THE SIGHT OF THE DEAD LEECHBEAR STRANGELY REASSURING. TRASS MUST BE UP TO THE TASK OF GETTING THROUGH LACROIX. ONE OF THESE IS HARD TO BRING DOWN, VOLK 380 OR NO.
I JUST HOPE THEY DIDN'T COME ACROSS THIS ONE'S--
--MATE.

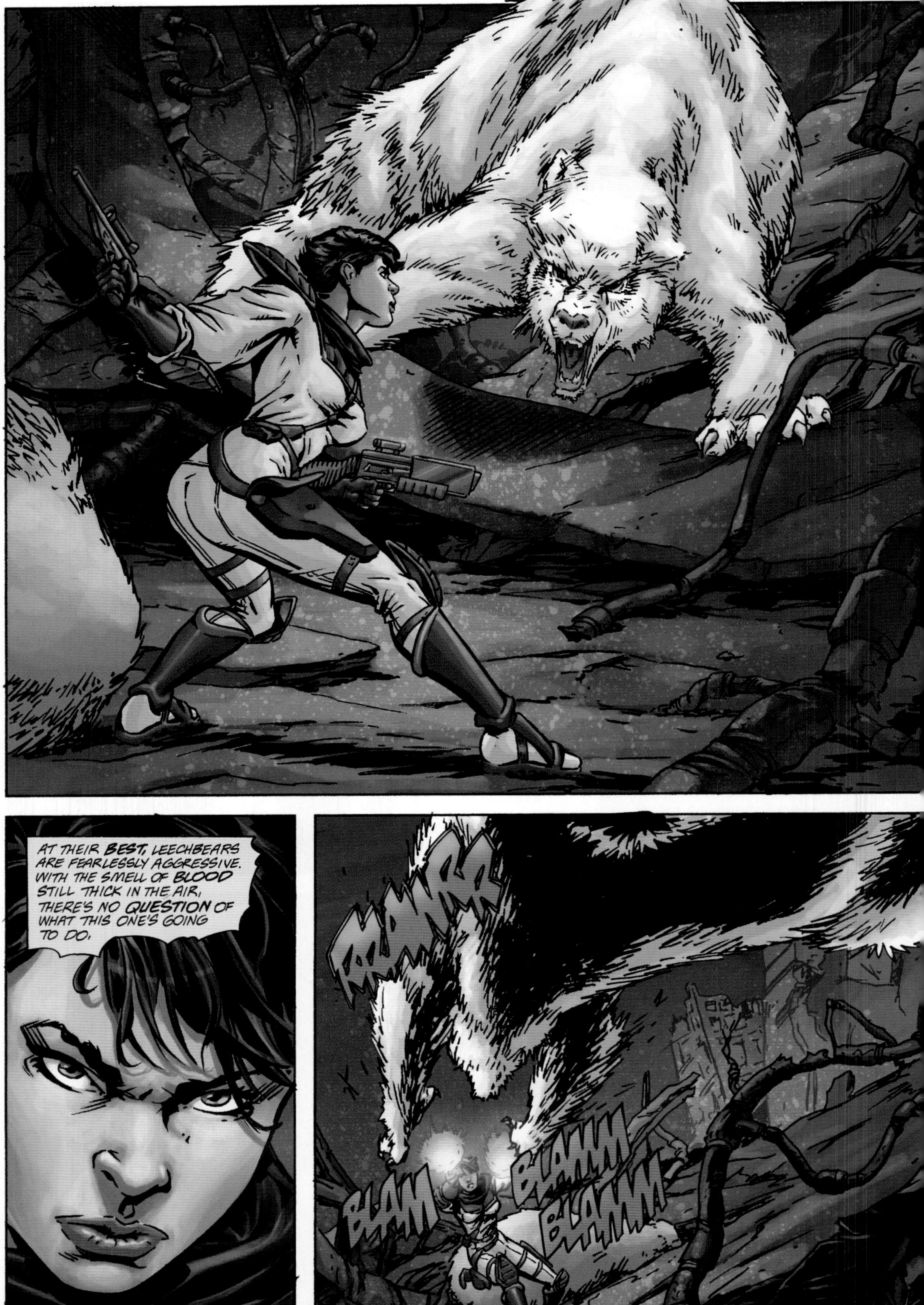
AT THEIR BEST, LEECHBEARS ARE FEARLESSLY AGGRESSIVE. WITH THE SMELL OF BLOOD STILL THICK IN THE AIR, THERE'S NO QUESTION OF WHAT THIS ONE'S GOING TO DO.
BLAM
BLAMM
BLAMM

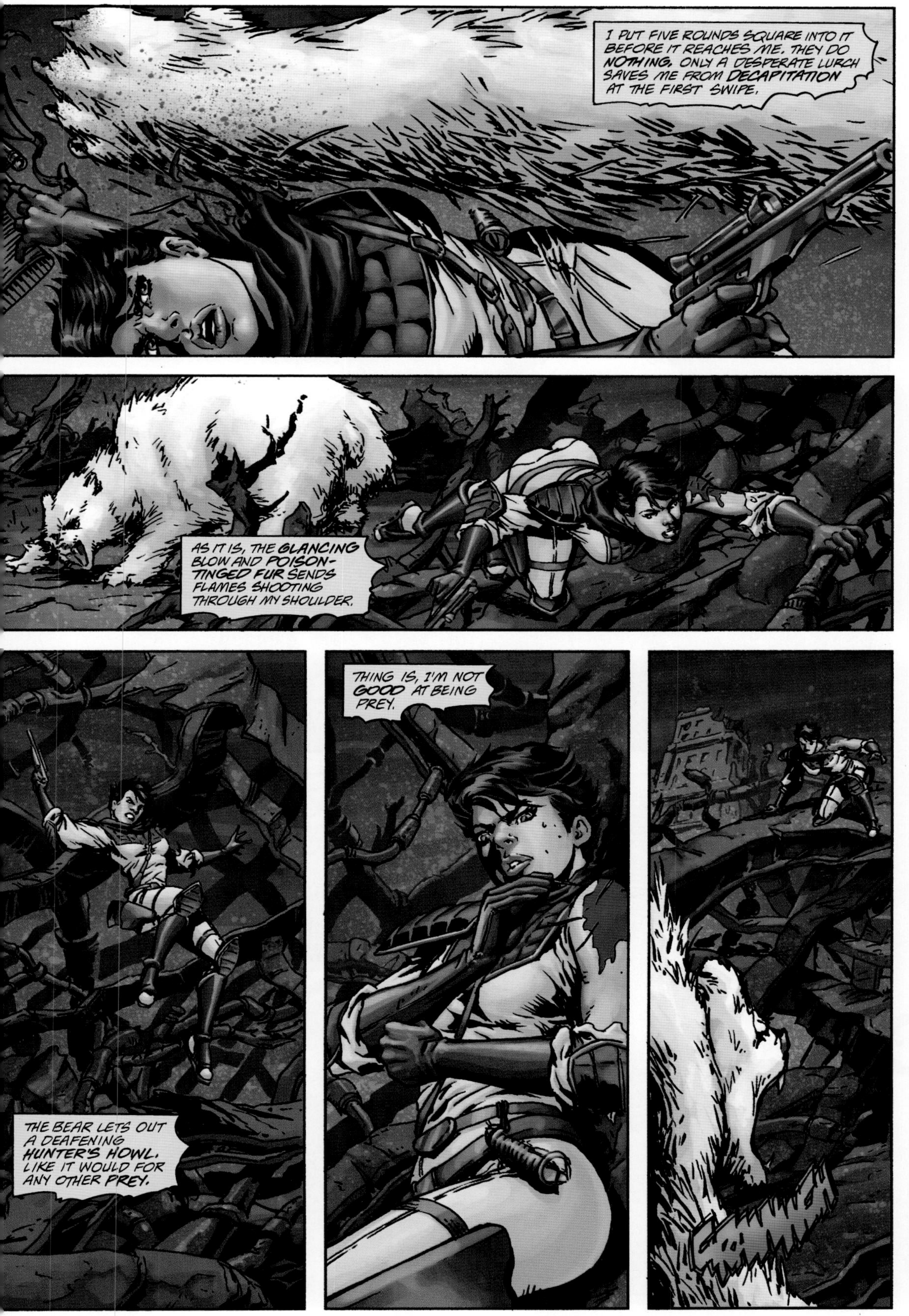
I PUT FIVE ROUNDS SQUARE INTO IT BEFORE IT REACHES ME. THEY DO NOTHING. ONLY A DESPERATE LURCH SAVES ME FROM DECAPITATION AT THE FIRST SWIPE.
AS IT IS, THE GLANCING BLOW AND POISON-TINGED FUR SENDS FLAMES SHOOTING THROUGH MY SHOULDER.
THE BEAR LETS OUT A DEAFENING HUNTER'S HOWL, LIKE IT WOULD FOR ANY OTHER PREY.
THING IS, I'M NOT GOOD AT BEING PREY.

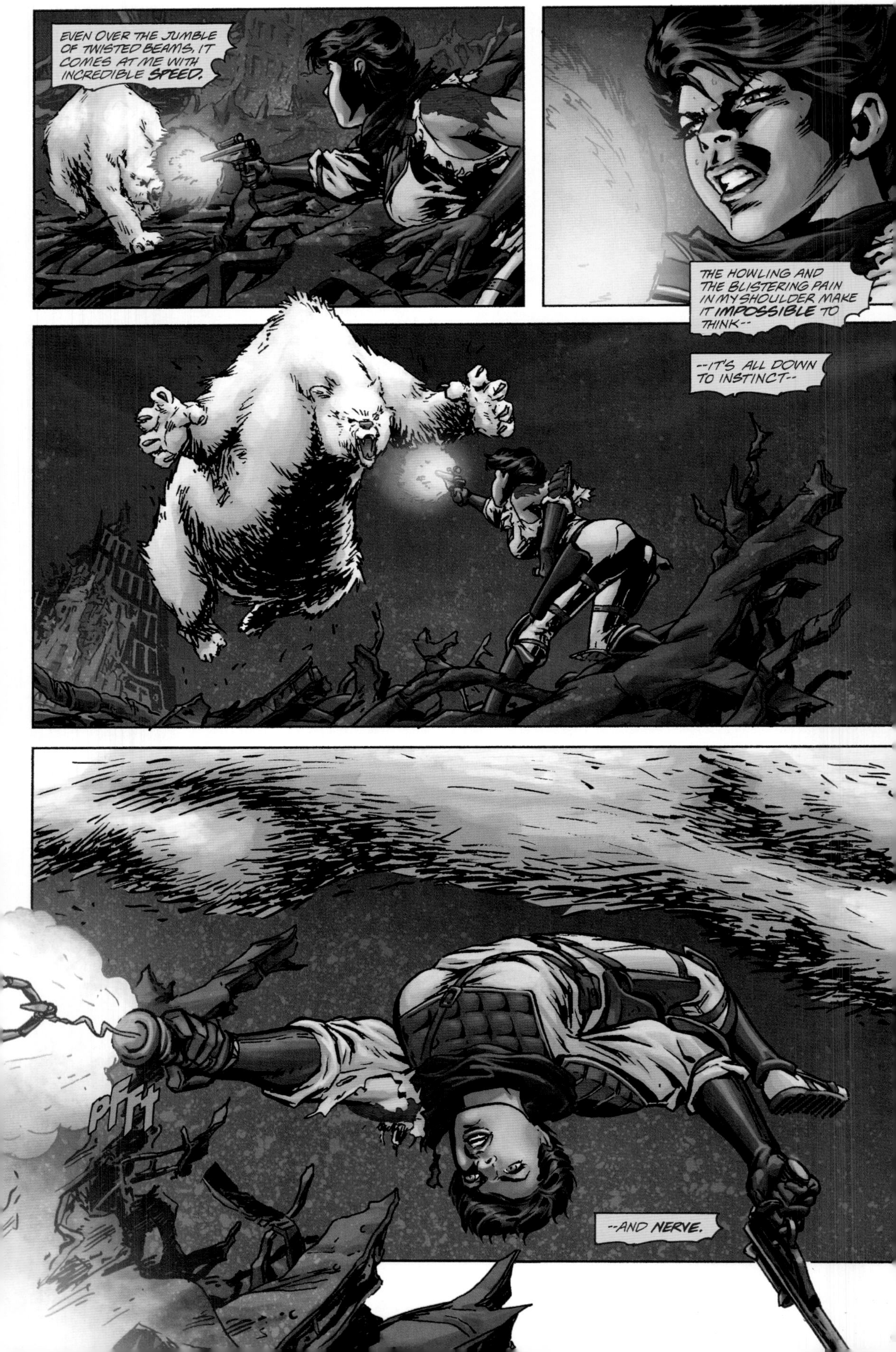
EVEN OVER THE JUMBLE OF TWISTED BEAMS, IT COMES AT ME WITH INCREDIBLE SPEED.
THE HOWLING AND THE BLISTERING PAIN IN MY SHOULDER MAKE IT IMPOSSIBLE TO THINK--
--IT'S ALL DOWN TO INSTINCT--
PFFT
--AND NERVE.

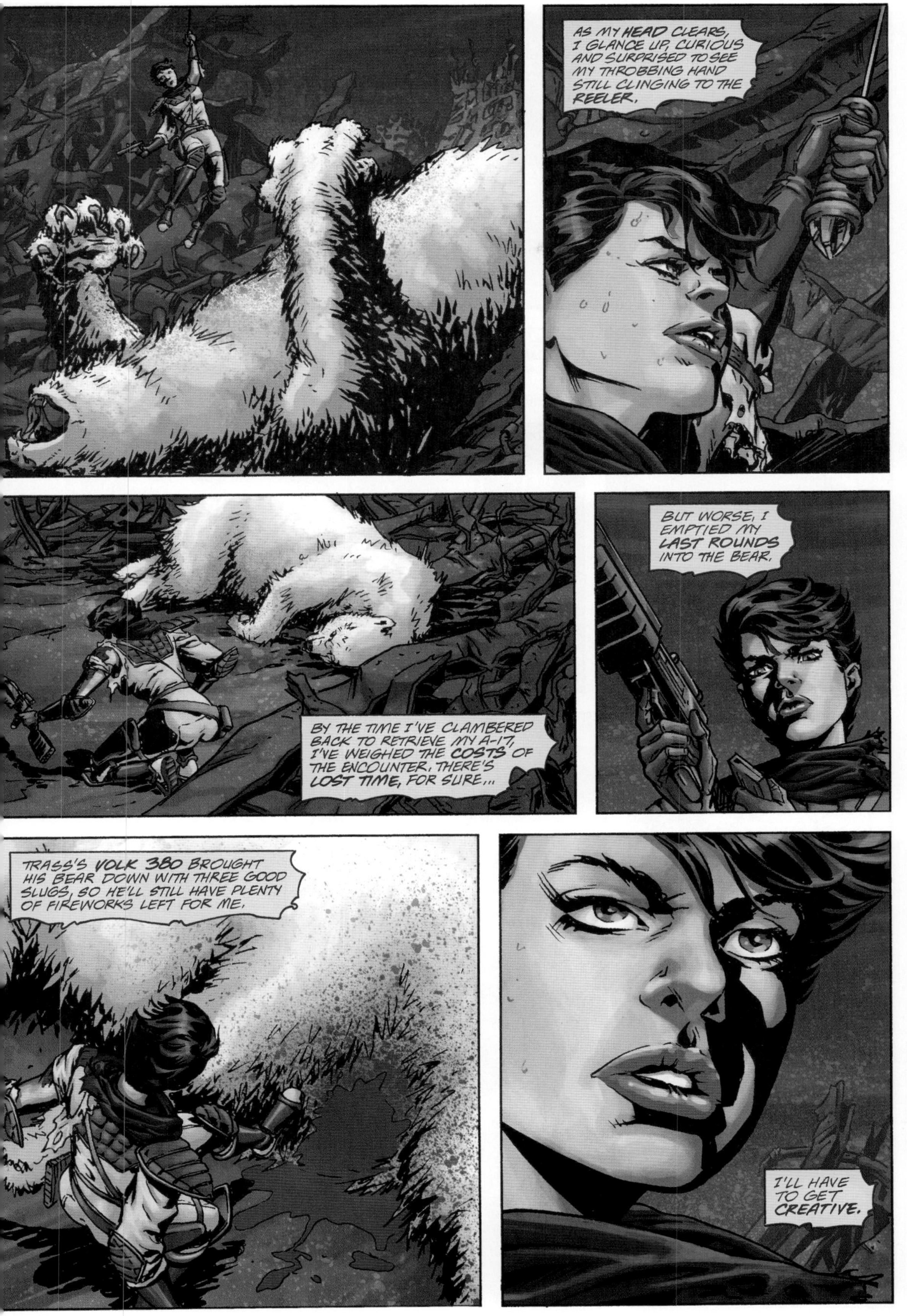
AS MY HEAD CLEARS, I GLANCE UP, CURIOUS AND SURPRISED TO SEE MY THROBBING HAND STILL CLINGING TO THE REELER.
BY THE TIME I'VE CLAMBERED BACK TO RETRIEVE MY A-17, I'VE WEIGHED THE COSTS OF THE ENCOUNTER. THERE'S LOST TIME, FOR SURE...
BUT WORSE, I EMPTIED MY LAST ROUNDS INTO THE BEAR.
TRASS'S VOLK 380 BROUGHT HIS BEAR DOWN WITH THREE GOOD SLUGS, SO HE'LL STILL HAVE PLENTY OF FIREWORKS LEFT FOR ME.
I'LL HAVE TO GET CREATIVE.

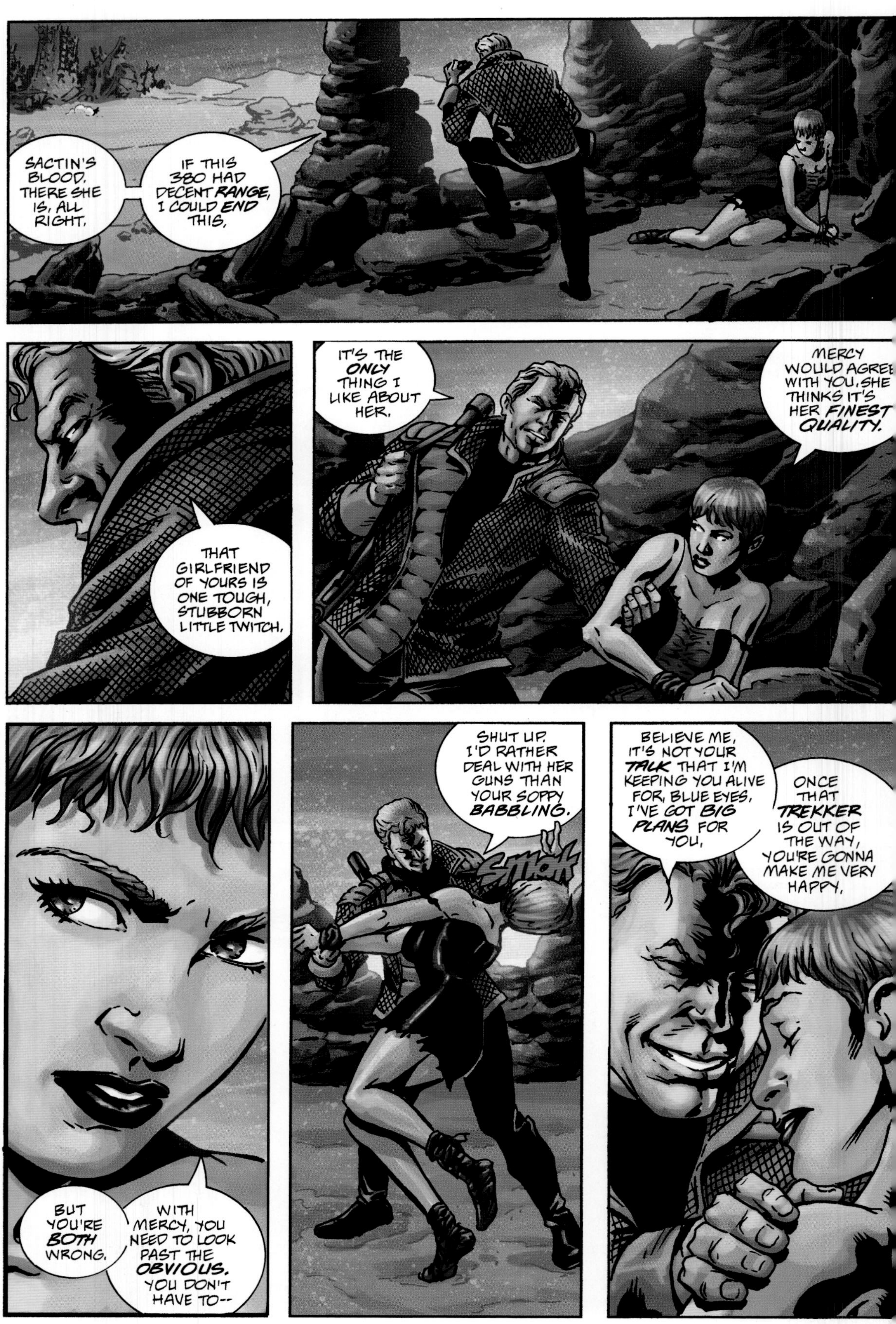

SACTIN'S BLOOD, THERE SHE IS, ALL RIGHT.
IF THIS 380 HAD DECENT *RANGE*, I COULD *END* THIS.
THAT GIRLFRIEND OF YOURS IS ONE TOUGH, STUBBORN LITTLE TWITCH.
IT'S THE *ONLY* THING I LIKE ABOUT HER.
MERCY WOULD AGREE WITH YOU. SHE THINKS IT'S HER *FINEST QUALITY.*
BUT YOU'RE *BOTH* WRONG.
WITH MERCY, YOU NEED TO LOOK PAST THE *OBVIOUS.* YOU DON'T HAVE TO--
SHUT UP. I'D RATHER DEAL WITH HER GUNS THAN YOUR SOPPY *BABBLING.*
SMACK
BELIEVE ME, IT'S NOT YOUR *TALK* THAT I'M KEEPING YOU ALIVE FOR, BLUE EYES. I'VE GOT *BIG PLANS* FOR YOU.
ONCE THAT *TREKKER* IS OUT OF THE WAY, YOU'RE GONNA MAKE ME VERY HAPPY.

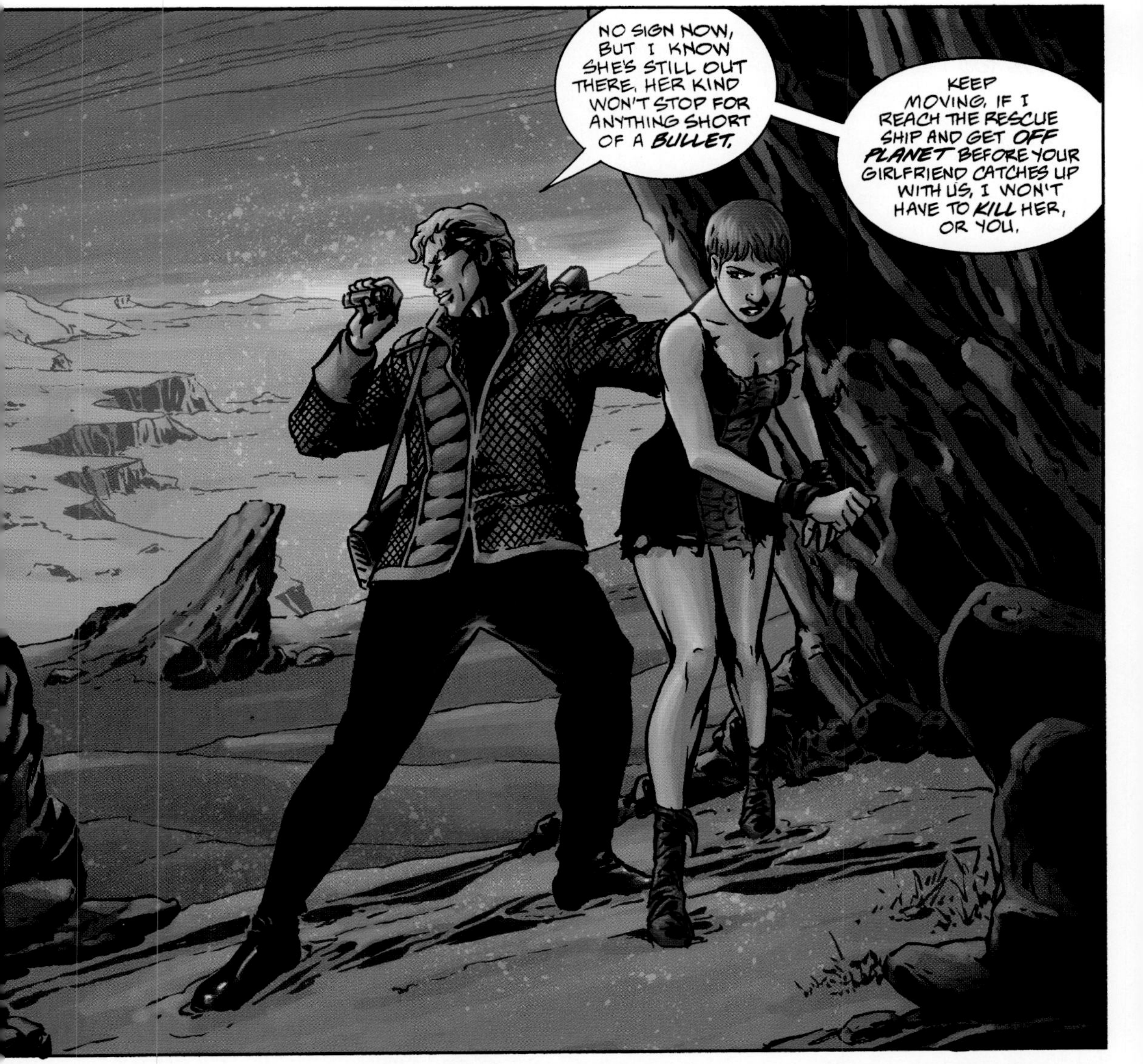
NO SIGN NOW, BUT I KNOW SHE'S STILL OUT THERE. HER KIND WON'T STOP FOR ANYTHING SHORT OF A BULLET.
KEEP MOVING. IF I REACH THE RESCUE SHIP AND GET OFF PLANET BEFORE YOUR GIRLFRIEND CATCHES UP WITH US, I WON'T HAVE TO KILL HER, OR YOU.

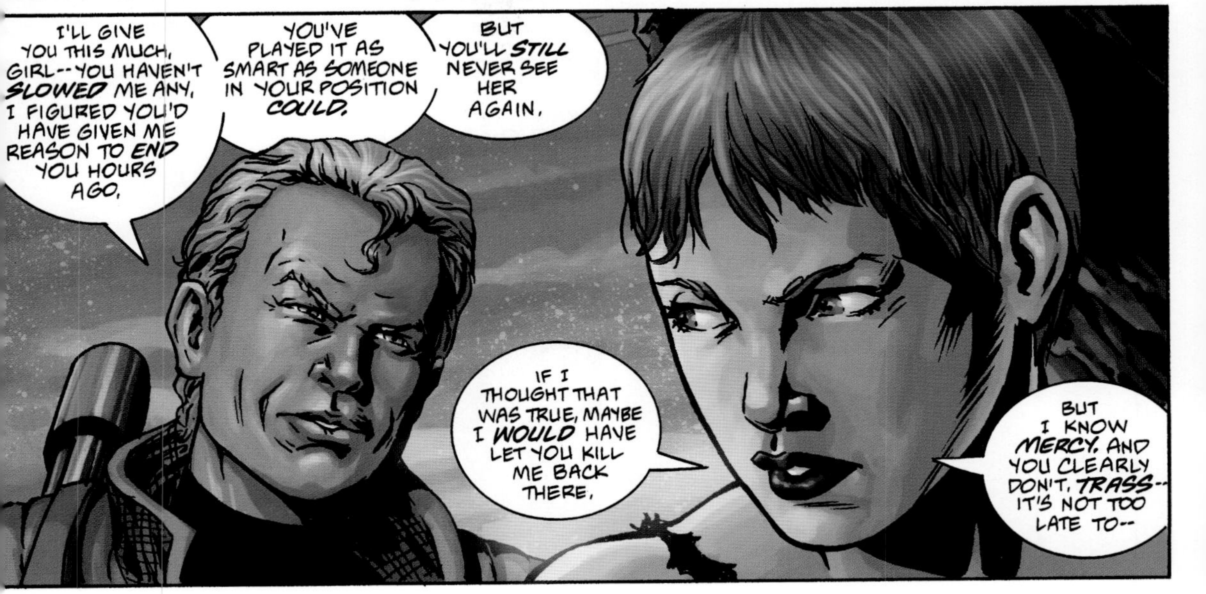
I'LL GIVE YOU THIS MUCH, GIRL-- YOU HAVEN'T SLOWED ME ANY. I FIGURED YOU'D HAVE GIVEN ME REASON TO END YOU HOURS AGO.
YOU'VE PLAYED IT AS SMART AS SOMEONE IN YOUR POSITION COULD.
BUT YOU'LL STILL NEVER SEE HER AGAIN.
IF I THOUGHT THAT WAS TRUE, MAYBE I WOULD HAVE LET YOU KILL ME BACK THERE.
BUT I KNOW MERCY. AND YOU CLEARLY DON'T, TRASS-- IT'S NOT TOO LATE TO--

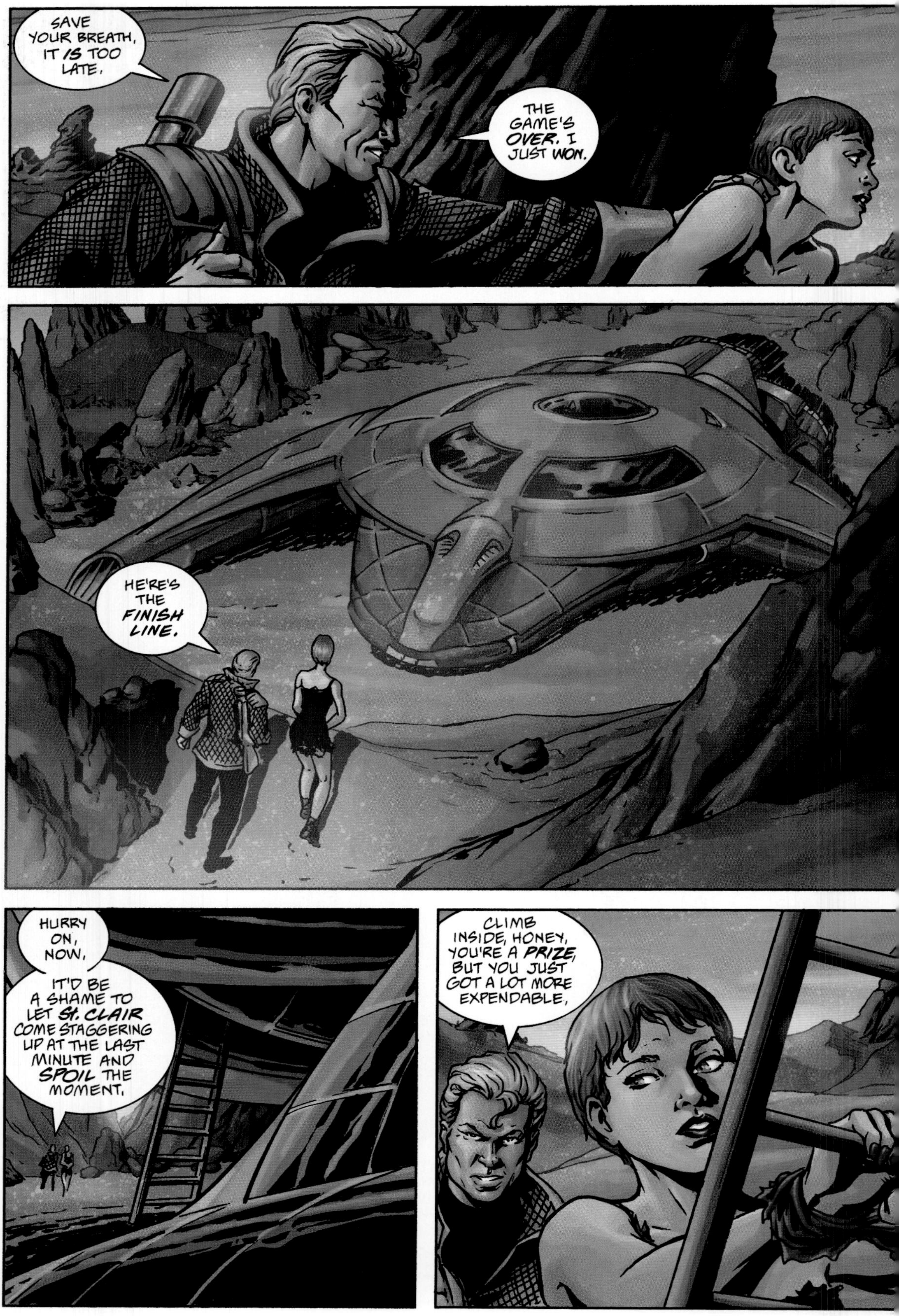

SAVE YOUR BREATH, IT IS TOO LATE.
THE GAME'S OVER. I JUST WON.
HE'RE'S THE FINISH LINE.
HURRY ON, NOW.
IT'D BE A SHAME TO LET St. CLAIR COME STAGGERING UP AT THE LAST MINUTE AND SPOIL THE MOMENT.
CLIMB INSIDE, HONEY. YOU'RE A PRIZE, BUT YOU JUST GOT A LOT MORE EXPENDABLE.

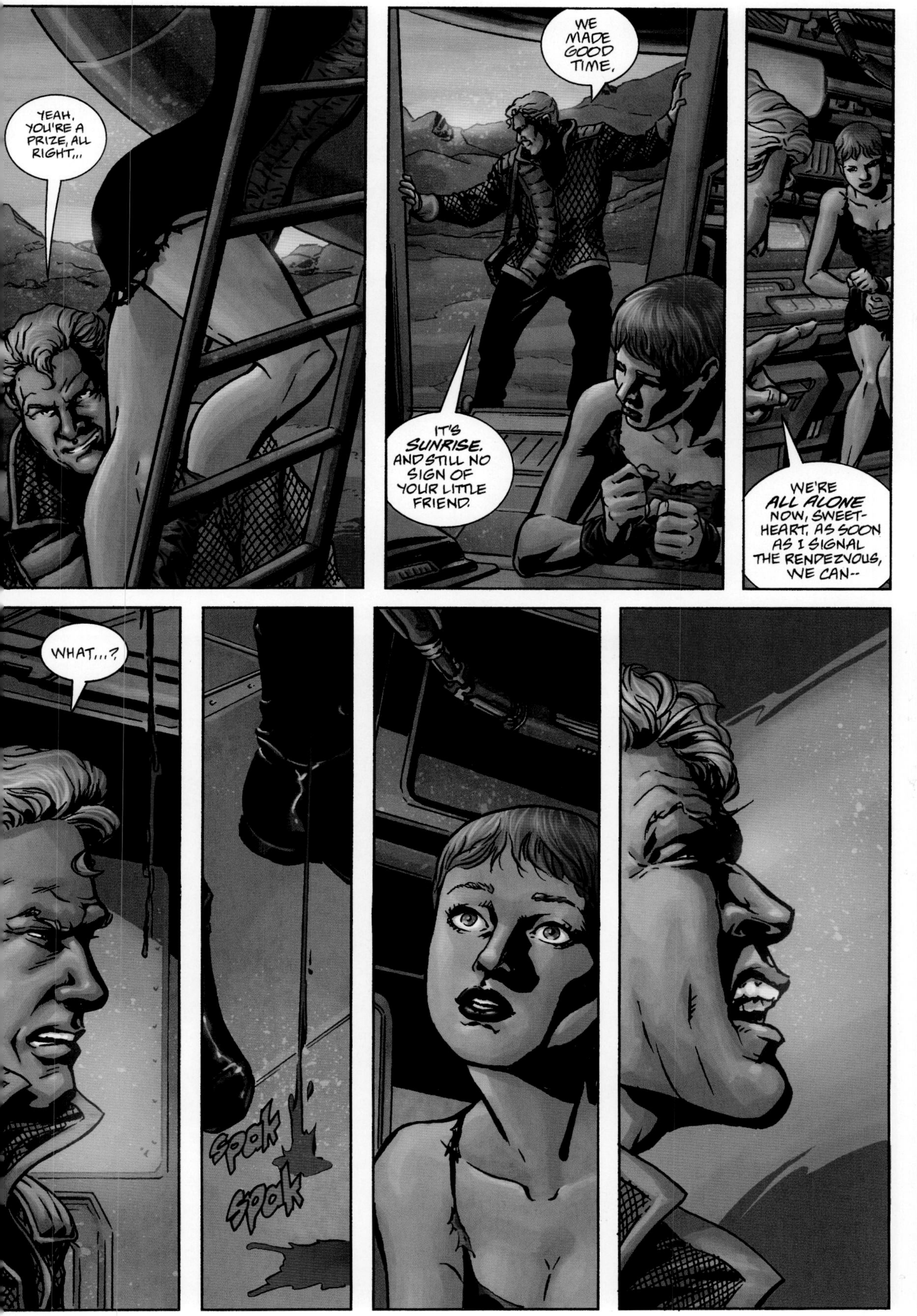
YEAH, YOU'RE A PRIZE, ALL RIGHT...
WE MADE GOOD TIME.
IT'S SUNRISE. AND STILL NO SIGN OF YOUR LITTLE FRIEND.
WE'RE ALL ALONE NOW, SWEET-HEART. AS SOON AS I SIGNAL THE RENDEZVOUS, WE CAN--
WHAT...?
SPAK
SPAK

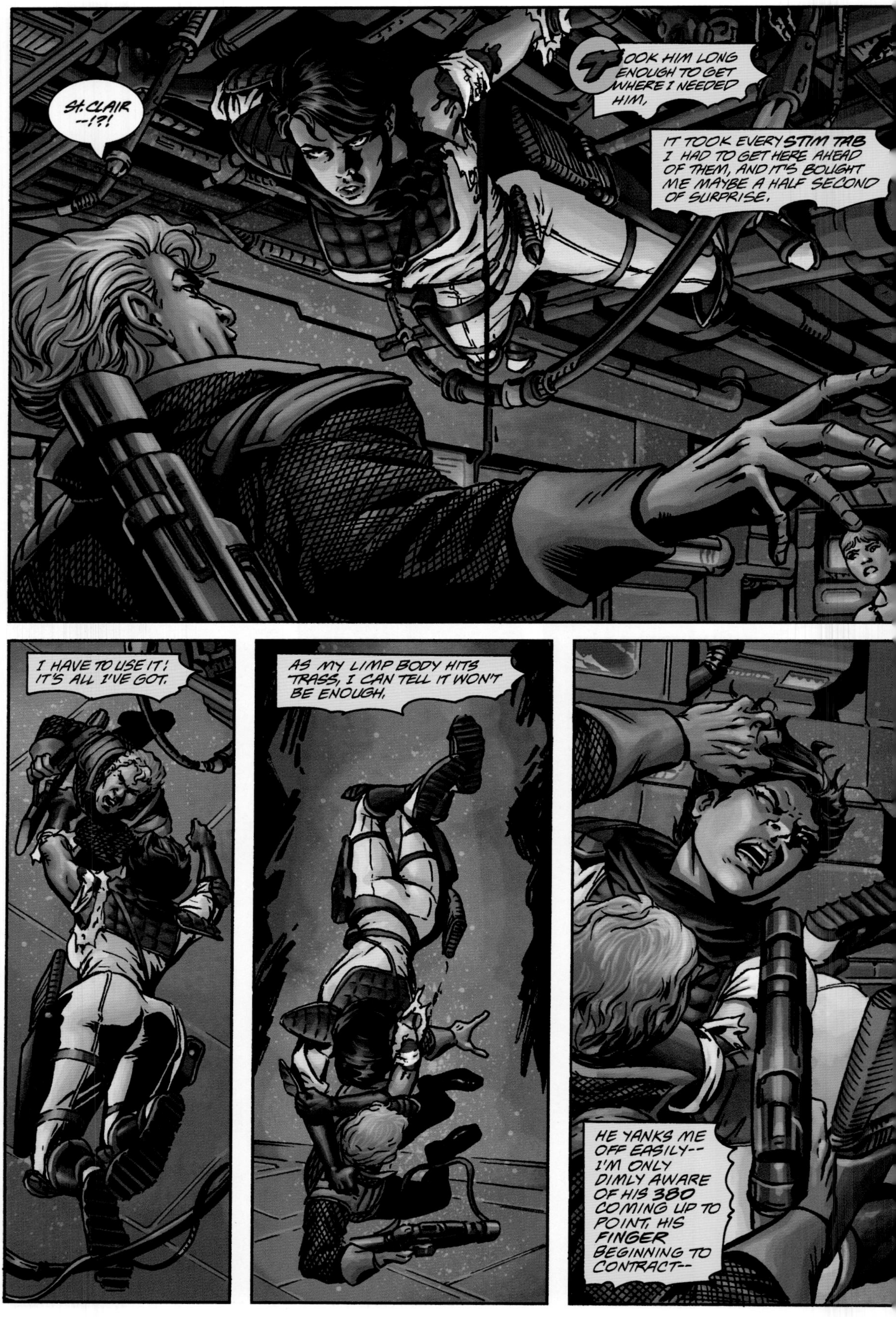
St. CLAIR --!?!
TOOK HIM LONG ENOUGH TO GET WHERE I NEEDED HIM.
IT TOOK EVERY STIM TAB I HAD TO GET HERE AHEAD OF THEM, AND IT'S BOUGHT ME MAYBE A HALF SECOND OF SURPRISE.
I HAVE TO USE IT! IT'S ALL I'VE GOT.
AS MY LIMP BODY HITS TRASS, I CAN TELL IT WON'T BE ENOUGH.
HE YANKS ME OFF EASILY-- I'M ONLY DIMLY AWARE OF HIS 380 COMING UP TO POINT, HIS FINGER BEGINNING TO CONTRACT--

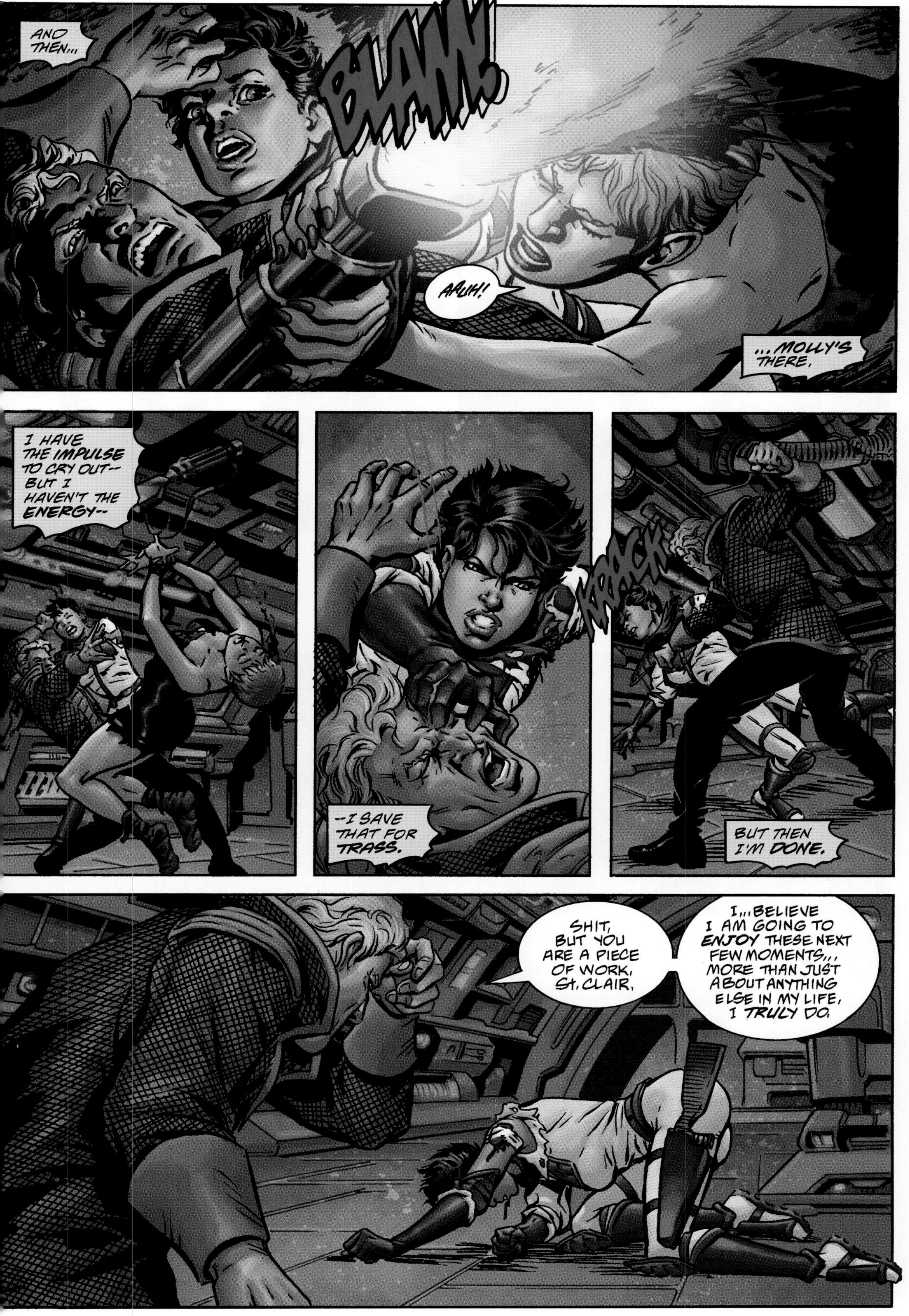

AND THEN...
BLAM!
AAUH!
...MOLLY'S THERE.
I HAVE THE IMPULSE TO CRY OUT-- BUT I HAVEN'T THE ENERGY--
--I SAVE THAT FOR TRASS.
KRAACK
BUT THEN I'M DONE.
SHIT, BUT YOU ARE A PIECE OF WORK, St. CLAIR.
I... BELIEVE I AM GOING TO ENJOY THESE NEXT FEW MOMENTS... MORE THAN JUST ABOUT ANYTHING ELSE IN MY LIFE. I TRULY DO.

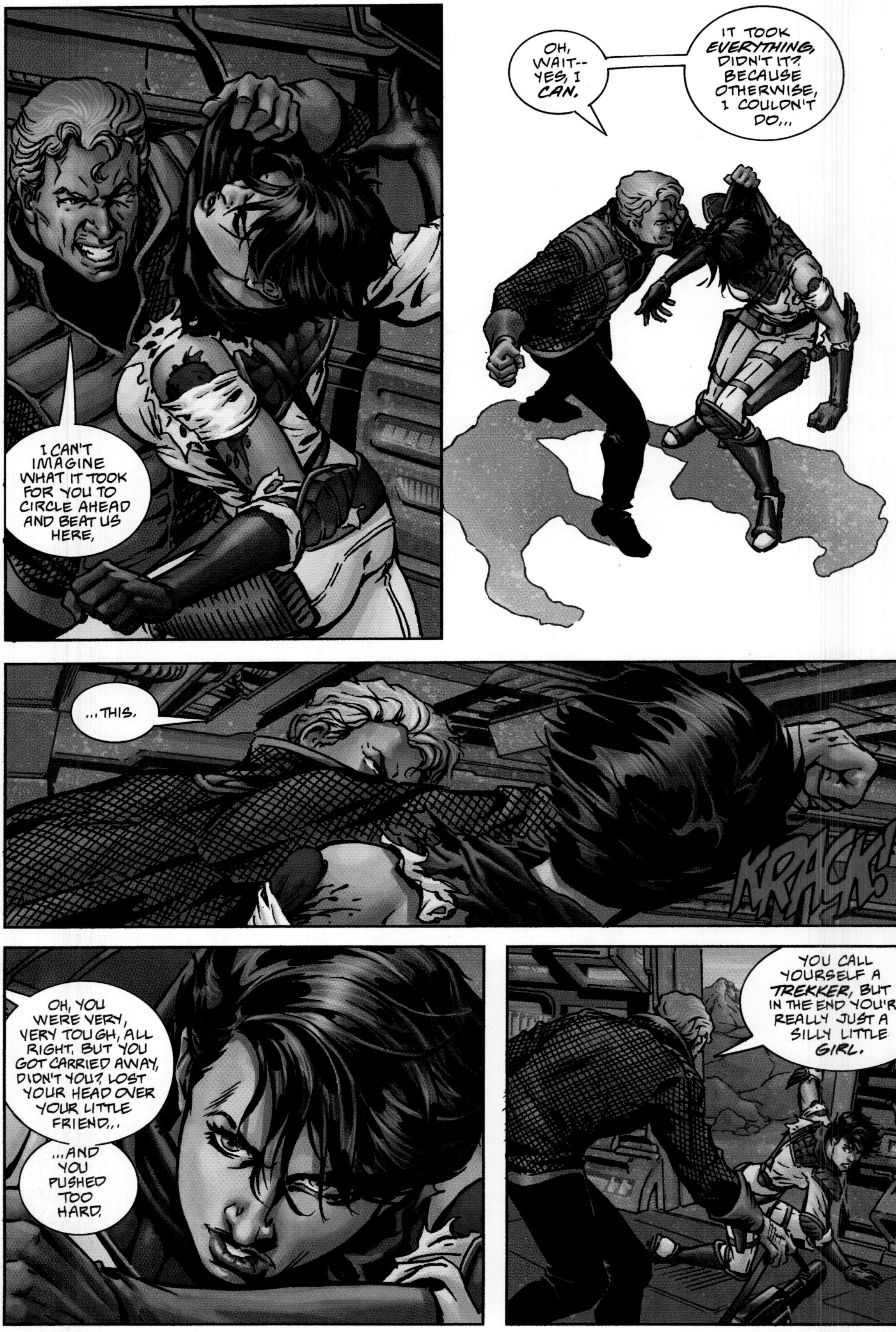
I CAN'T IMAGINE WHAT IT TOOK FOR YOU TO CIRCLE AHEAD AND BEAT US HERE,
OH, WAIT-- YES, I CAN.
IT TOOK EVERYTHING, DIDN'T IT? BECAUSE OTHERWISE, I COULDN'T DO...
...THIS.
KRACK!
OH, YOU WERE VERY, VERY TOUGH, ALL RIGHT, BUT YOU GOT CARRIED AWAY, DIDN'T YOU? LOST YOUR HEAD OVER YOUR LITTLE FRIEND...
...AND YOU PUSHED TOO HARD.
YOU CALL YOURSELF A TREKKER, BUT IN THE END YOU'RE REALLY JUST A SILLY LITTLE GIRL.

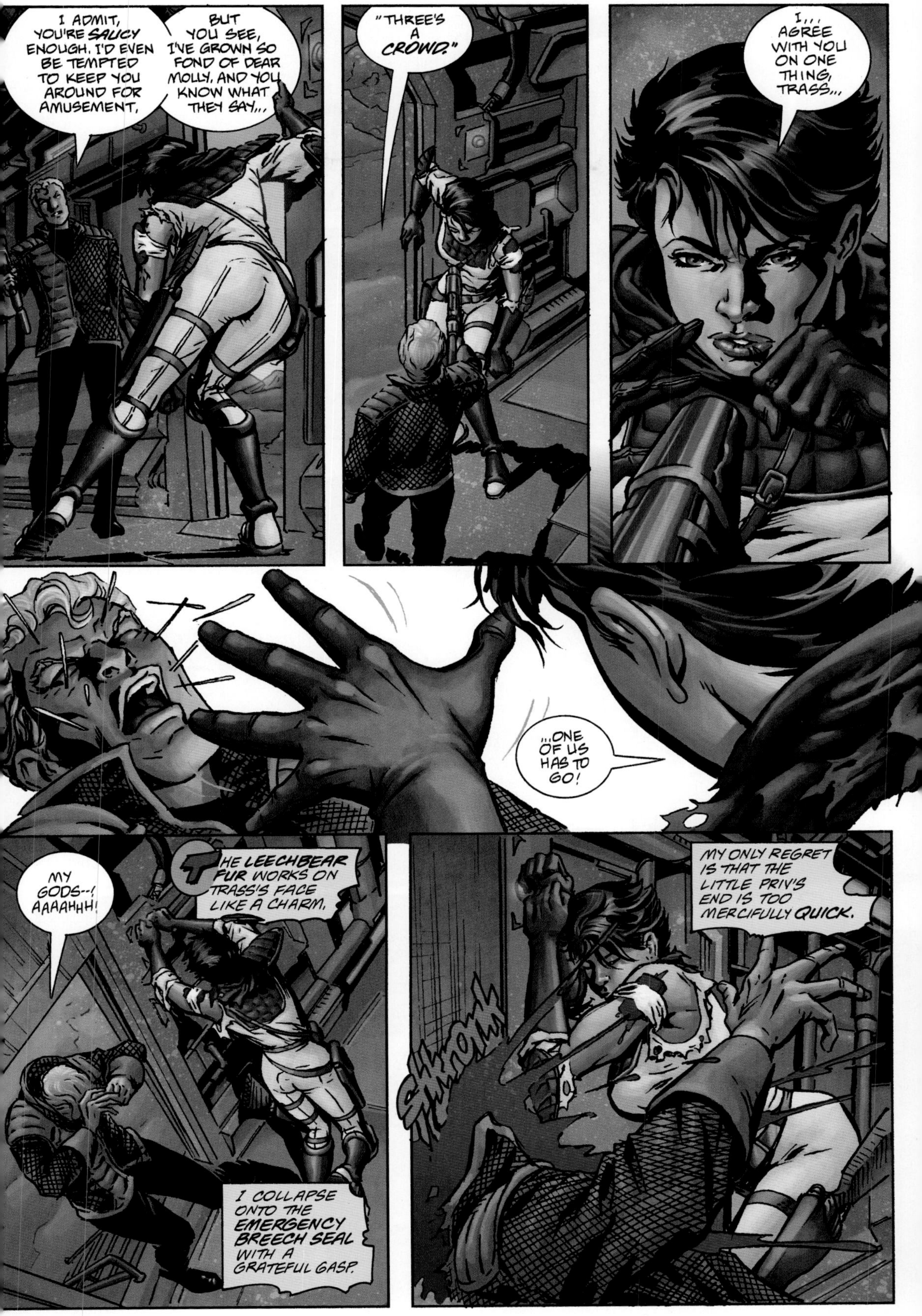
I ADMIT, YOU'RE SAUCY ENOUGH. I'D EVEN BE TEMPTED TO KEEP YOU AROUND FOR AMUSEMENT,
BUT YOU SEE, I'VE GROWN SO FOND OF DEAR MOLLY, AND YOU KNOW WHAT THEY SAY...
"THREE'S A CROWD."
I... AGREE WITH YOU ON ONE THING, TRASS...
...ONE OF US HAS TO GO!
MY GODS--! AAAAHHH!
THE LEECHBEAR FUR WORKS ON TRASS'S FACE LIKE A CHARM.
I COLLAPSE ONTO THE EMERGENCY BREECH SEAL WITH A GRATEFUL GASP.
MY ONLY REGRET IS THAT THE LITTLE PRIV'S END IS TOO MERCIFULLY QUICK.
SHTHOWN

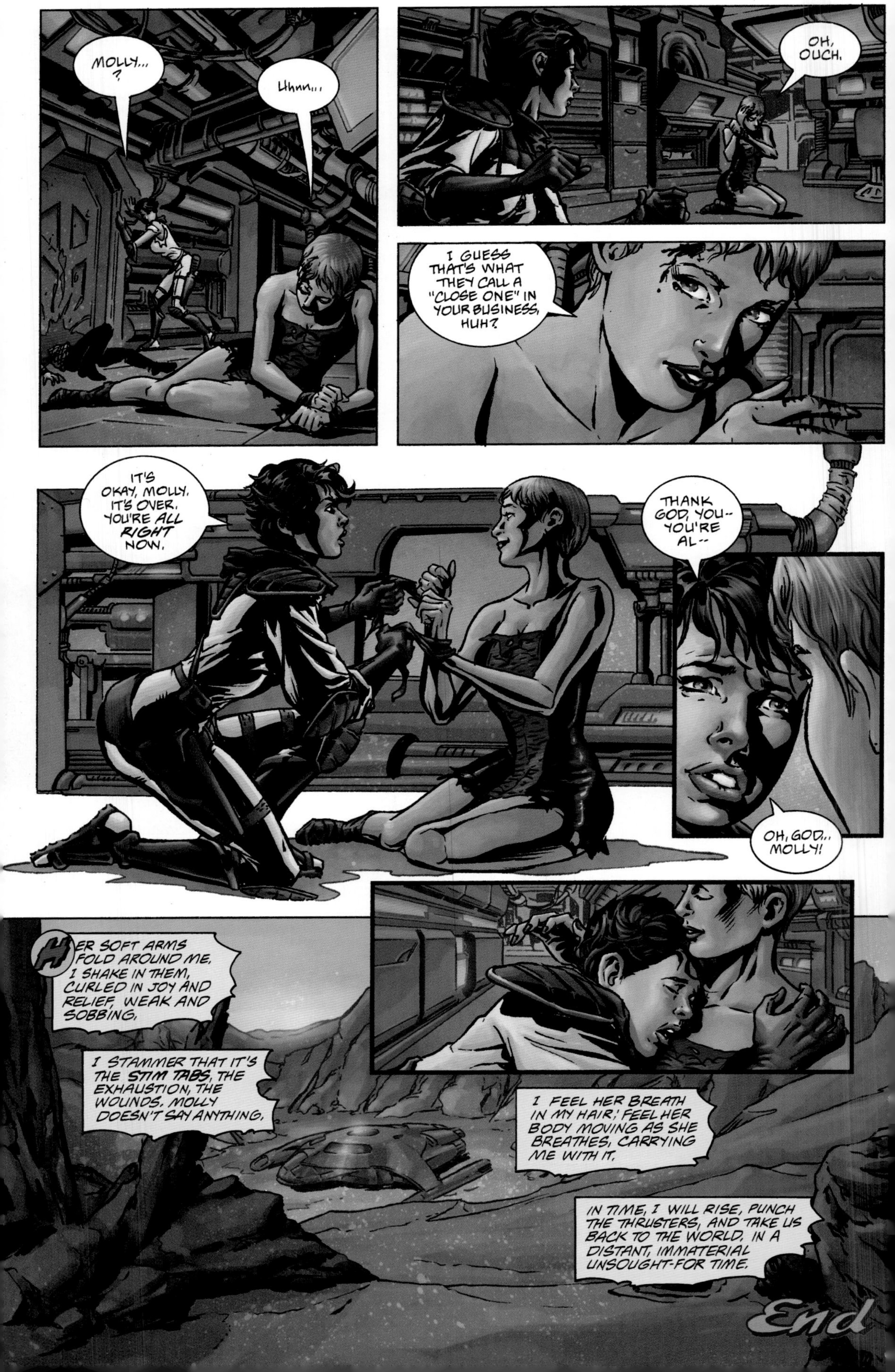
MOLLY... ?
Uhnn...
OH, OUCH.
I GUESS THAT'S WHAT THEY CALL A "CLOSE ONE" IN YOUR BUSINESS, HUH?
IT'S OKAY, MOLLY. IT'S OVER. YOU'RE ALL RIGHT NOW.
THANK GOD, YOU-- YOU'RE AL--
OH, GOD... MOLLY!
HER SOFT ARMS FOLD AROUND ME. I SHAKE IN THEM, CURLED IN JOY AND RELIEF, WEAK AND SOBBING.
I STAMMER THAT IT'S THE STIM TABS, THE EXHAUSTION, THE WOUNDS. MOLLY DOESN'T SAY ANYTHING.
I FEEL HER BREATH IN MY HAIR; FEEL HER BODY MOVING AS SHE BREATHES, CARRYING ME WITH IT.
IN TIME, I WILL RISE, PUNCH THE THRUSTERS, AND TAKE US BACK TO THE WORLD. IN A DISTANT, IMMATERIAL UNSOUGHT-FOR TIME.
End

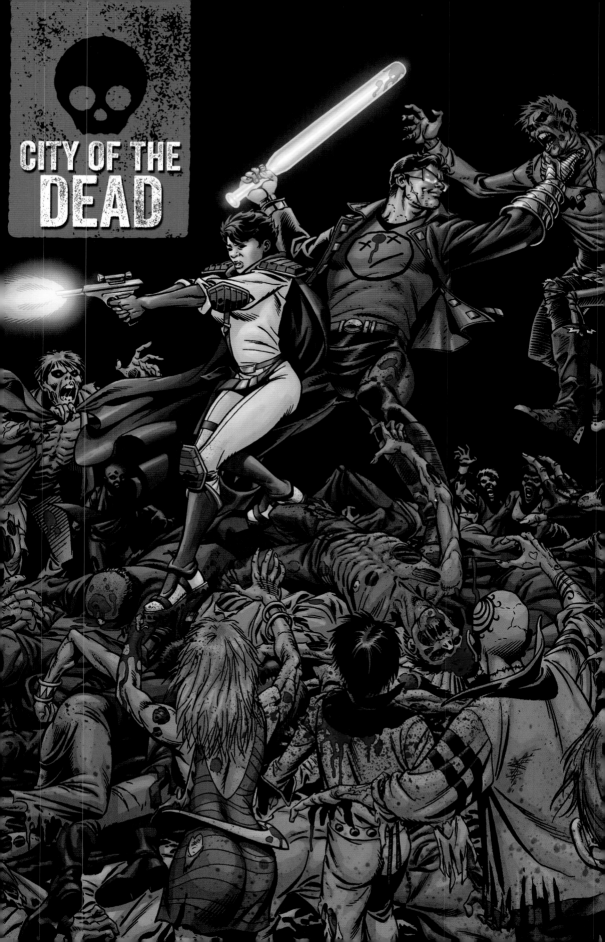

CITY OF THE
DEAD

MERCY ST. CLAIR AND ZOMBIES? When Karl Kesel contacted me about a one-off story where Mercy could cross paths with his semifolkloric Johnny Zombie, I was pretty skeptical. That is, until I finished hearing his idea. Then it just sounded like too much fun to resist. Karl built a plausible tale where these characters from two completely different worlds could reasonably coexist, at least for the length of this one special story. If you like this print version, you can find the story in its original unique, digital form at Thrillbent.com.

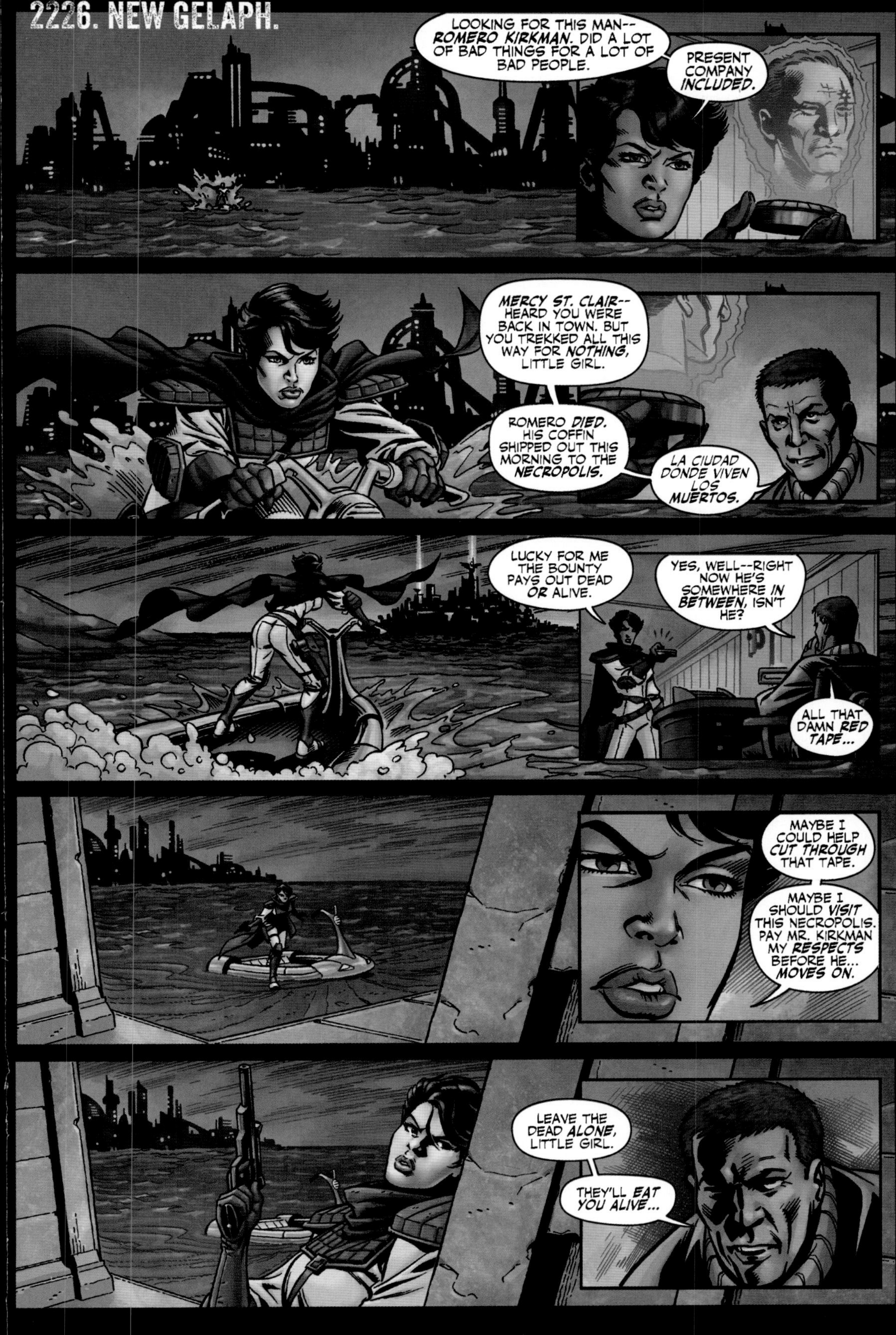
2226. NEW GELAPH.
LOOKING FOR THIS MAN-- ROMERO KIRKMAN. DID A LOT OF BAD THINGS FOR A LOT OF BAD PEOPLE.
PRESENT COMPANY INCLUDED.
MERCY ST. CLAIR-- HEARD YOU WERE BACK IN TOWN. BUT YOU TREKKED ALL THIS WAY FOR NOTHING, LITTLE GIRL.
ROMERO DIED. HIS COFFIN SHIPPED OUT THIS MORNING TO THE NECROPOLIS.
LA CIUDAD DONDE VIVEN LOS MUERTOS.
LUCKY FOR ME THE BOUNTY PAYS OUT DEAD OR ALIVE.
YES, WELL--RIGHT NOW HE'S SOMEWHERE IN BETWEEN, ISN'T HE?
ALL THAT DAMN RED TAPE...
MAYBE I COULD HELP CUT THROUGH THAT TAPE.
MAYBE I SHOULD VISIT THIS NECROPOLIS. PAY MR. KIRKMAN MY RESPECTS BEFORE HE... MOVES ON.
LEAVE THE DEAD ALONE, LITTLE GIRL.
THEY'LL EAT YOU ALIVE...

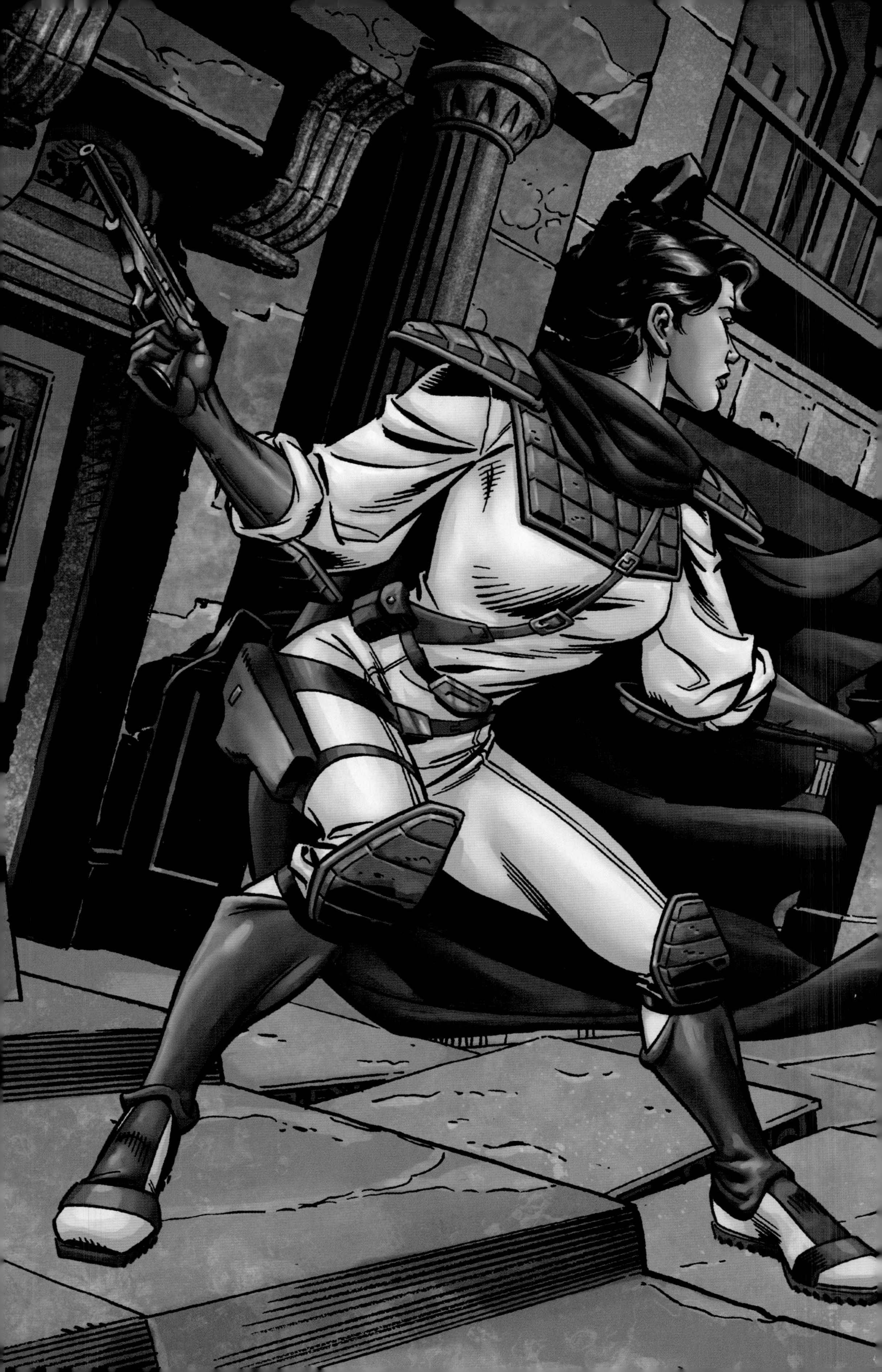

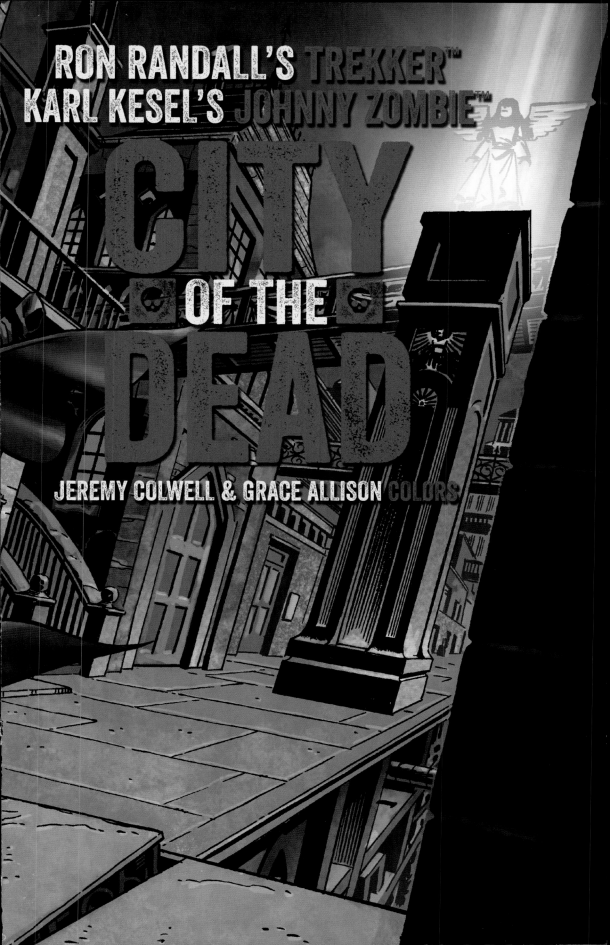

RON RANDALL'S TREKKER™
KARL KESEL'S JOHNNY ZOMBIE™

CITY OF THE DEAD

JEREMY COLWELL & GRACE ALLISON COLORS

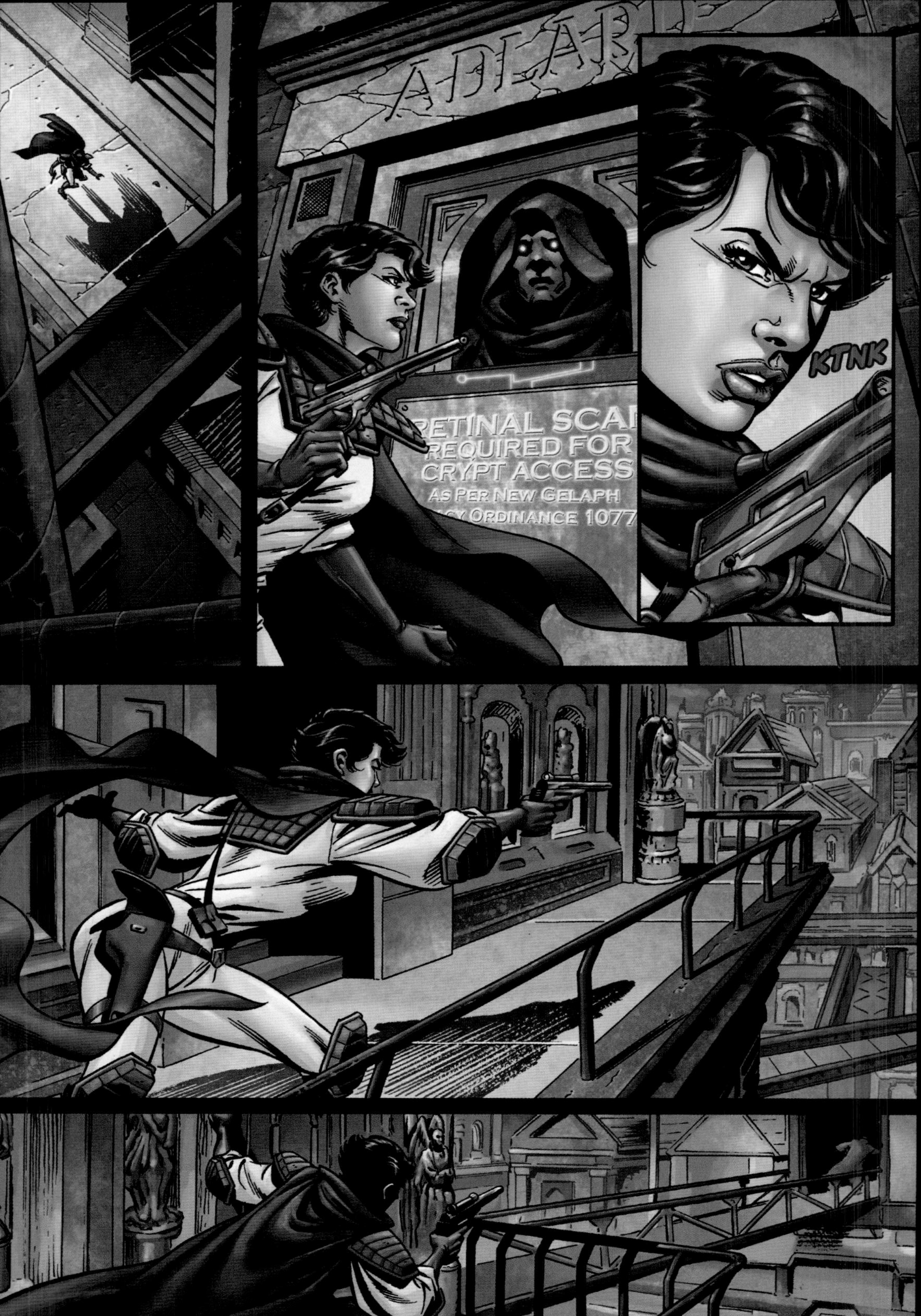
ADLAR
RETINAL SCA
REQUIRED FOR
CRYPT ACCESS
As Per New Gelaph
Ordinance 1077
KTNK

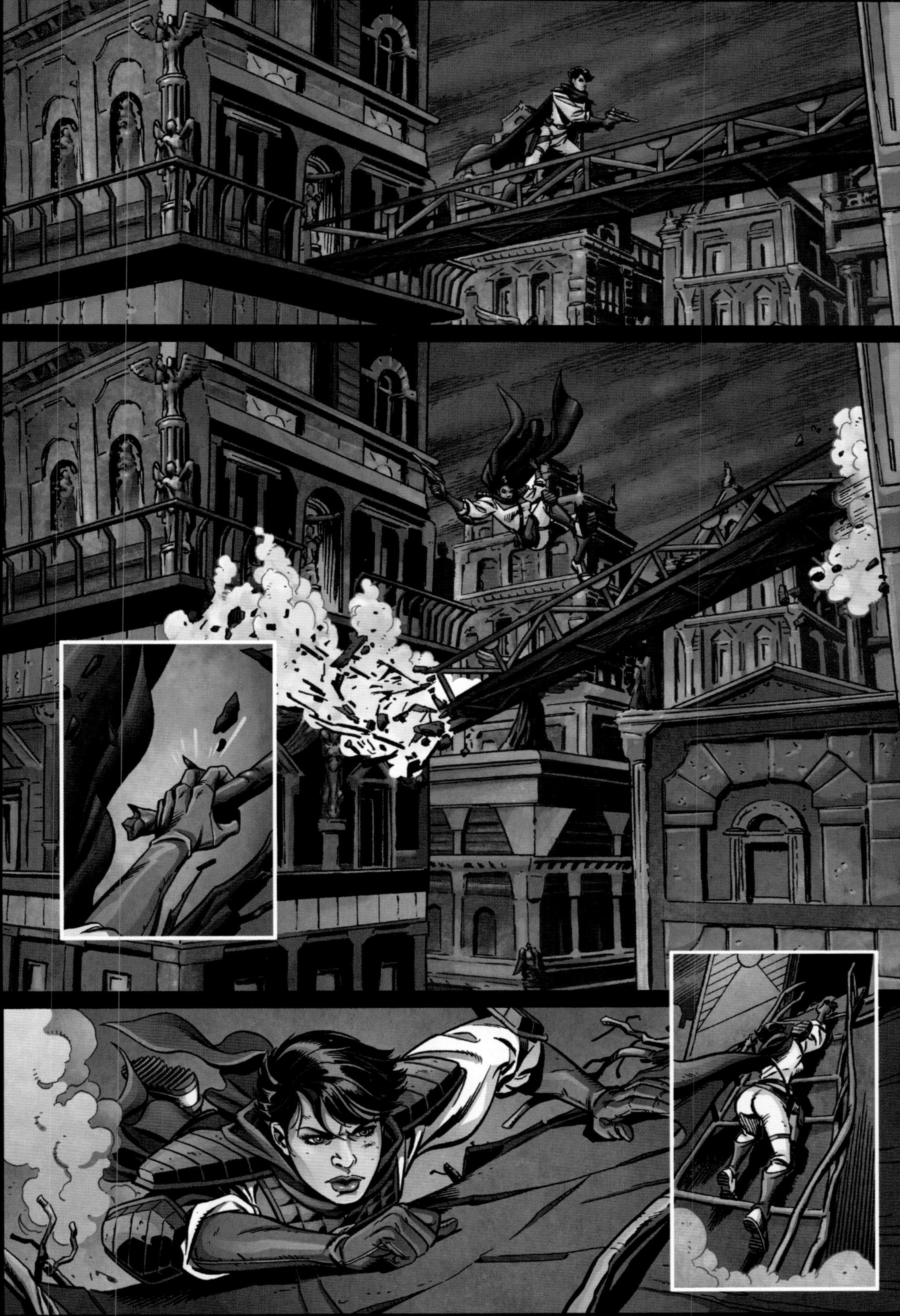

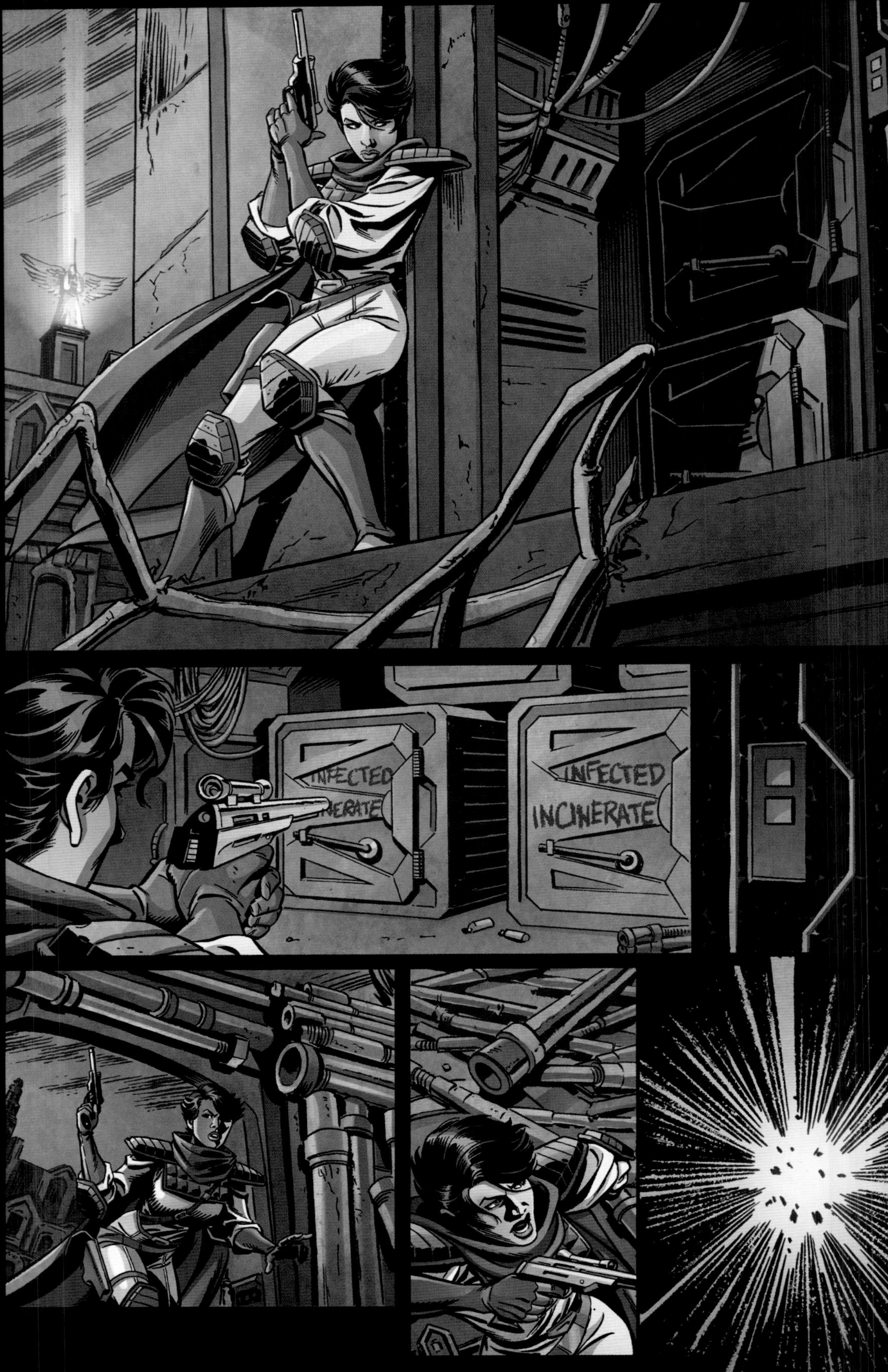
INFECTED
INCINERATE

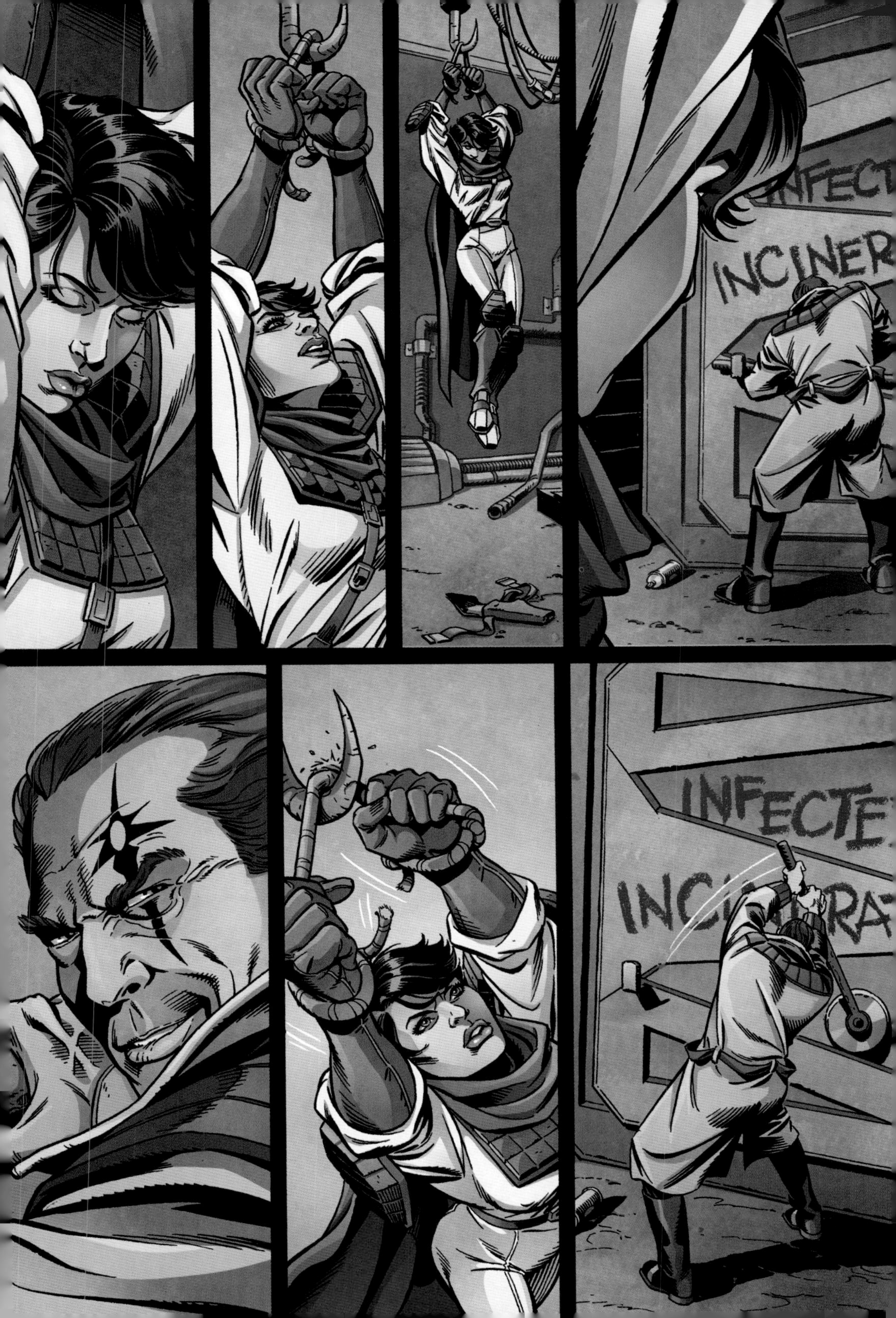
INCINER
INFECTE

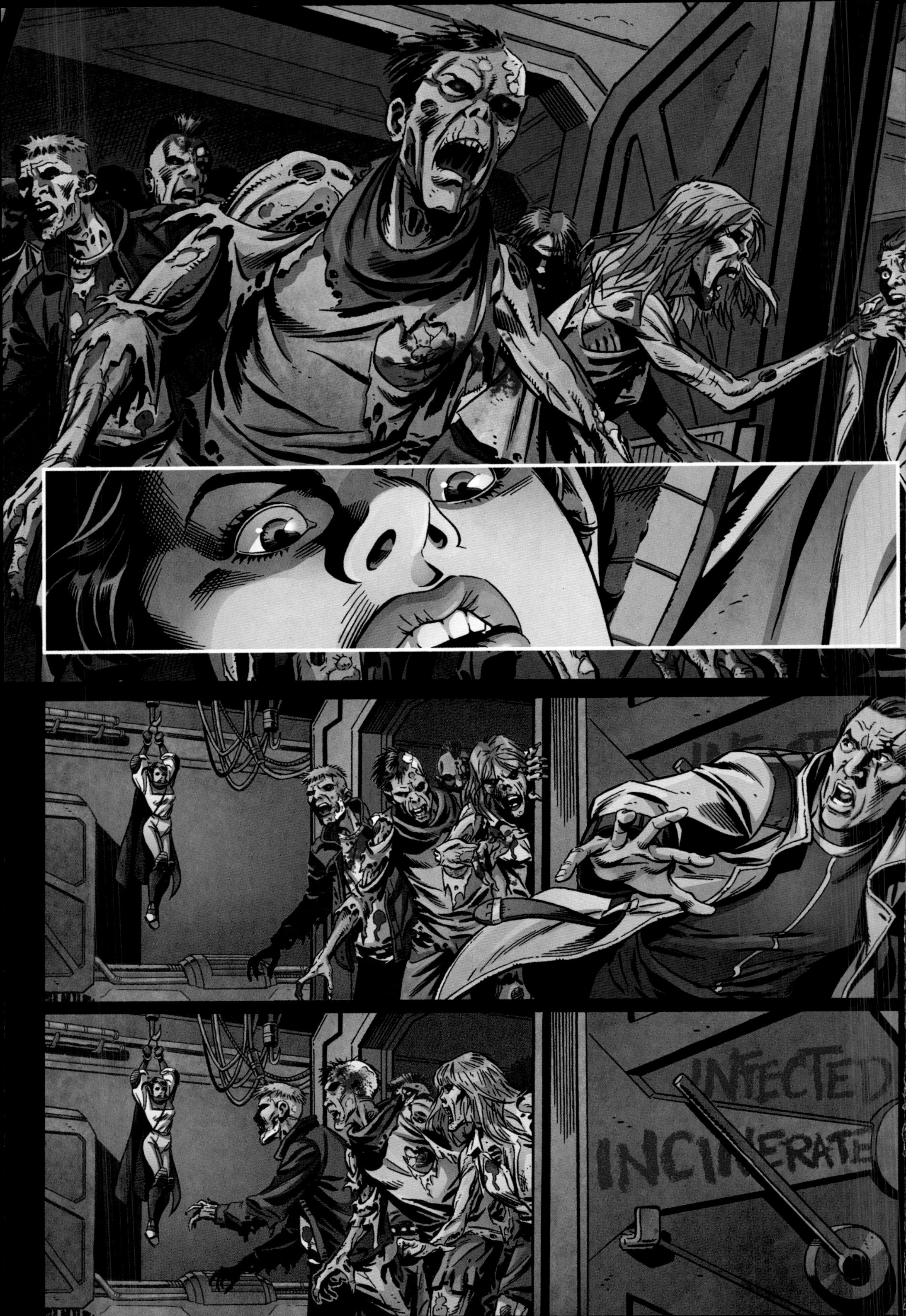
INFECTED
INCINERATE

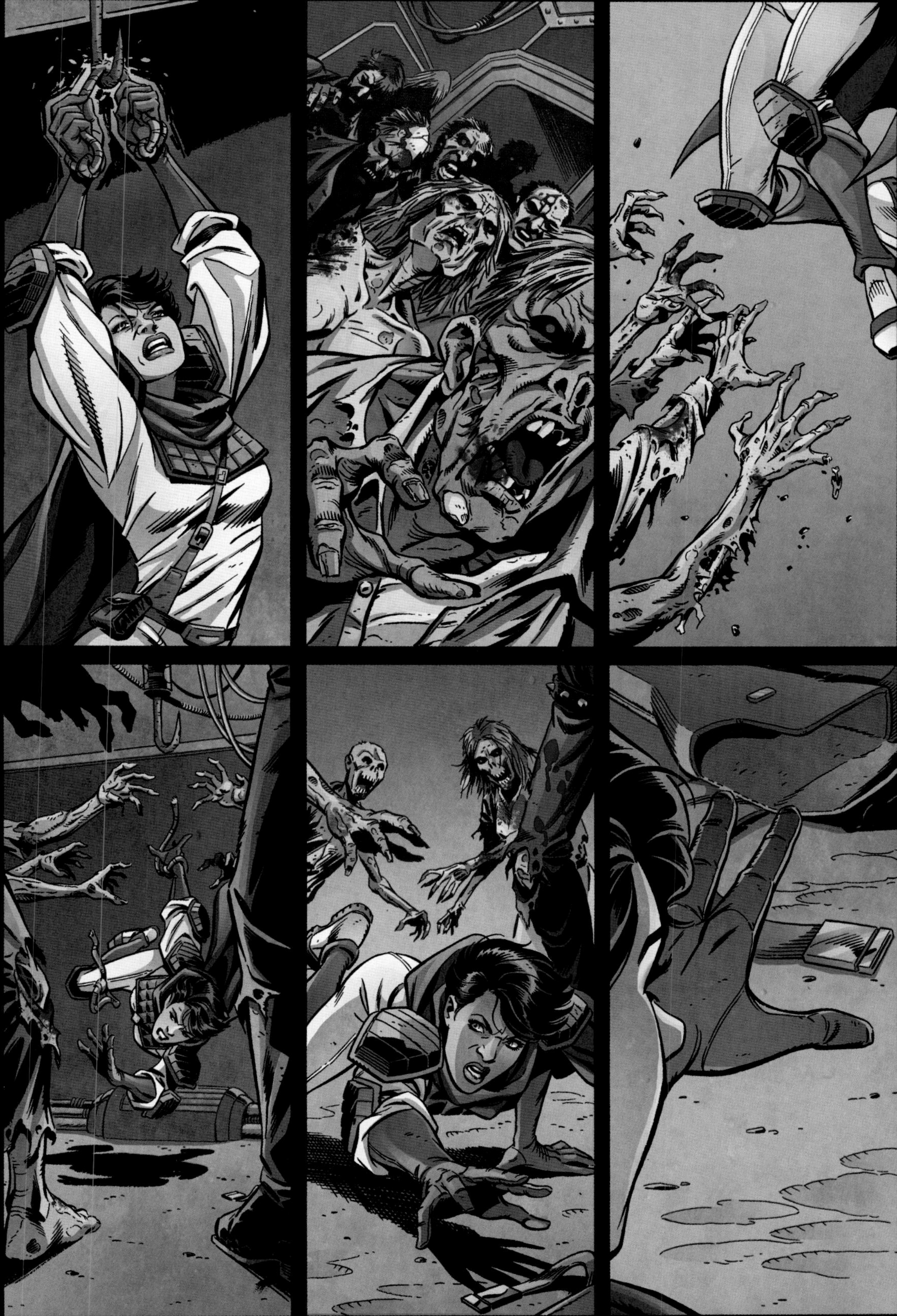

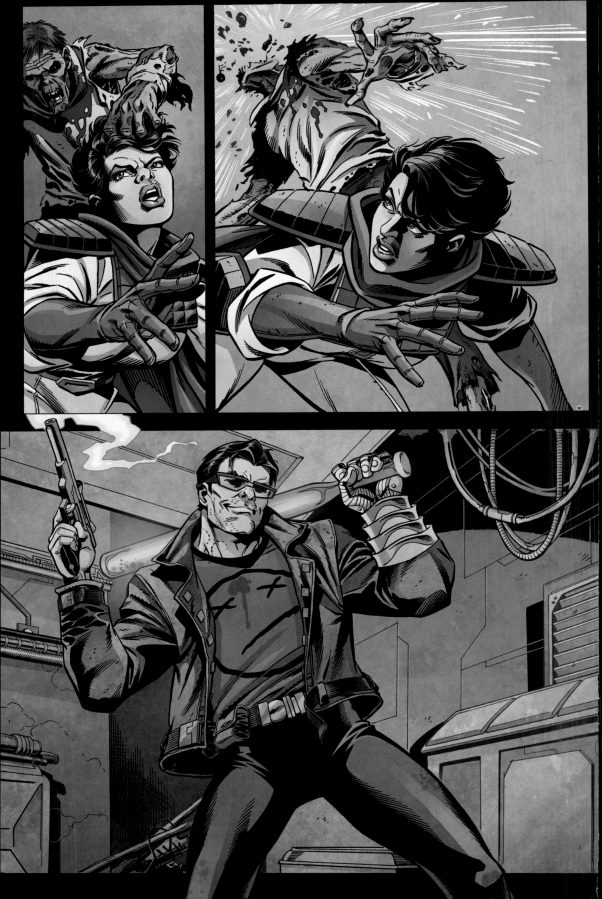

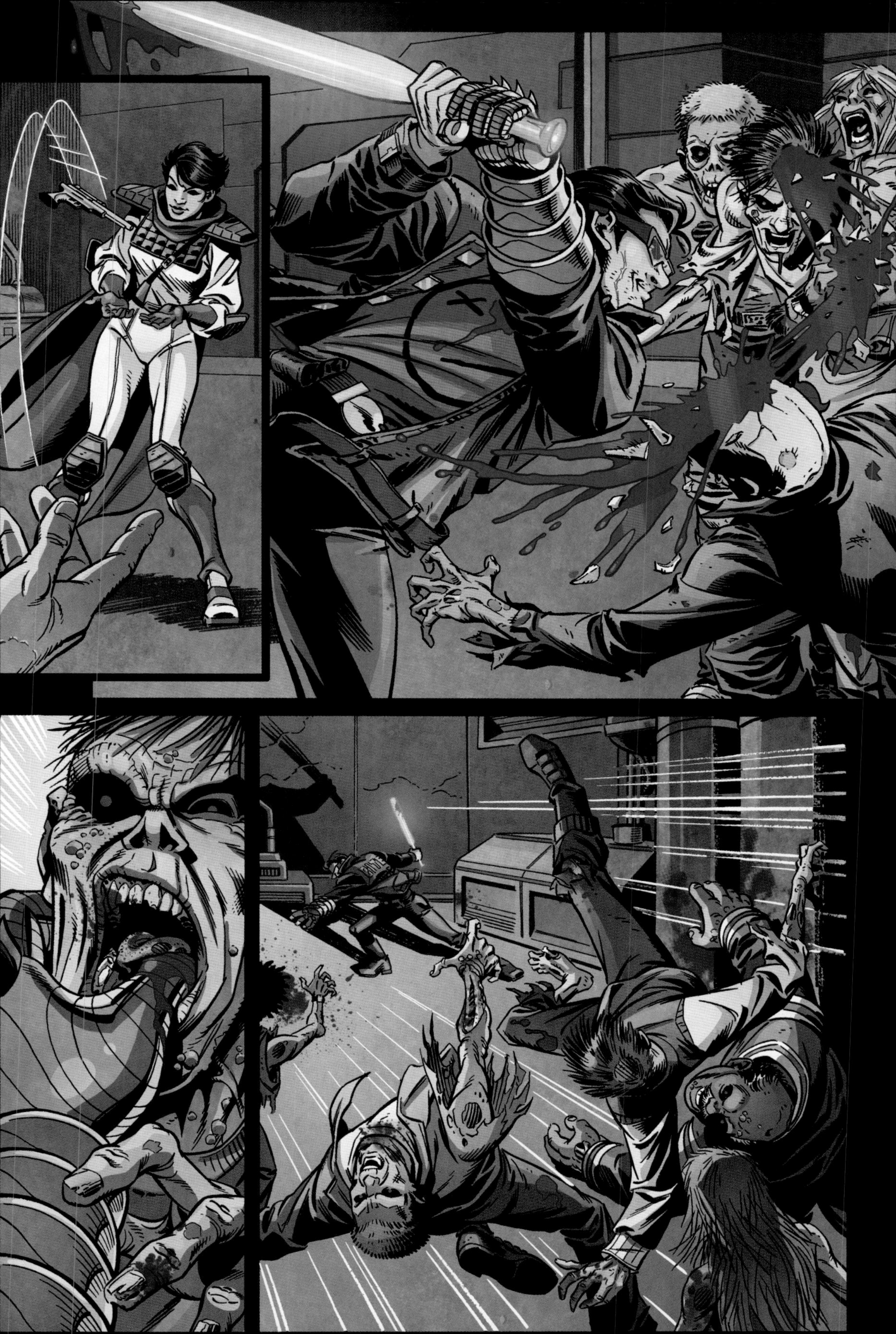

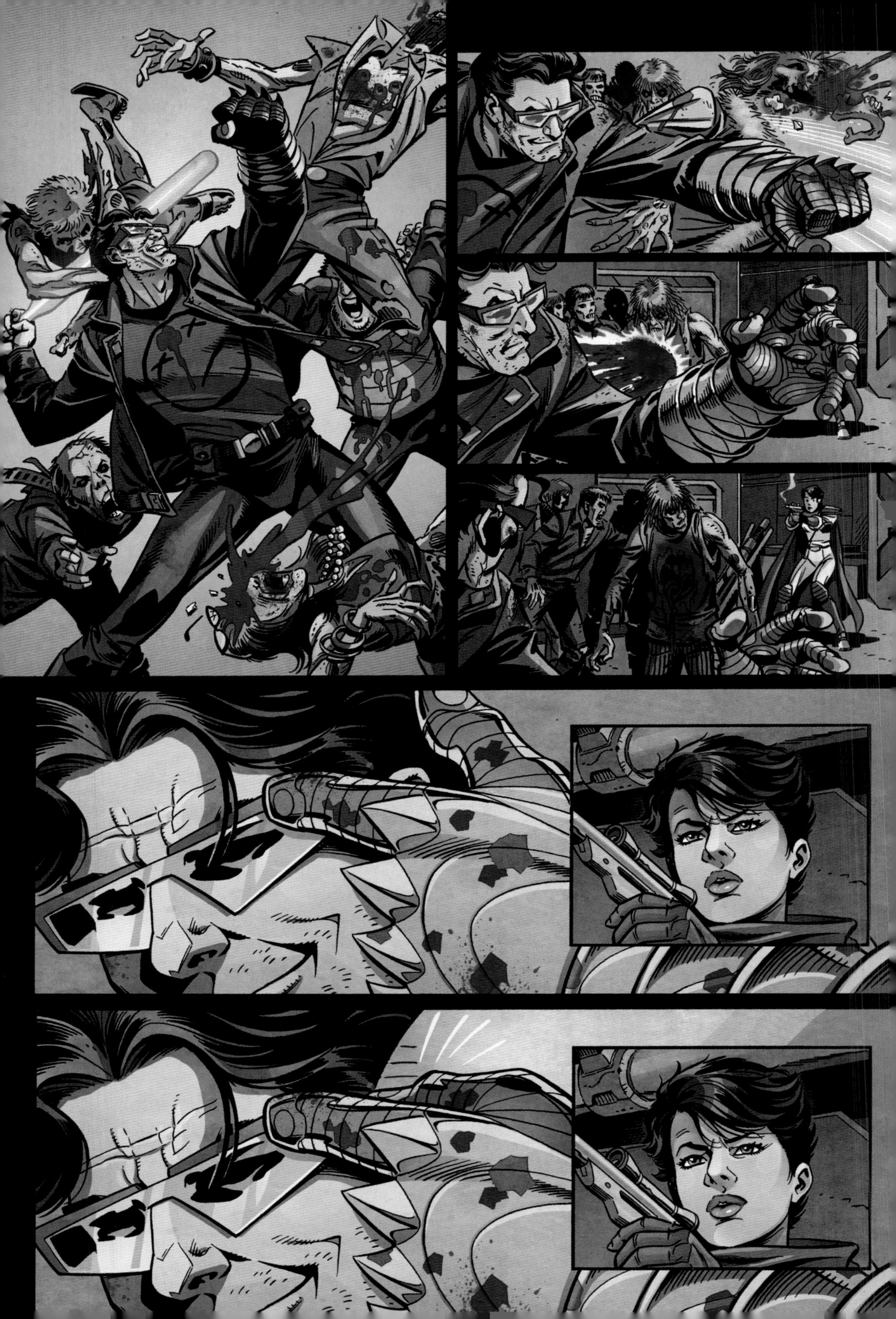

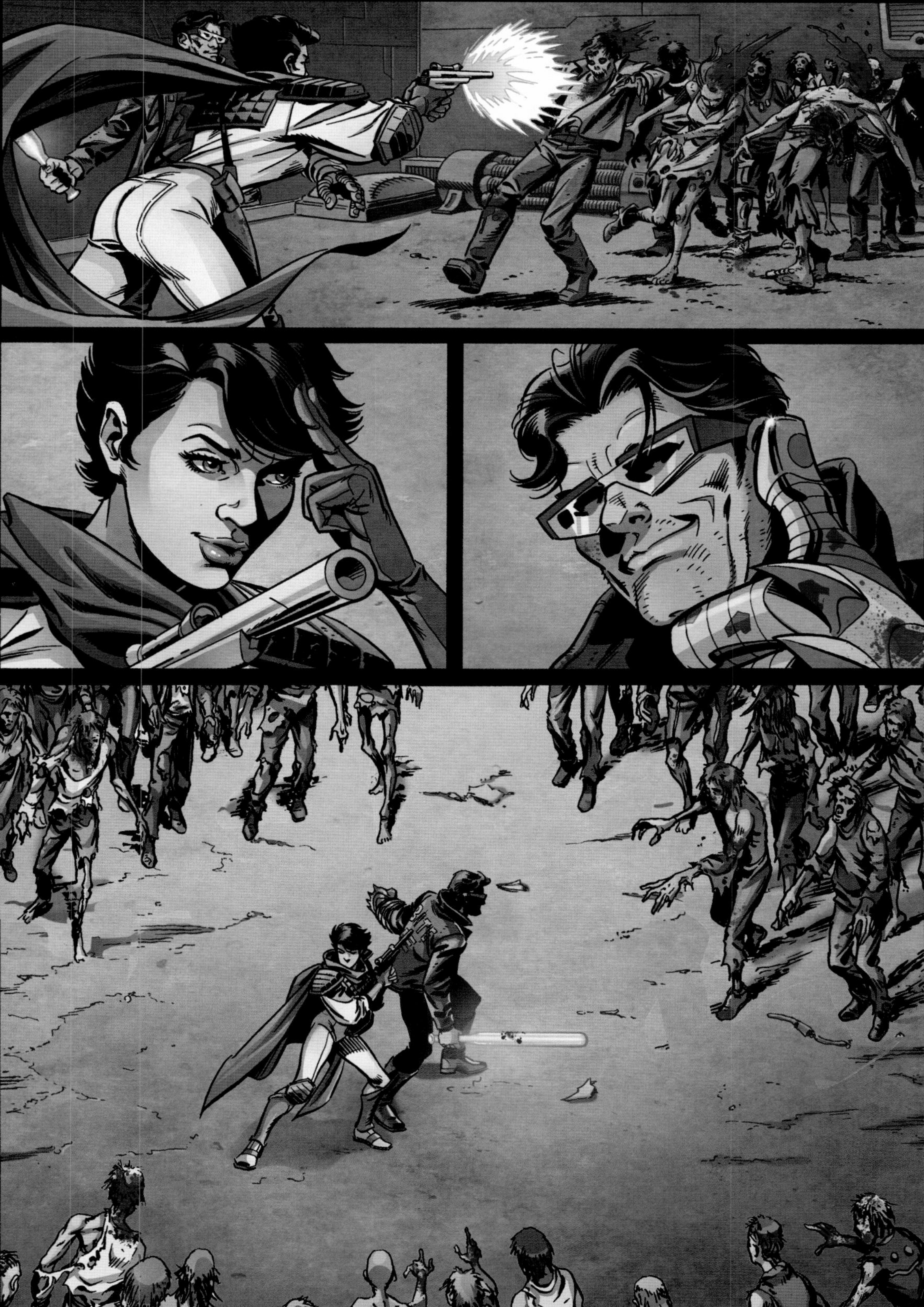

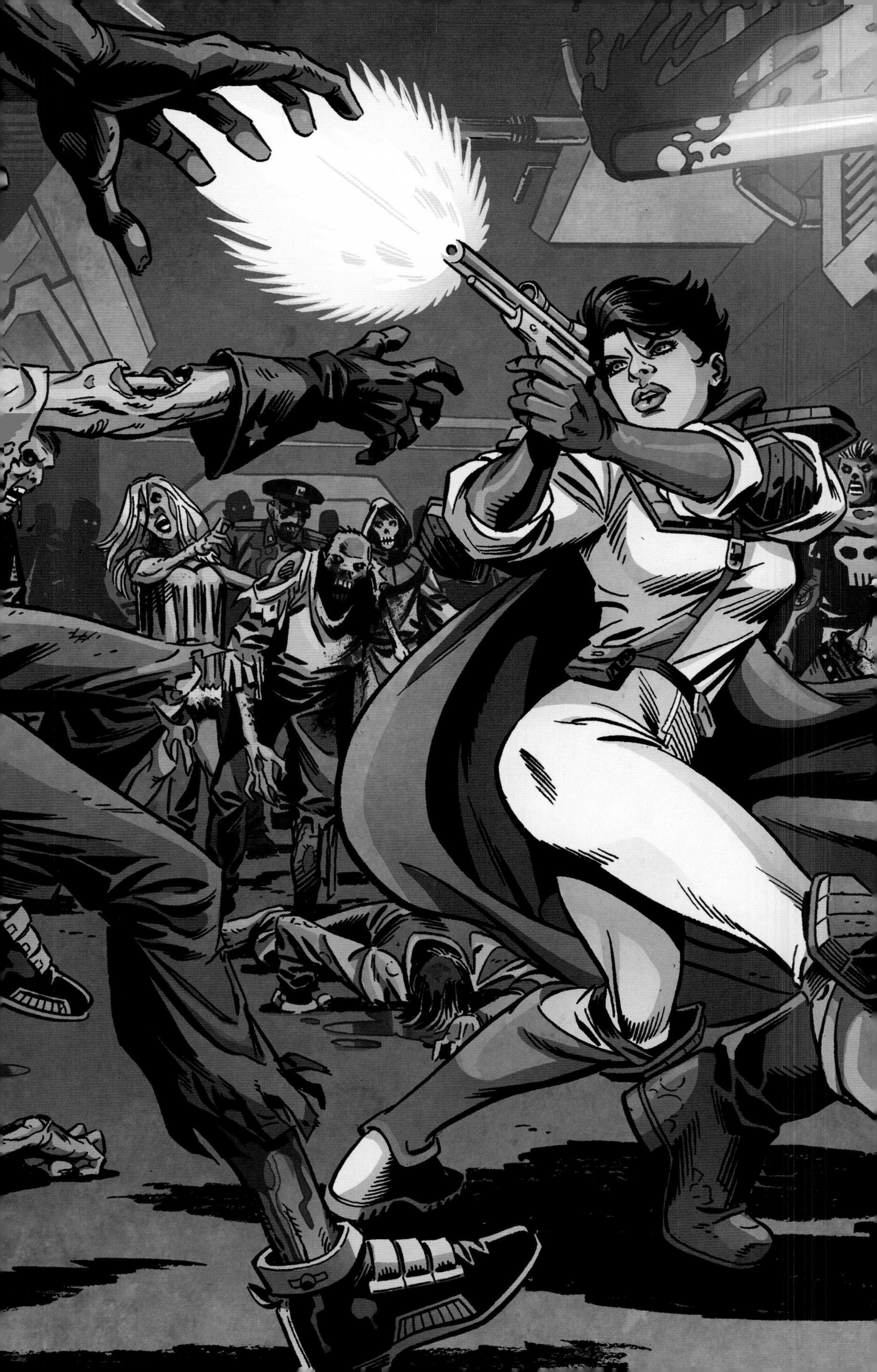

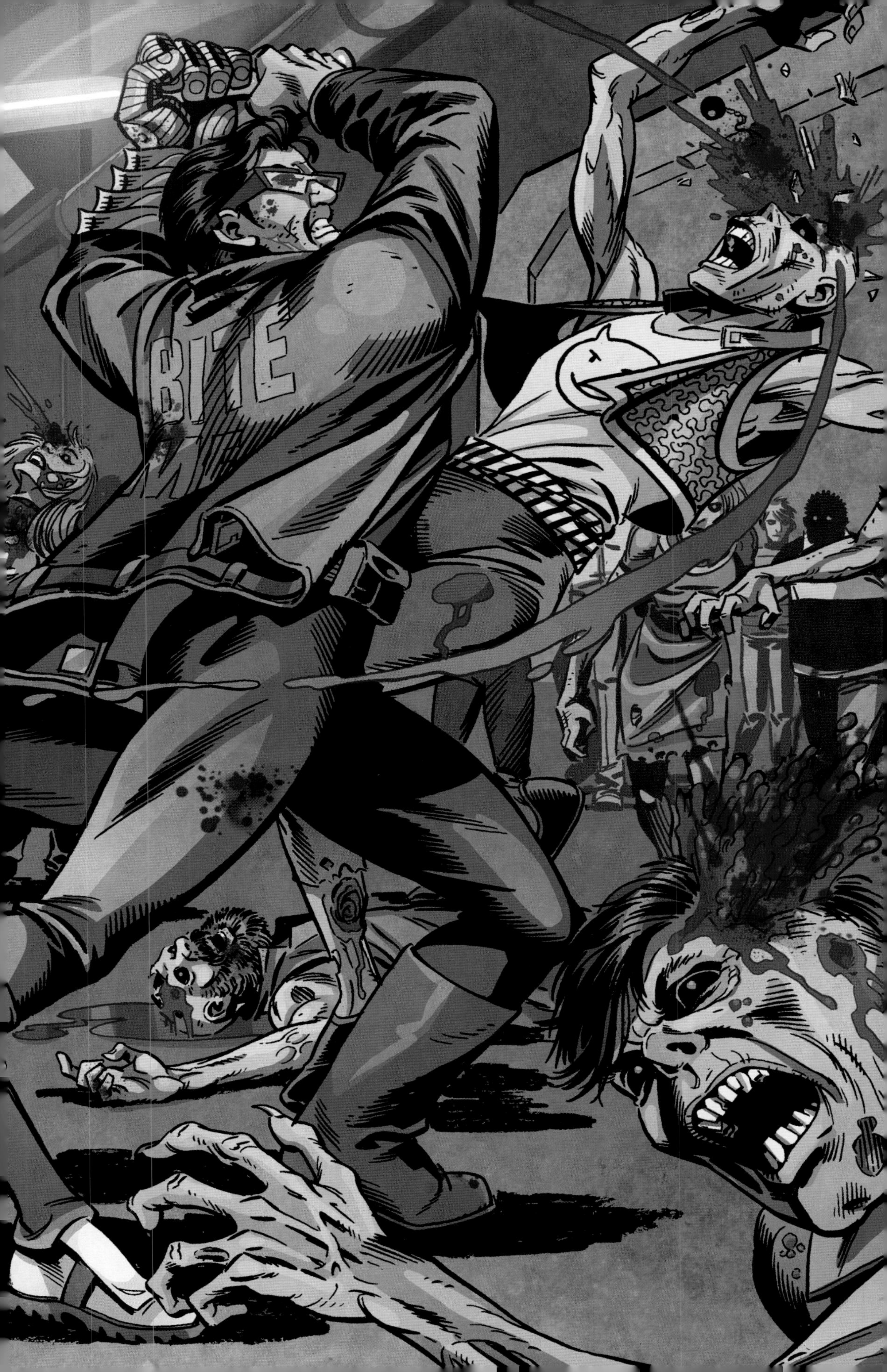
BITE

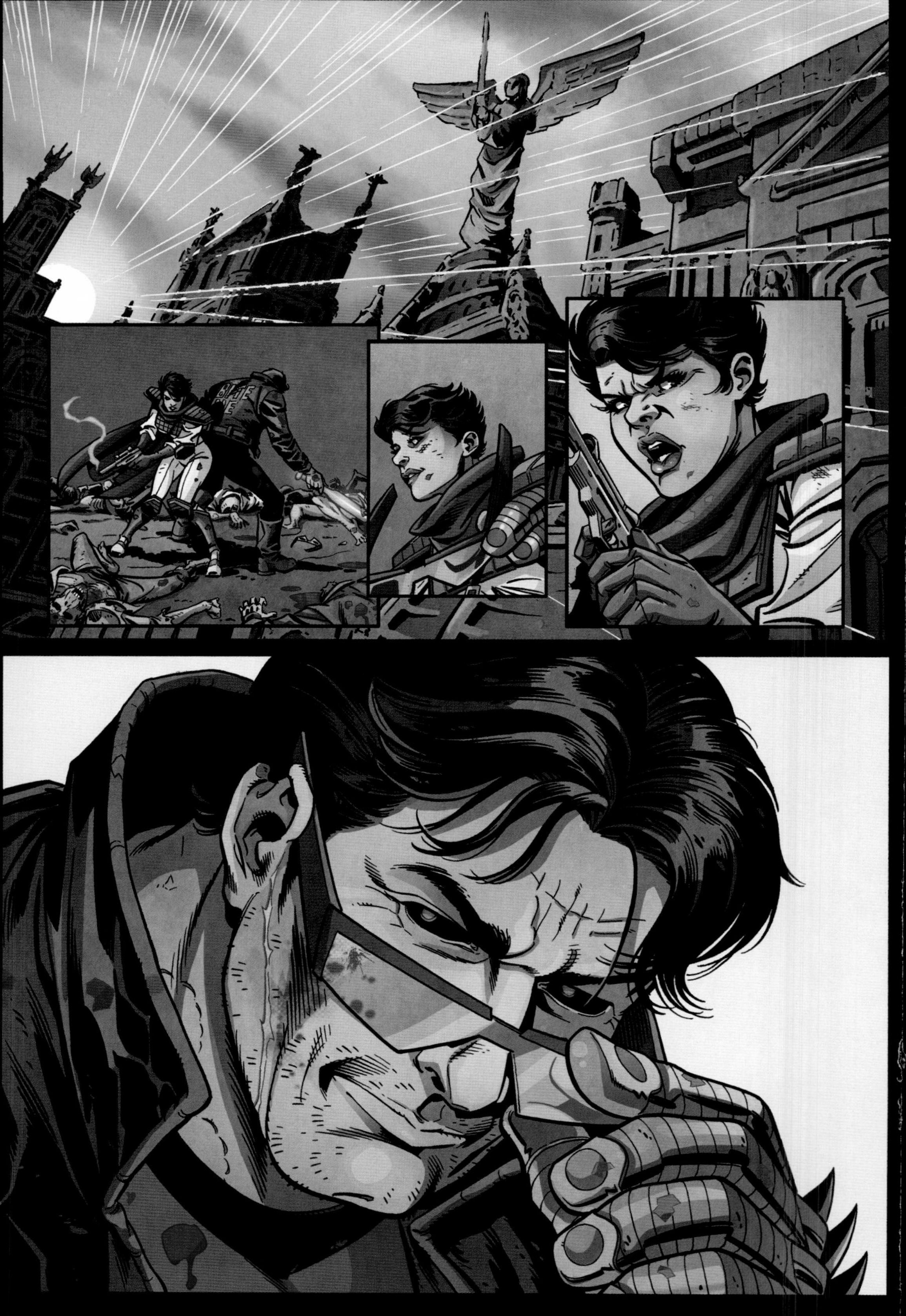

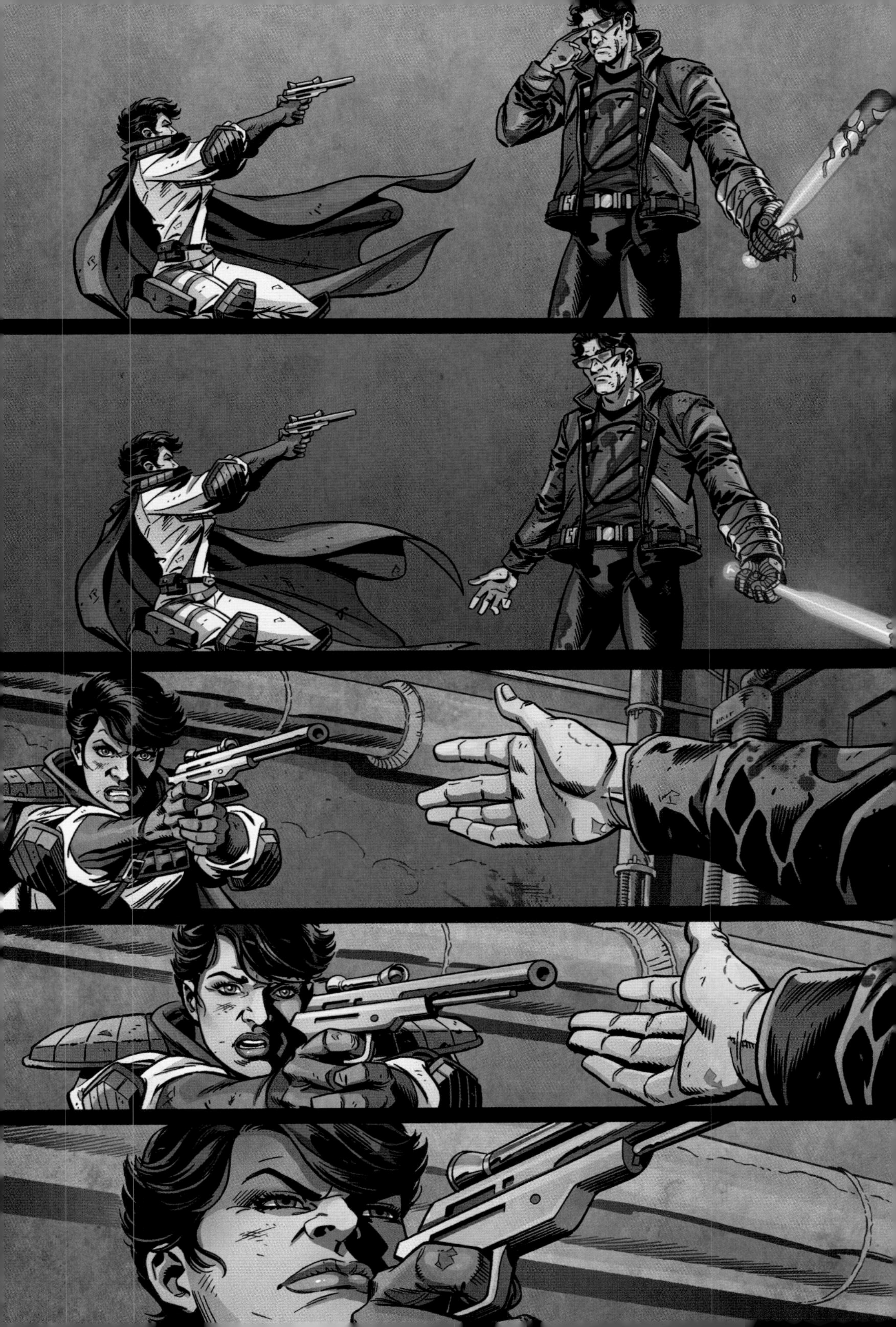

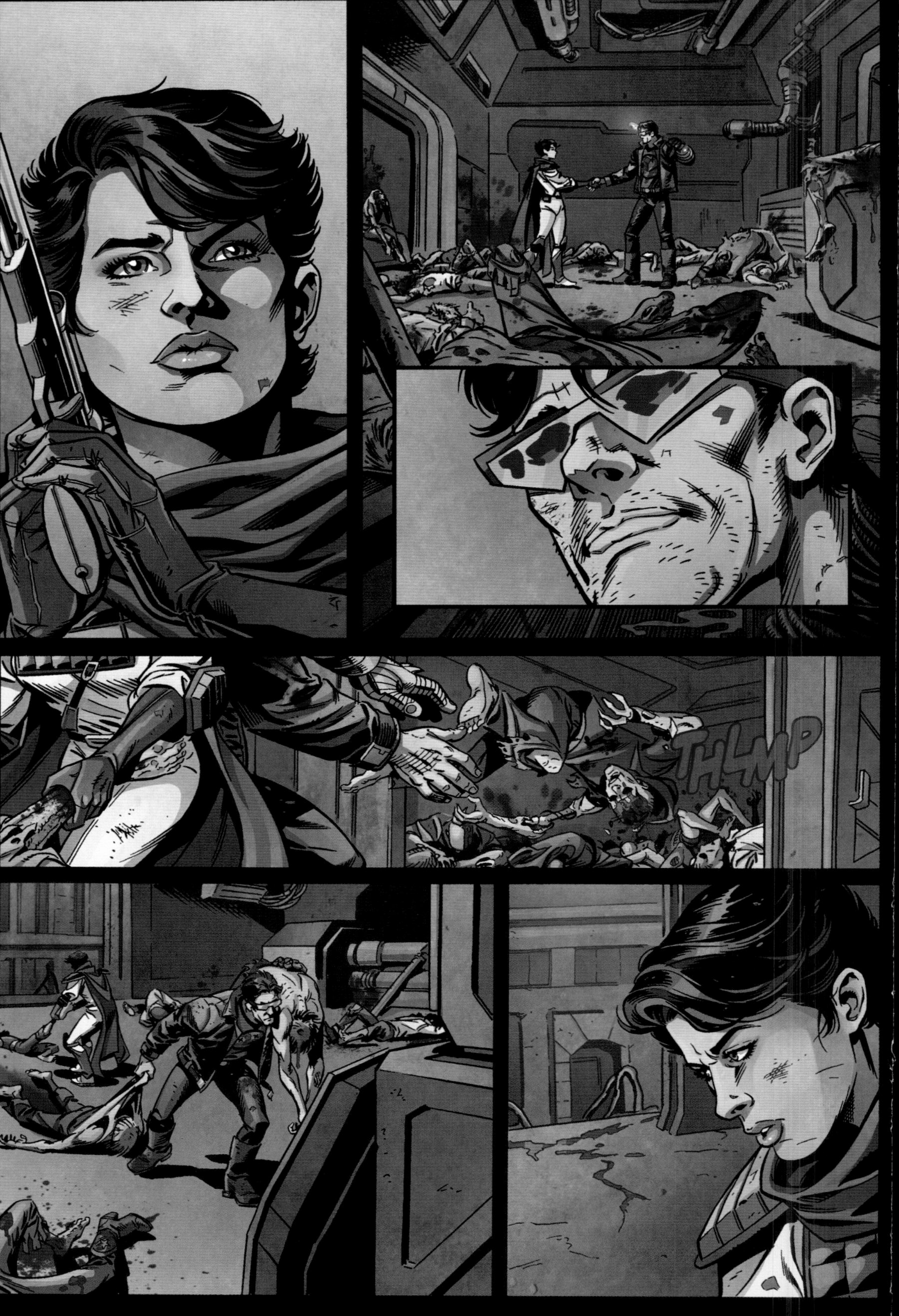
THUMP

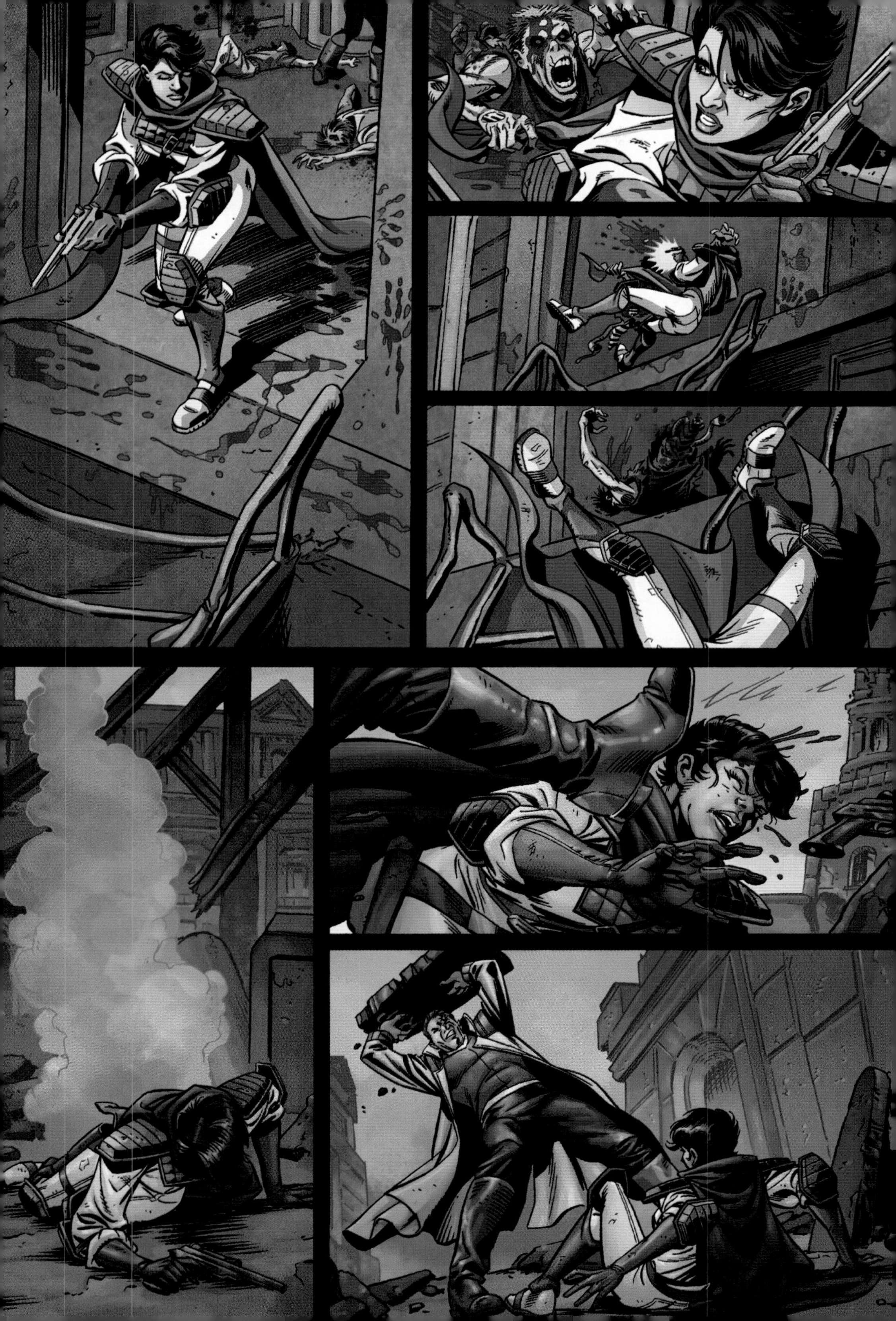

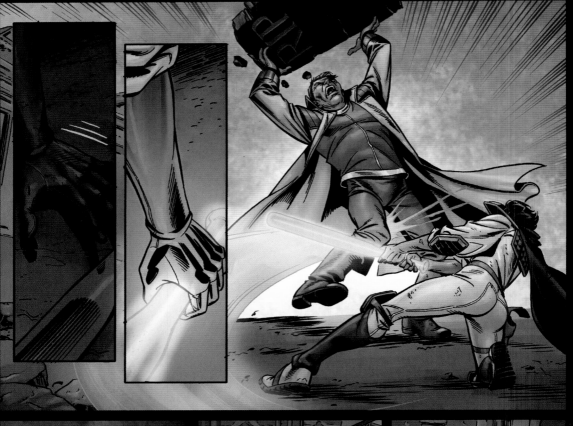

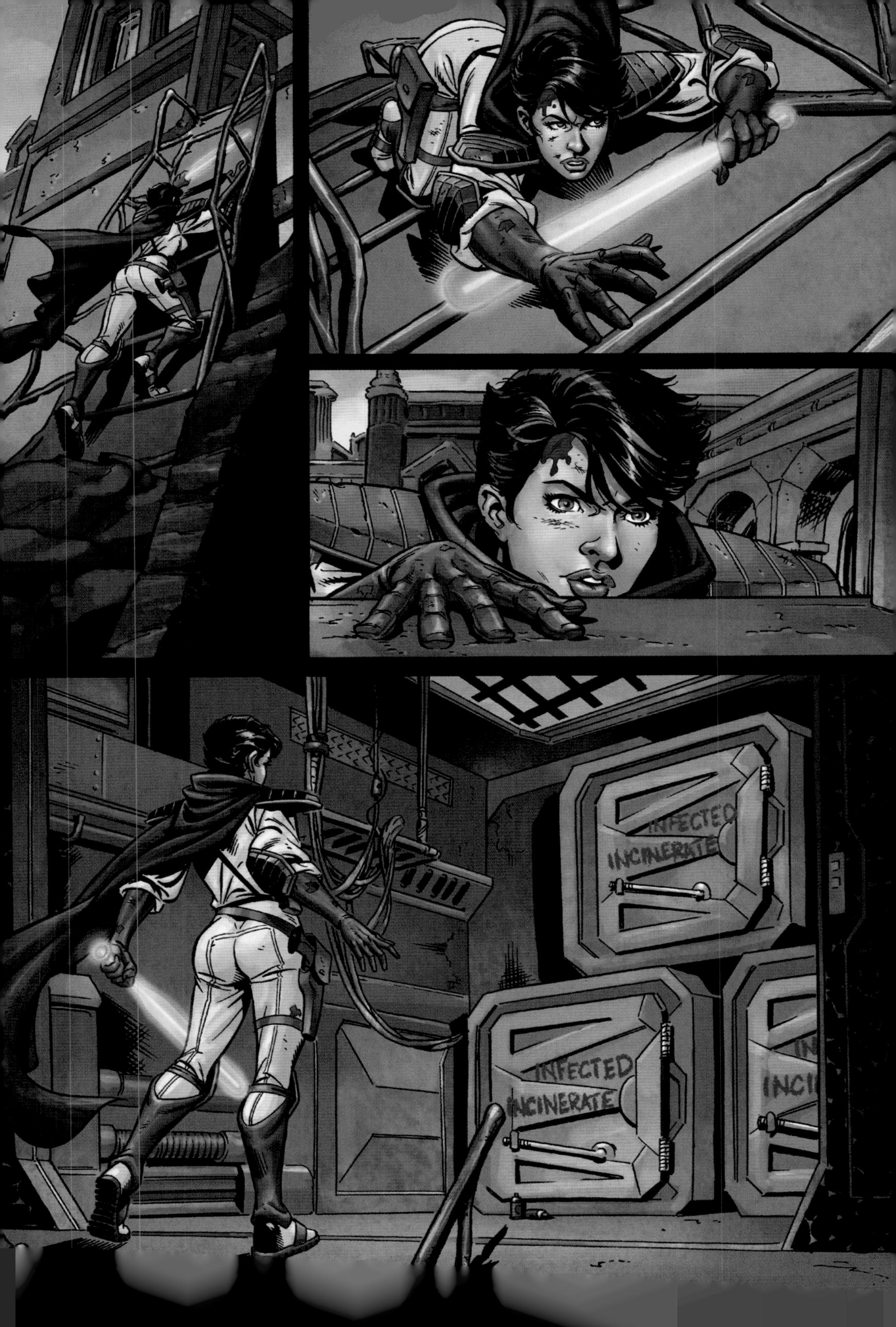
INFECTED
INCINERATE
INFECTED
INCINERATE

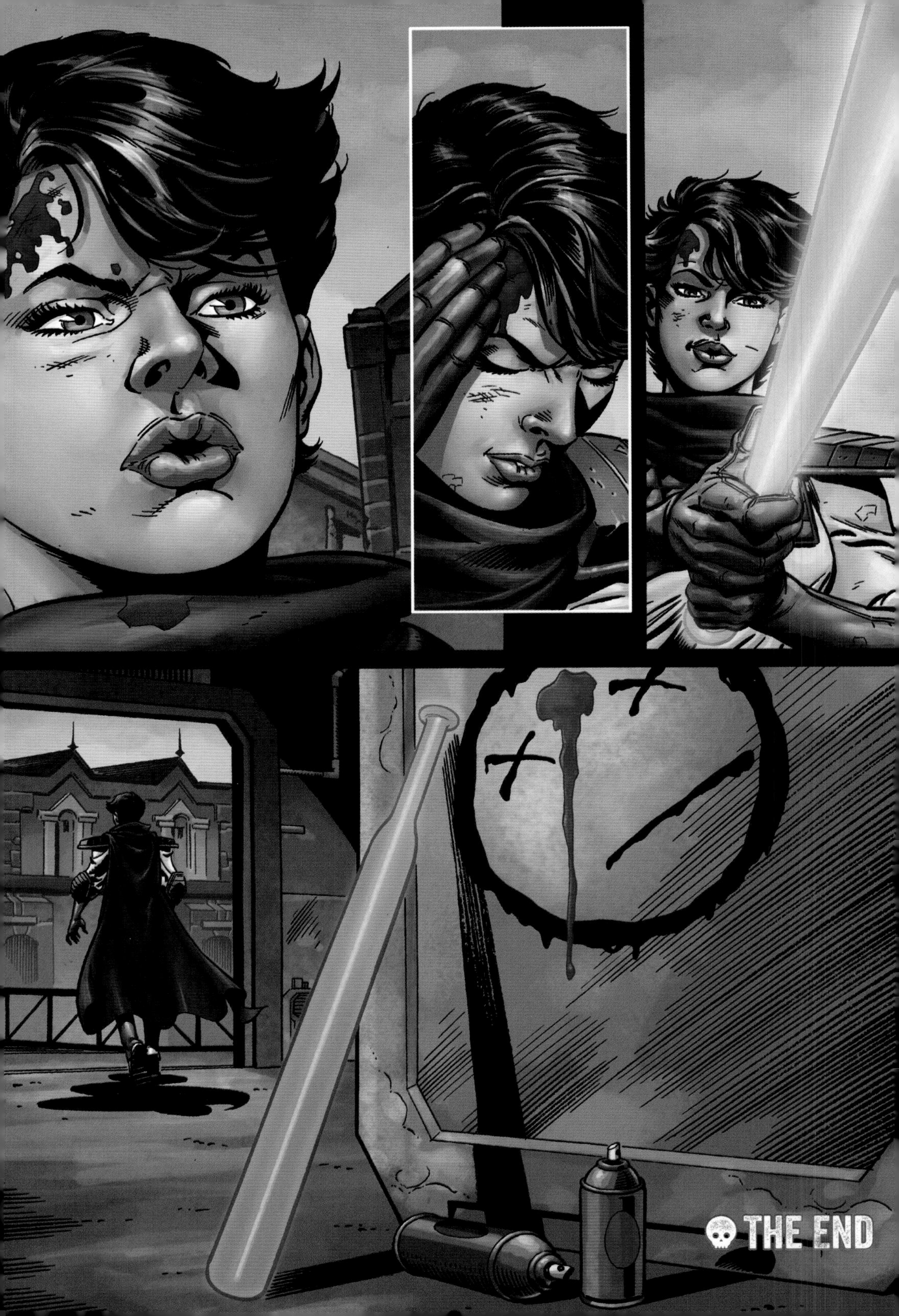
THE END

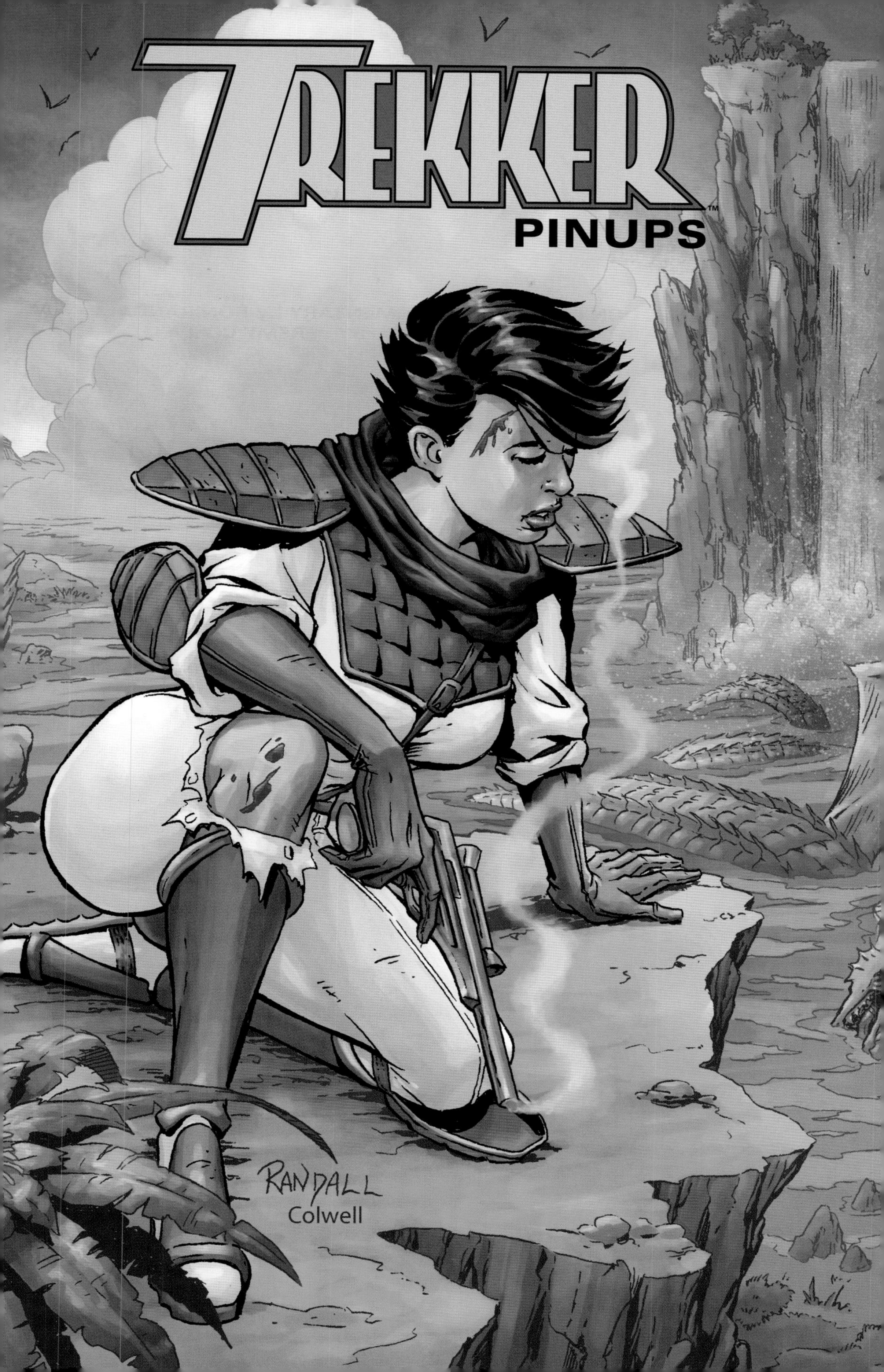
TREKKER™
PINUPS
RANDALL
Colwell

PINUP SECTION COVER AND COMMENTARY BY RON RANDALL
PINUP SECTION COVER COLORS BY JEREMY COLWELL

When I put out a call to many fellow artists to contribute "sketches" of Mercy for this volume, I didn't know I'd be hit with such a fantastic wave of images. These selections could just as well serve as a particularly awesome-looking list of thank-yous, since virtually every artist represented here has served as a source of inspiration, advice, and/or support along the path of *Trekker*'s return. I advise you all to seek out the work of each of them—you will find yourself richly rewarded.

PINUPS BY

Mark Schultz
Jonathan Case
Thomas Yeates
Dustin Weaver
Ben Bates
Steve Lieber
Pete Woods
Paul Guinan
Karl Kesel
Ron Chan
Cat Farris
Aaron McConnell
Rich Ellis
Colleen Coover
Grace Allison
Jesse Hamm

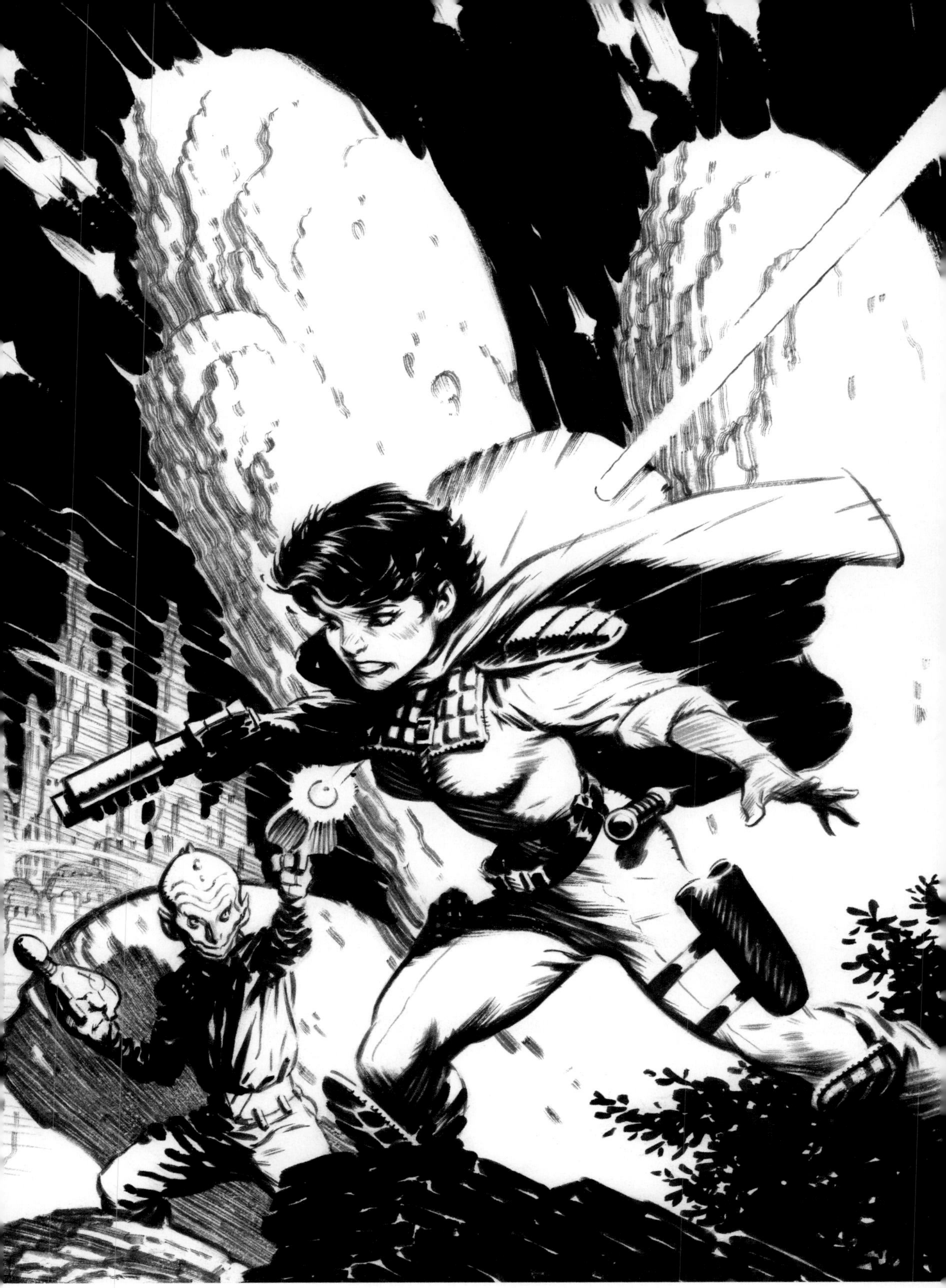

MARK SCHULTZ

Creator of the legendary *Xenozoic Tales*, Mark has a superhuman level of craft and a mastery of classic adventure that have been untouchable from his very first strip.

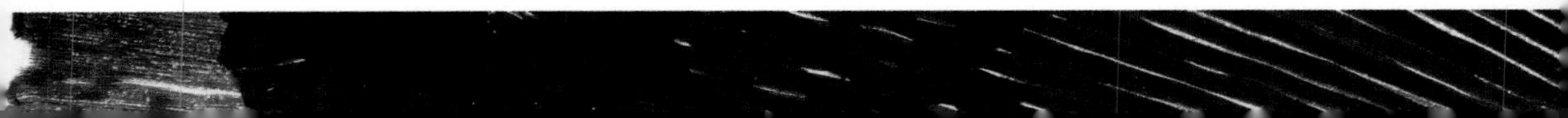

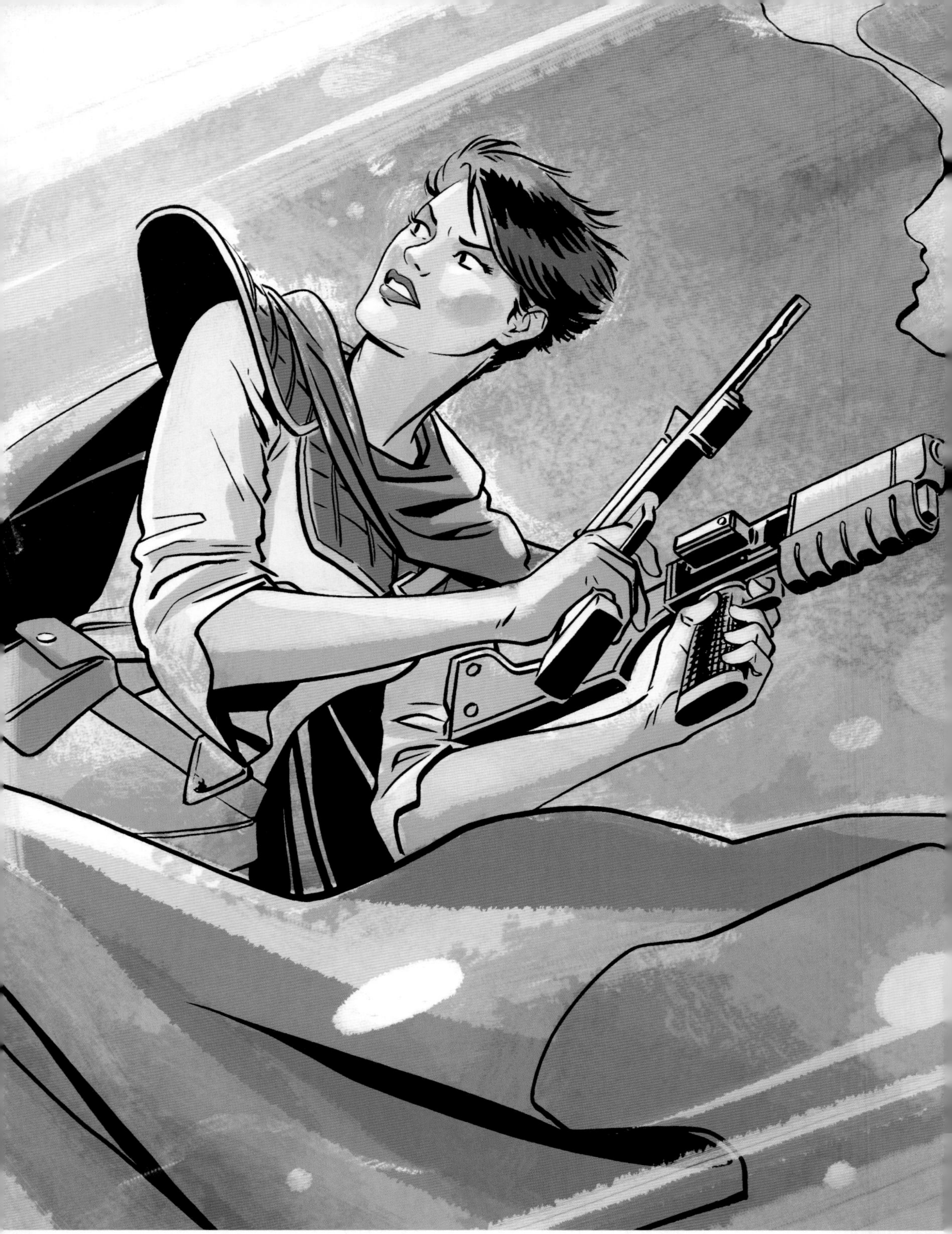

JONATHAN CASE

From his stunning debut with the graphic novel *Dear Creature* to his Eisner-winning *Green River Killer* to his current best-selling stint on *Batman '66*, Jonathan has rapidly generated a string of breathtaking works. And he's just getting started.

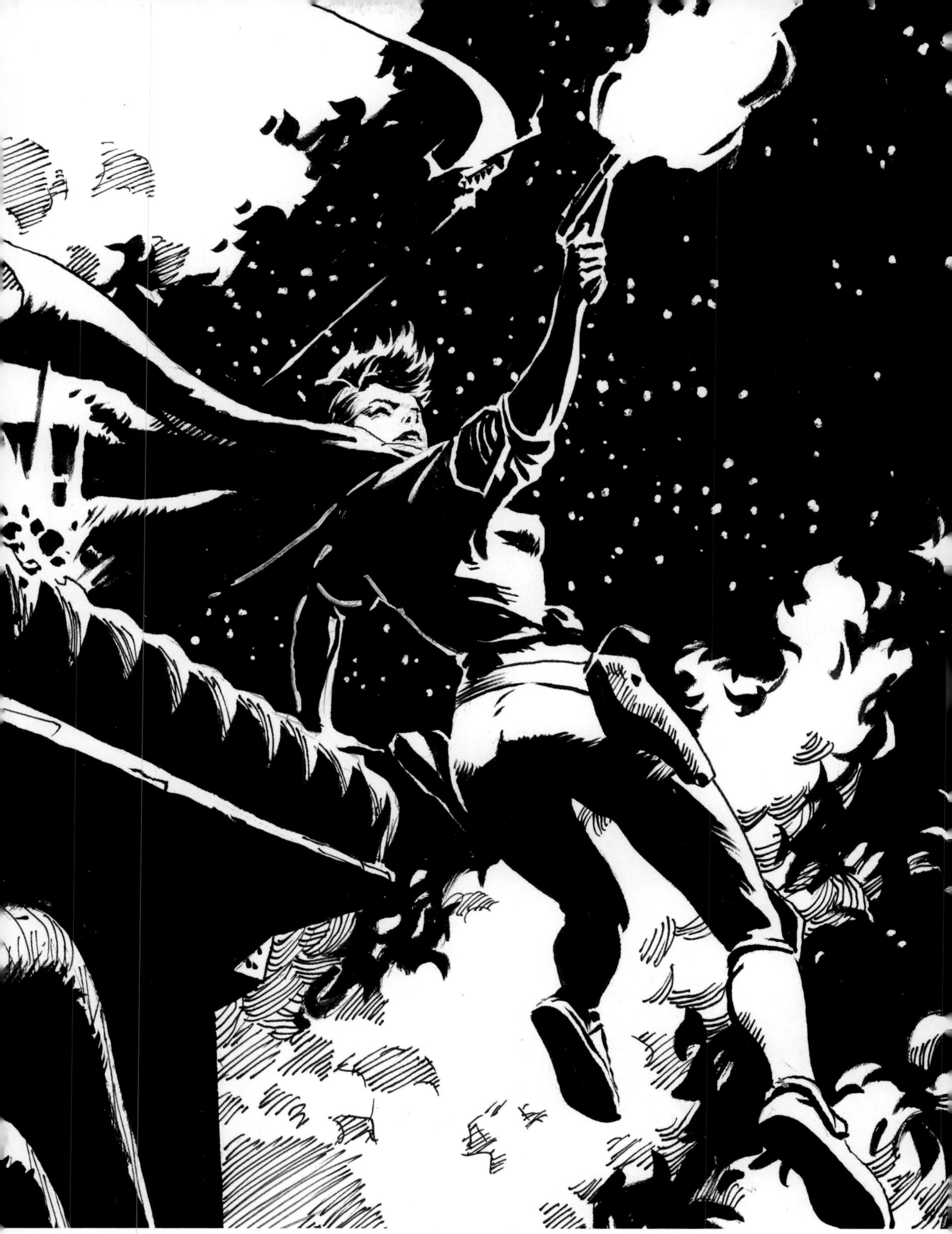

THOMAS YEATES

I met Tom at the Joe Kubert School, where he was in the class above me. I immediately began to learn from him, because he was already mastering the approach of many of the classic adventure illustrators that I was enthralled by. Following his own elegant contributions to *Swamp Thing*, *Zorro*, and *Tarzan*, among many others, Tom is now bringing a vintage, classically Fosteresque feel to *Prince Valiant* in newspapers every Sunday!

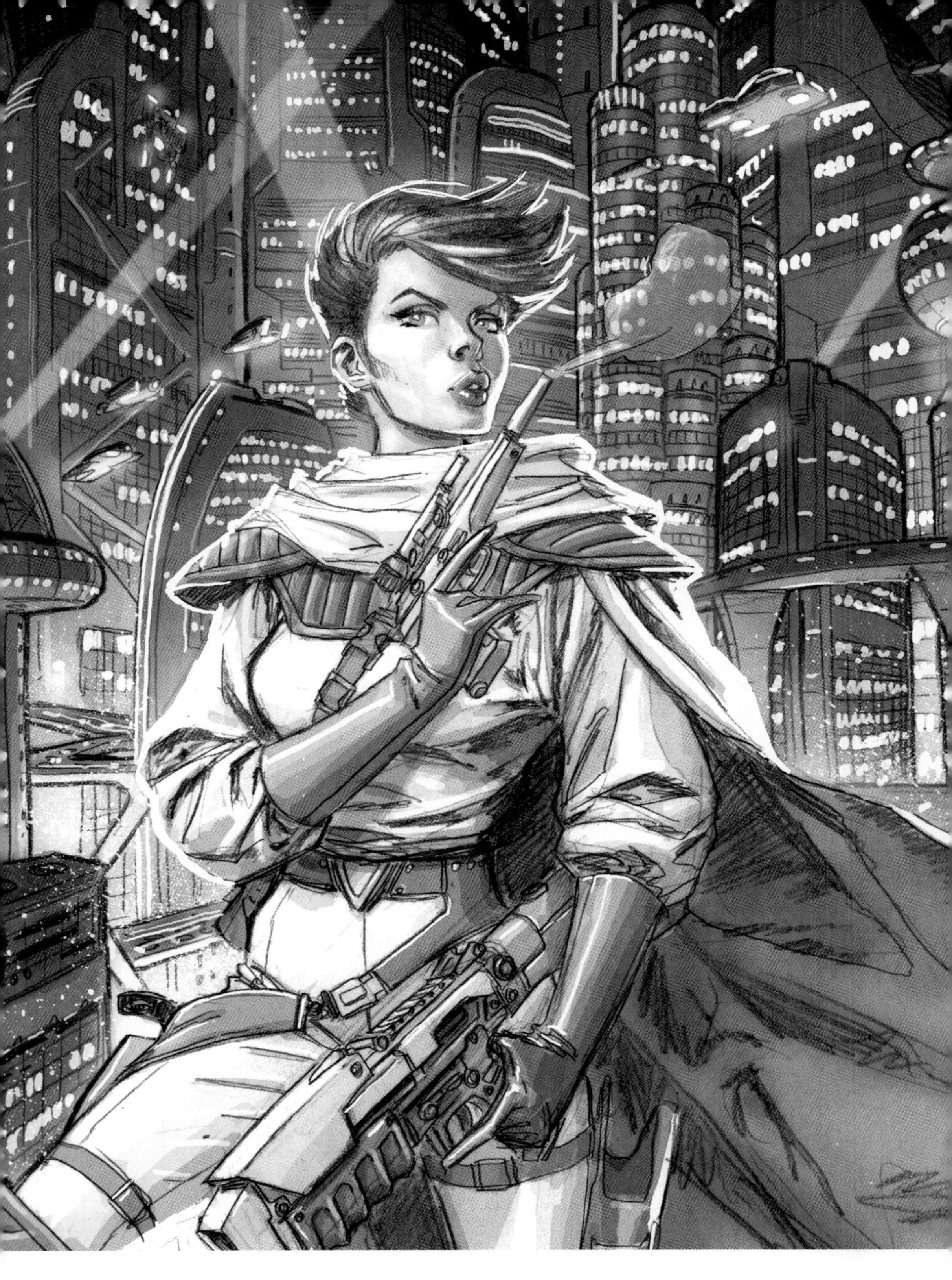

DUSTIN WEAVER

Dustin is just possibly not completely human. Who could produce such intensely realized work over such a span of top-shelf projects? Between *Star Wars: Knights of the Old Republic*, *Avengers*, *S.H.I.E.L.D.*, and now even *TMNT*'s *Bebop & Rocksteady*, there seems to be no stopping him.

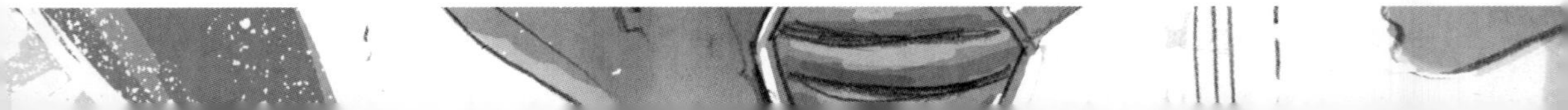

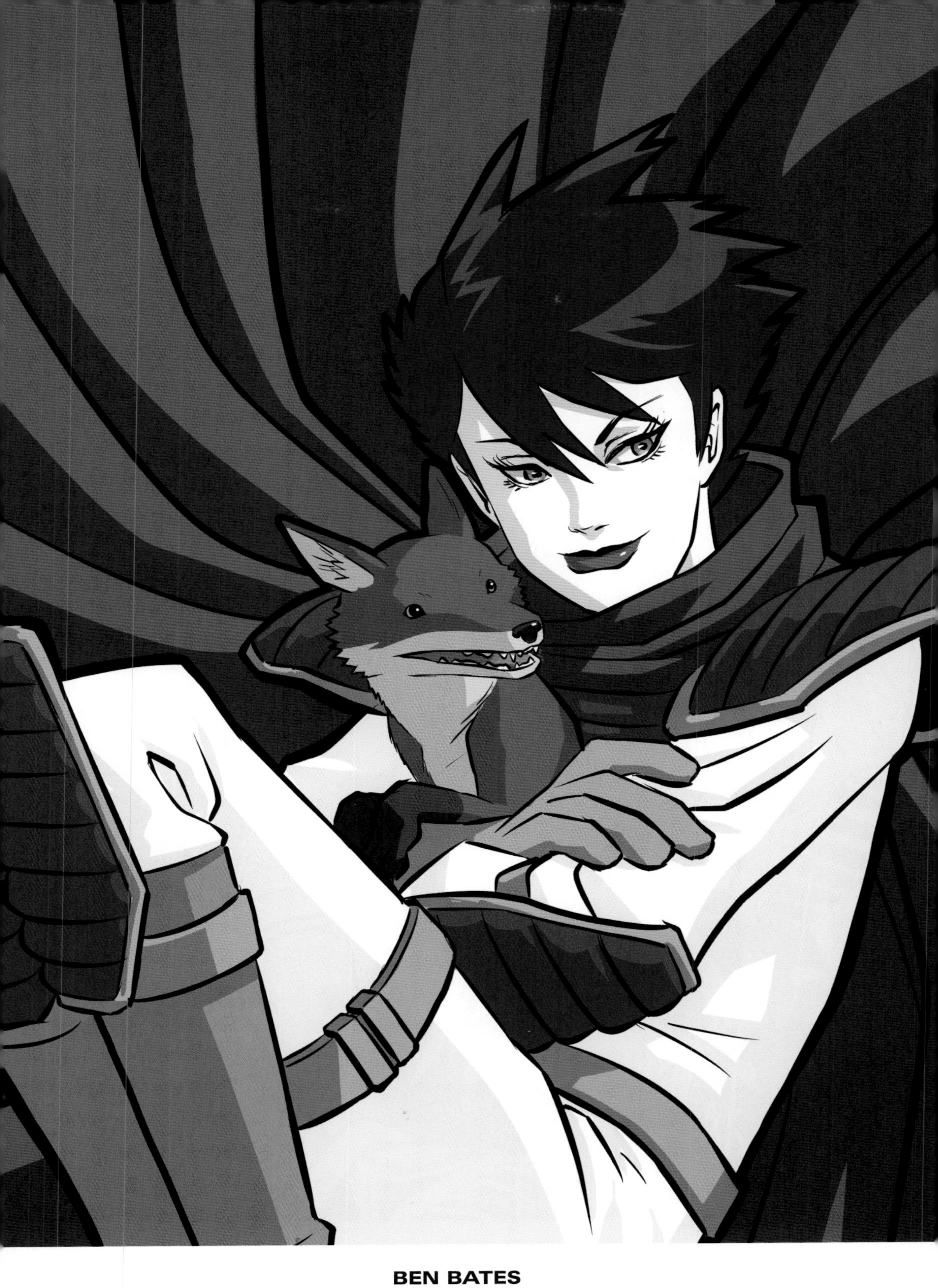

BEN BATES

Ben came into the industry with a single-minded focus that was truly scary. Since then, he has realized his dreams by conquering one coveted project after another: With *Sonic*, *Teenage Mutant Ninja Turtles*, *Star Wars*, and teaming up with Dustin on *Bebop & Rocksteady*, everything Ben turns his hand to leaps into energetic and enthusiastic life!

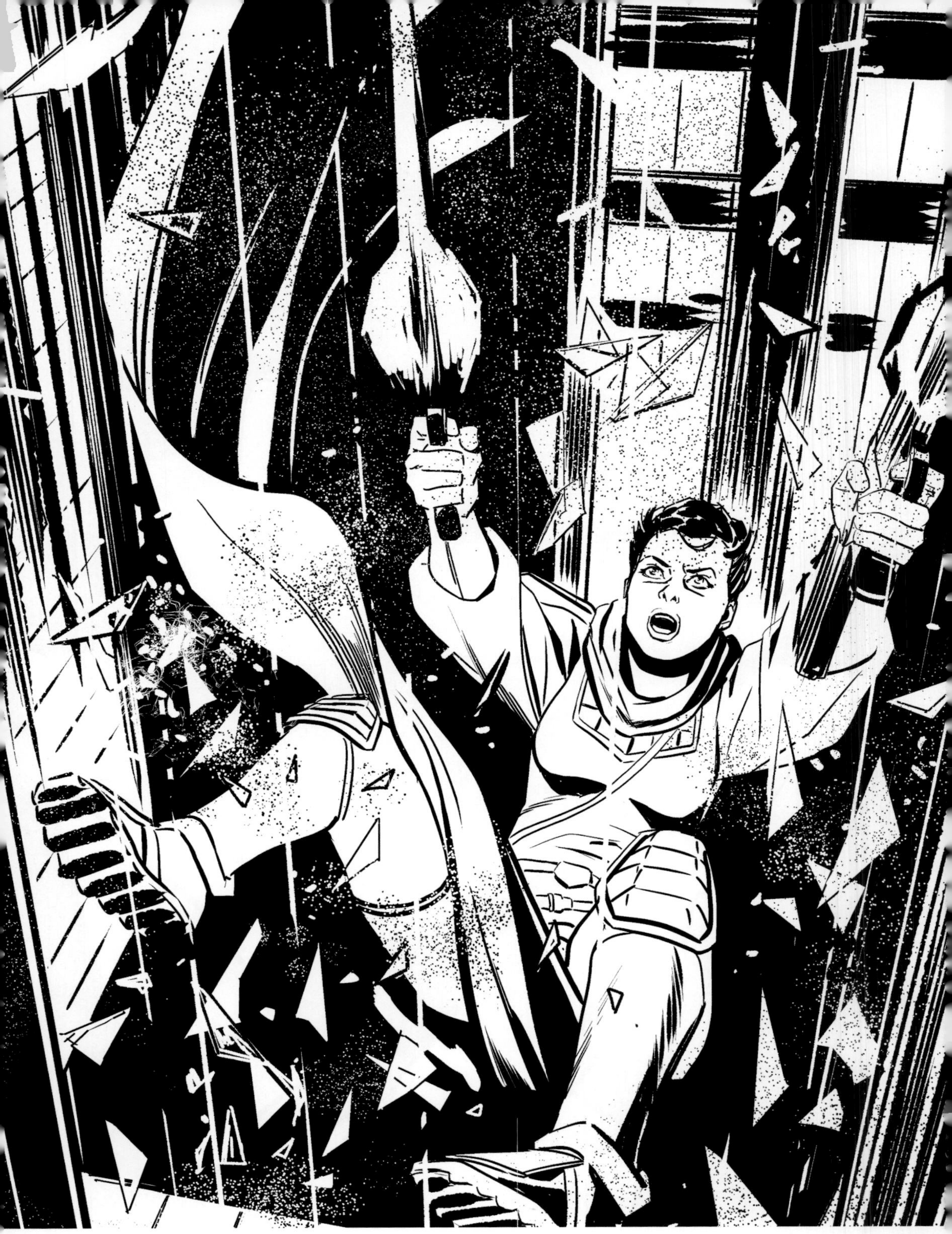

STEVE LIEBER

If you don't know about Steve Lieber, I don't know what to say to you. Steve is a peerless draftsman and storyteller as well as a passionate scholar of virtually every aspect of the art of comics. His sterling career spans from early work on *Hawkman* to the Eisner-winning graphic novel *Whiteout,* and the equally stunning graphic novel *Underground* to the groundbreaking *Alabaster*. Steve is currently subverting the industry from within as the cowriter and artist on *The Superior Foes of Spider-Man*.

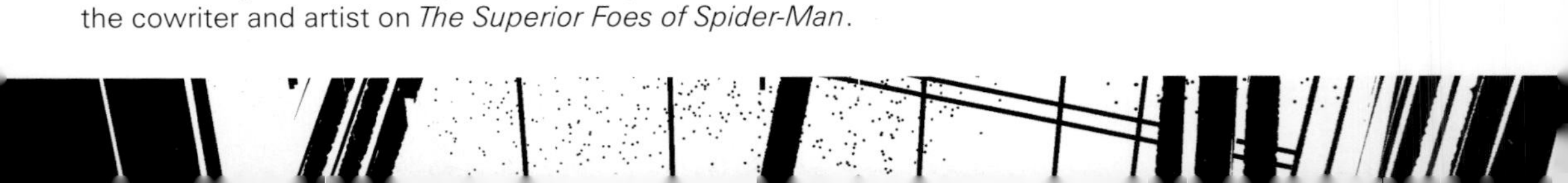

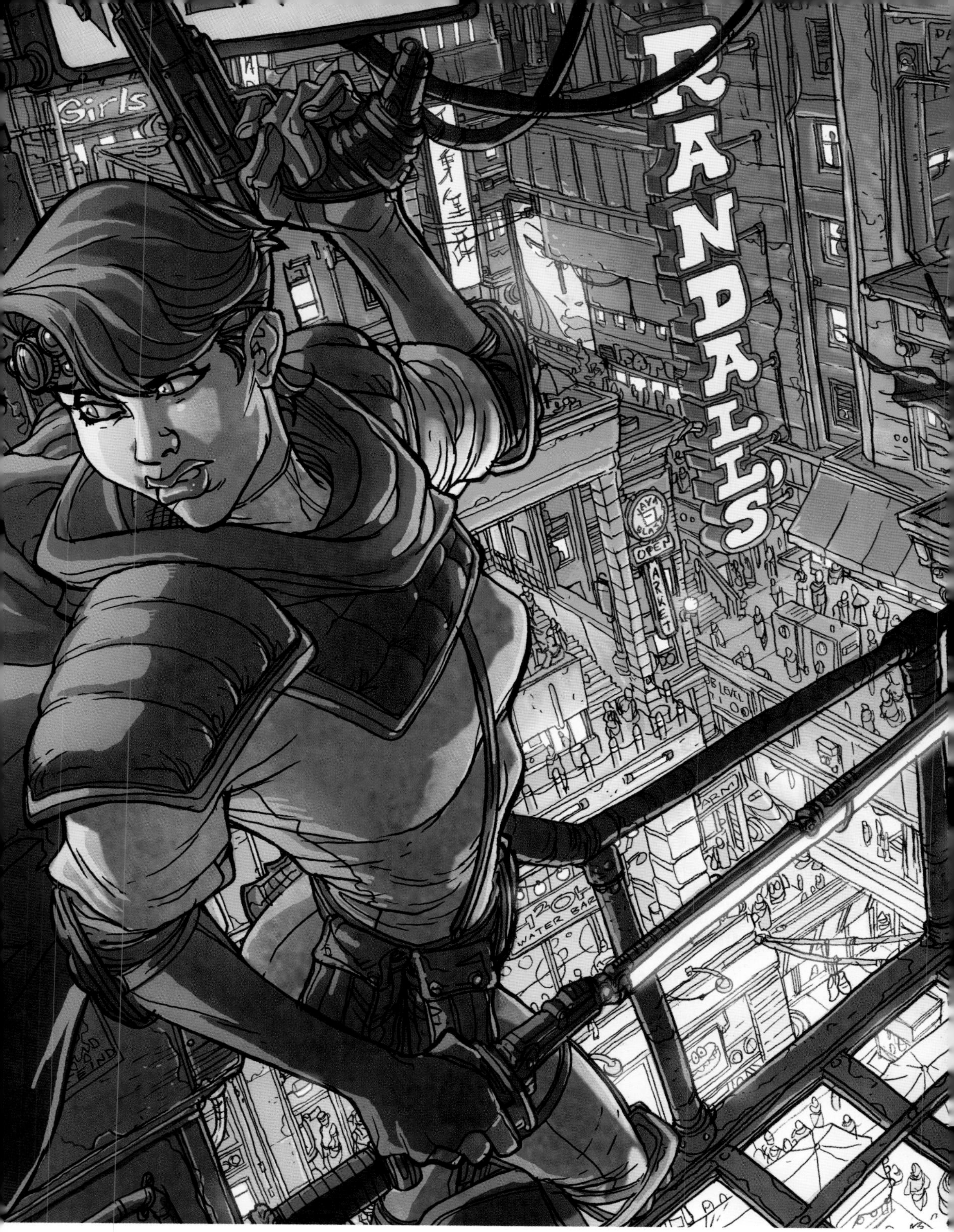
Girls
OPEN
WATER BAR

PETE WOODS

Pete is a world unto himself. Pete's work always seems to arrive effortlessly at the most direct line to a powerful image that tells his story with absolute mastery. You cannot pass by or overlook any of his arresting work from his acclaimed runs on *Deadpool*, *Robin*, *Superman: World of New Krypton*, and recently *Vibe*. Pete always delivers the goods.

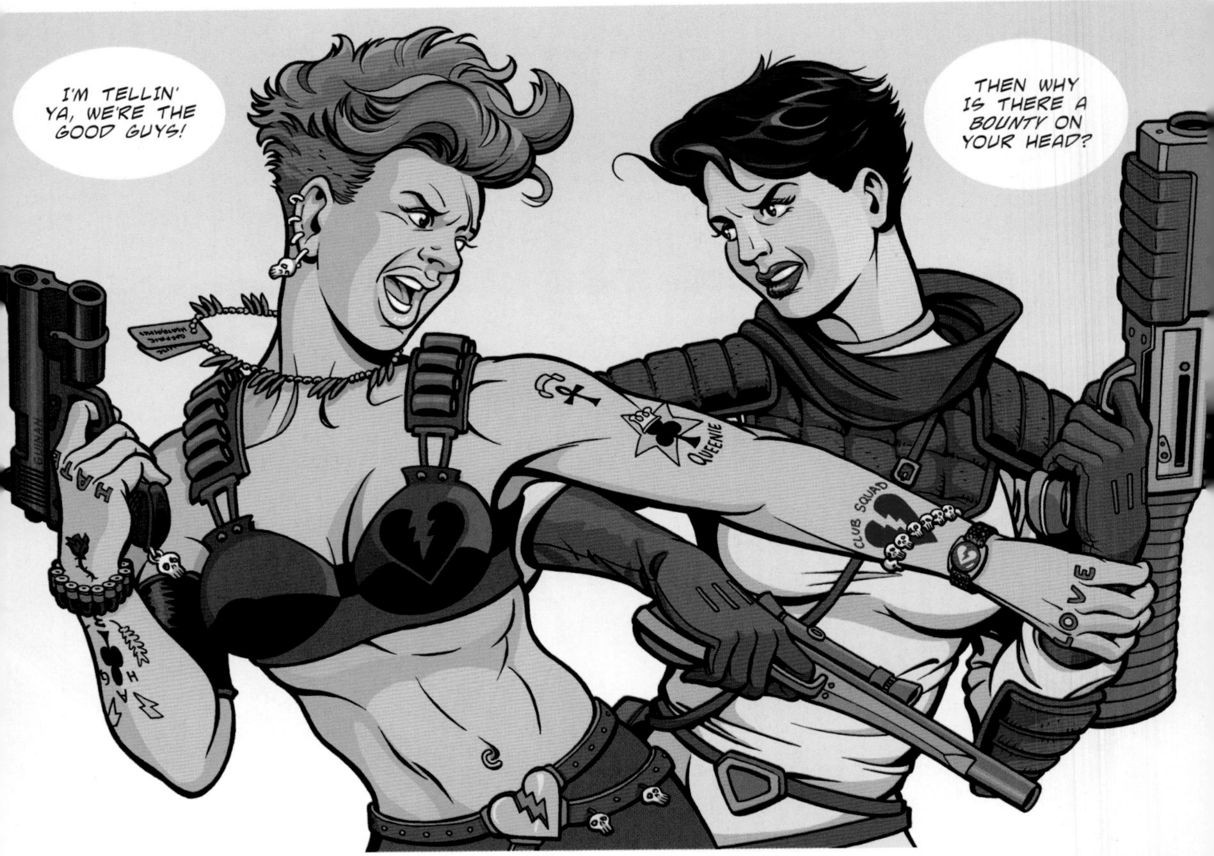
I'M TELLIN' YA, WE'RE THE GOOD GUYS!
THEN WHY IS THERE A BOUNTY ON YOUR HEAD?

PAUL GUINAN

Paul has created several groundbreaking comics in his career: his own sci-fi epic *Heartbreakers*, the DC series *Chronos*, and the steampunk sensation *Boilerplate* are all completely unique works of vision and passion.

KARL KESEL

Karl instantly established himself as one of comics' premier inkers with his early work on titles such as *Suicide Squad*. Then he went on to breathe fresh life into classic characters with his writing on *Hawk and Dove* and *Superboy*, as well as being part of the writing team that revitalized *Superman* in the nineties. Since then he has continued to ply the field as writer, penciler, and/or inker on little-known titles like *Spider-Man*, *Minimum Carnage*, and *Fantastic Four*.

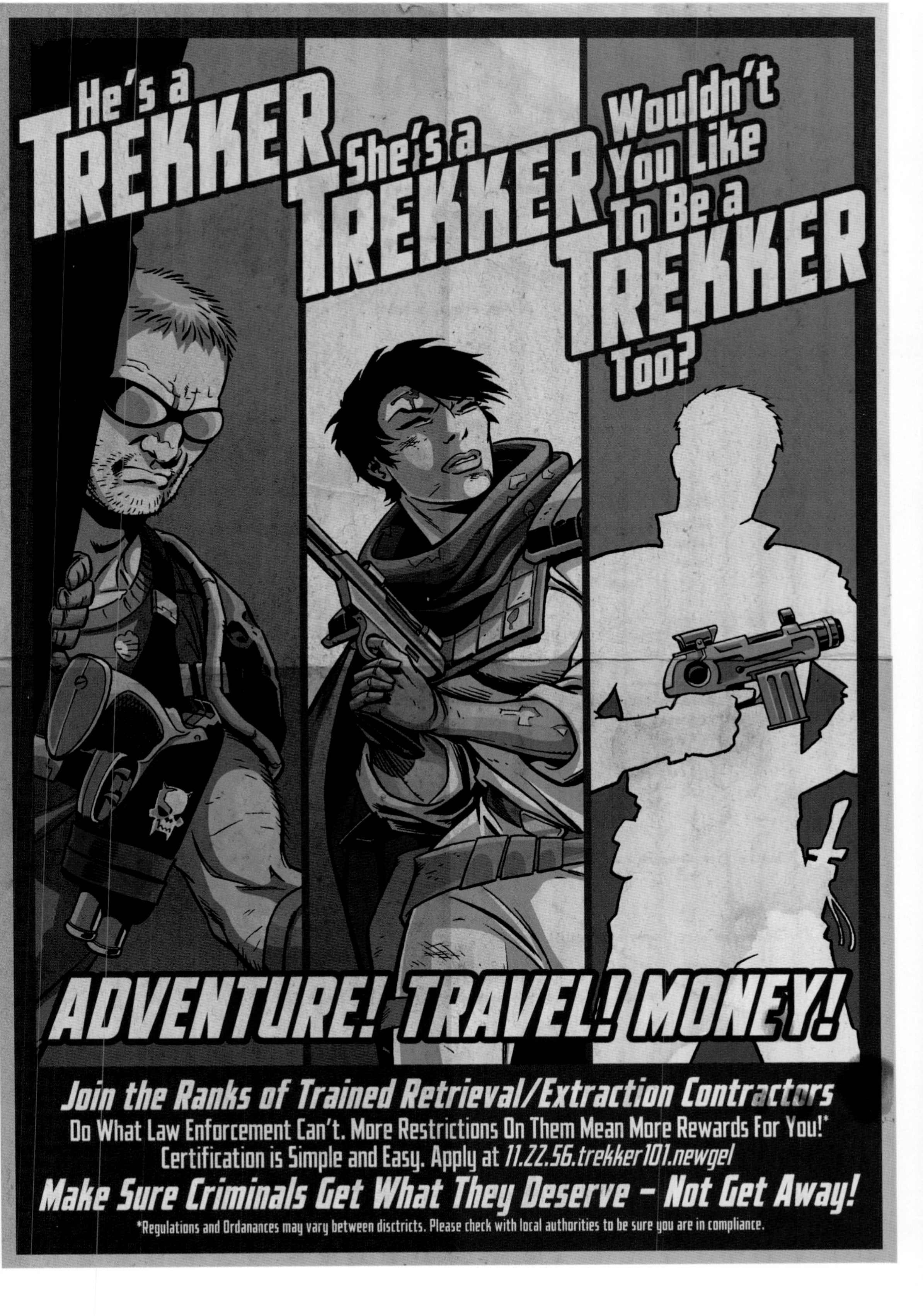
He's a TREKKER
She's a TREKKER
Wouldn't You Like To Be a TREKKER Too?
ADVENTURE! TRAVEL! MONEY!
Join the Ranks of Trained Retrieval/Extraction Contractors
Do What Law Enforcement Can't. More Restrictions On Them Mean More Rewards For You!*
Certification is Simple and Easy. Apply at 11.22.56.trekker101.newgel
Make Sure Criminals Get What They Deserve – Not Get Away!
*Regulations and Ordanances may vary between disctricts. Please check with local authorities to be sure you are in compliance.

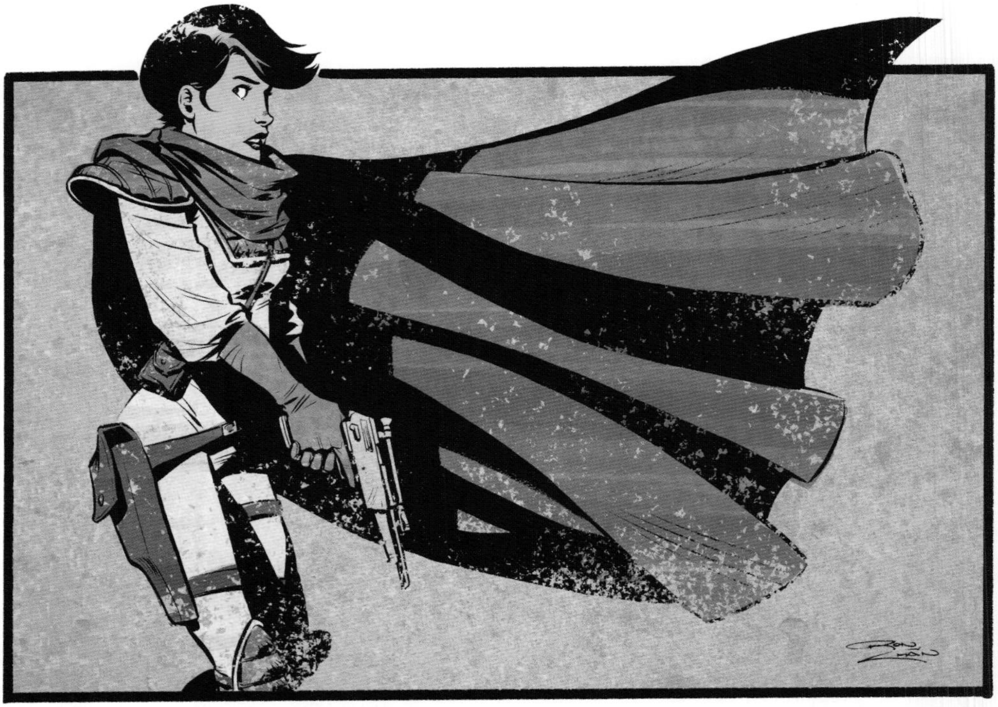

RON CHAN

Ron is a staggeringly brilliant storyboard artist who has also made a comics name for himself with attention-grabbing work on *Guy Ritchie's Gamekeeper*, *Husbands*, and *Plants vs. Zombies: Lawnmageddon*.

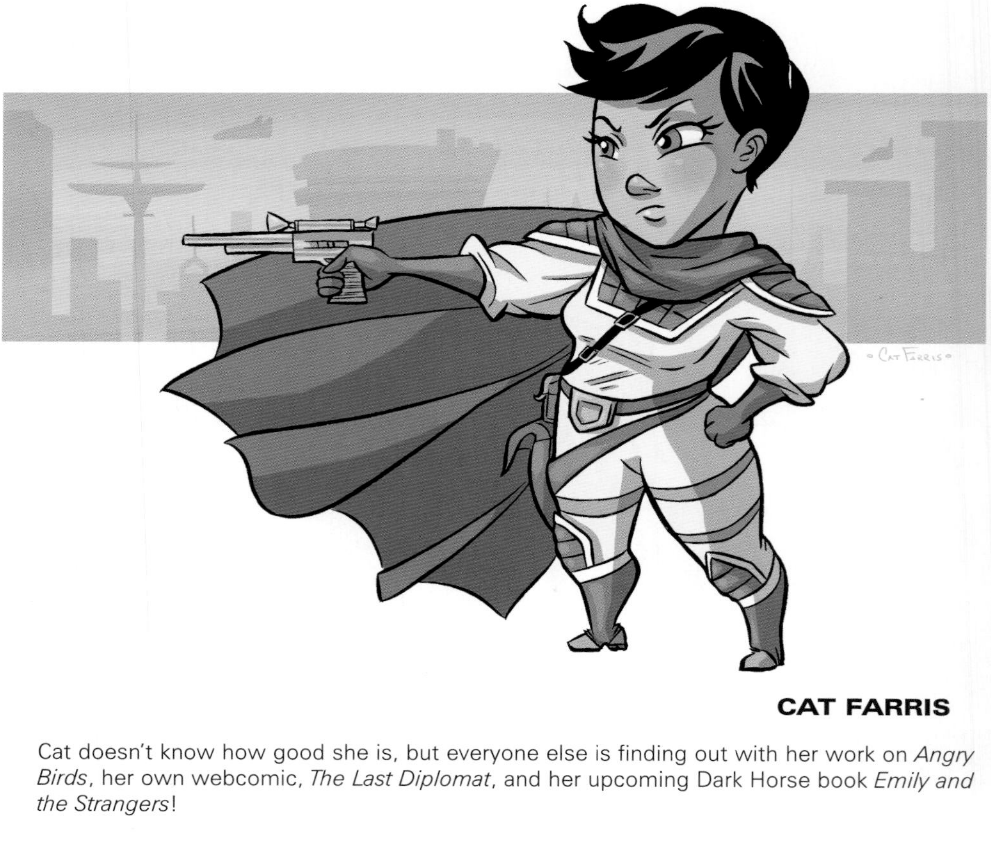
CAT FARRIS

CAT FARRIS

Cat doesn't know how good she is, but everyone else is finding out with her work on *Angry Birds*, her own webcomic, *The Last Diplomat*, and her upcoming Dark Horse book *Emily and the Strangers*!

AARON McCONNELL

Aaron's brilliantly eclectic work can be found in the critically acclaimed graphic novels *The Gettysburg Address* and *The United States Constitution*, the high-fantasy RPG *13th Age*, and Dark Horse's *Robert E. Howard's Savage Sword*.

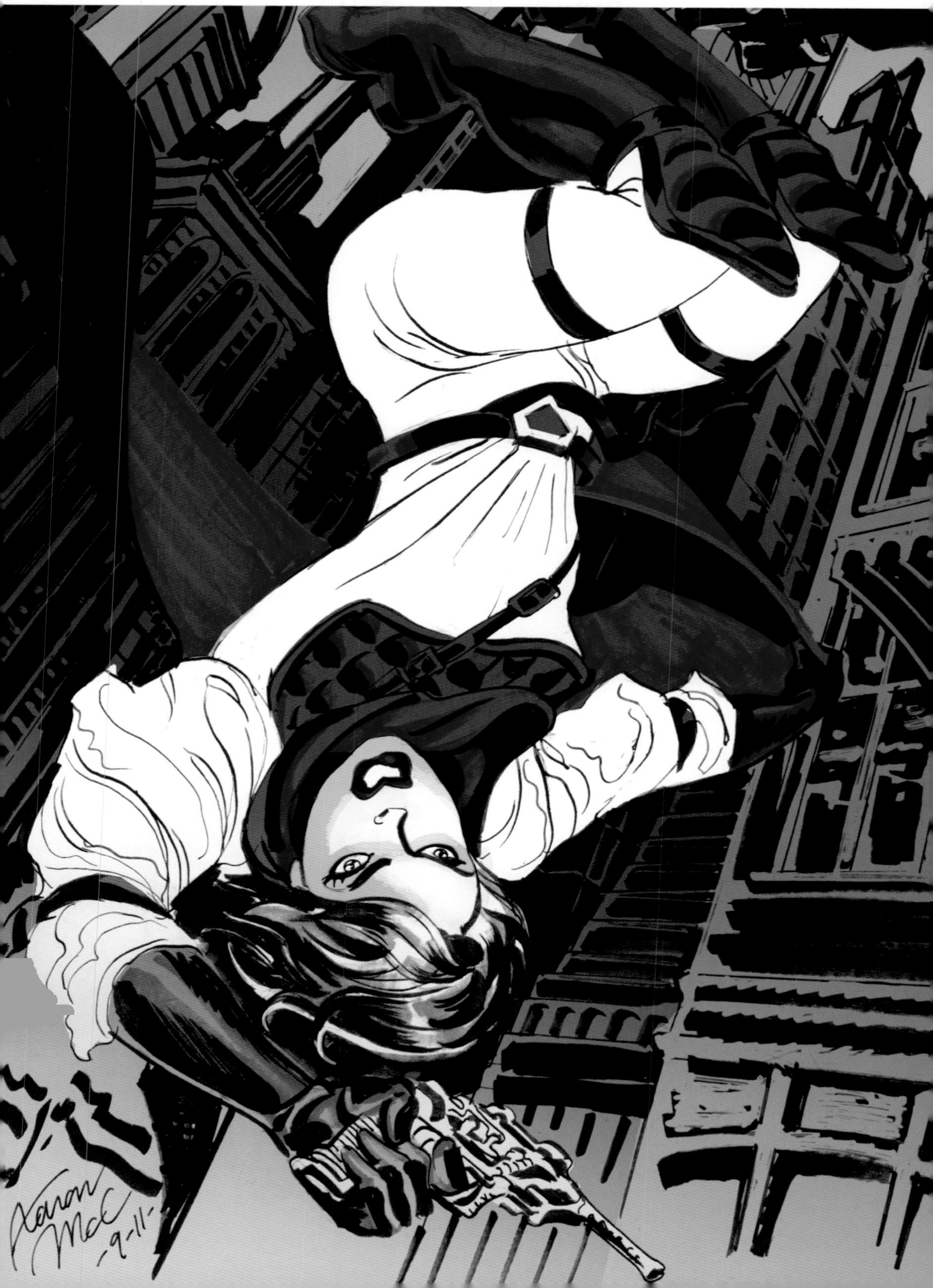

RICH ELLIS

Rich made a name for himself quickly as the artist/cocreator of the epic fantasy-adventure comic *Memorial* for IDW. Currently he is cooking up his own hardcore sci-fi series *Triton* through Monkeybrain that will turn your head upside down. Stay tuned!

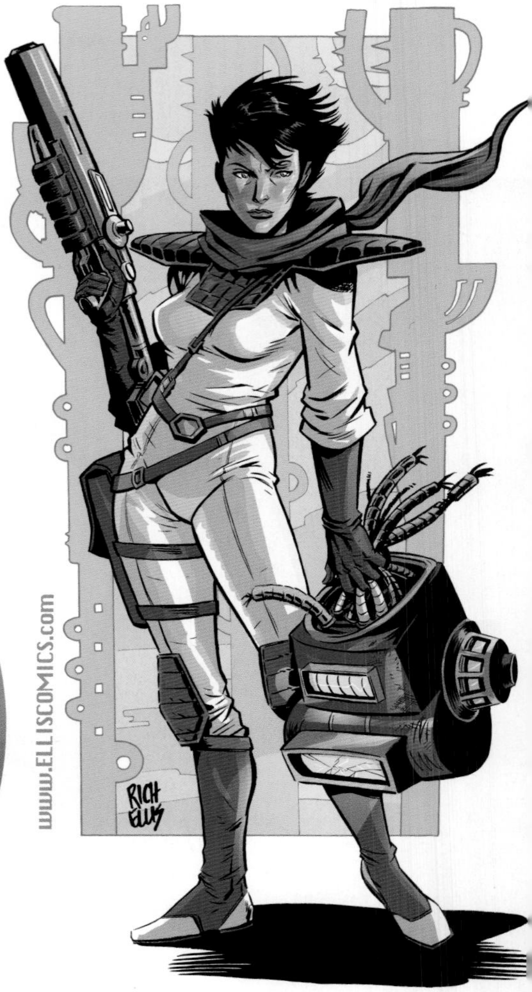
www.ELLISCOMICS.com
RICH ELLIS

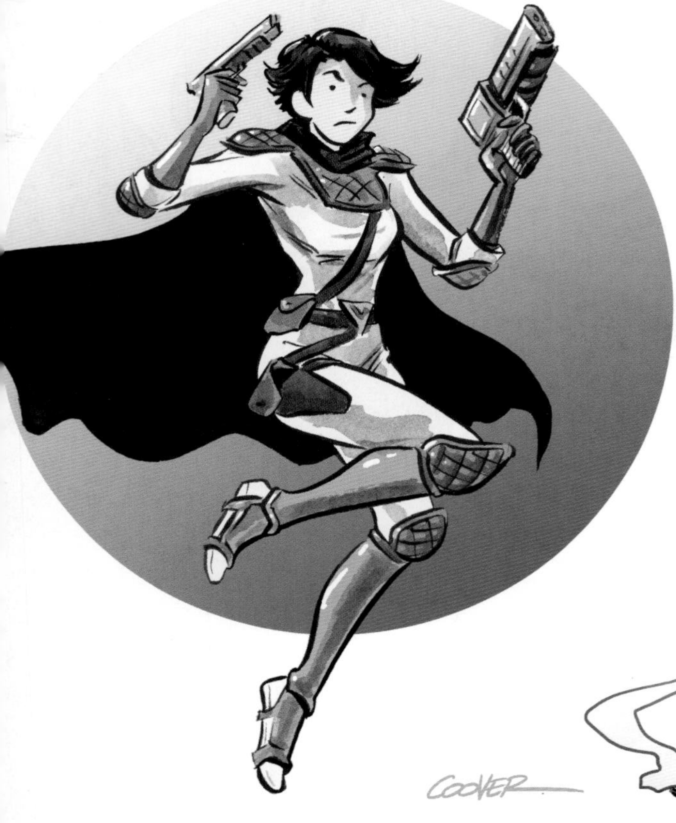
COOVER

COLLEEN COOVER

Colleen's art will charm the pants off of you, regardless of what she is working on. Whether you're reading a groundbreaking adult title like *Small Favors* or *Gingerbread Girl*, all-ages work like *Banana Sunday*, or her Eisner-winning strip, *Bandette*, just be prepared to be enchanted.

GRACE ALLISON

Grace is fashioning her own digital series, *Wander*, through Comixology when she isn't busy lending her gorgeous coloring work to projects from *Johnny Zombie* to *Memorial*.

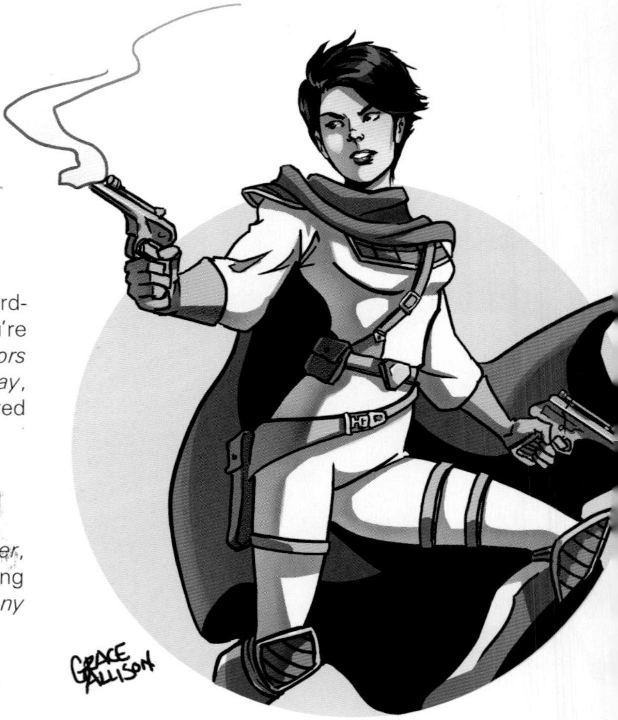
GRACE ALLISON

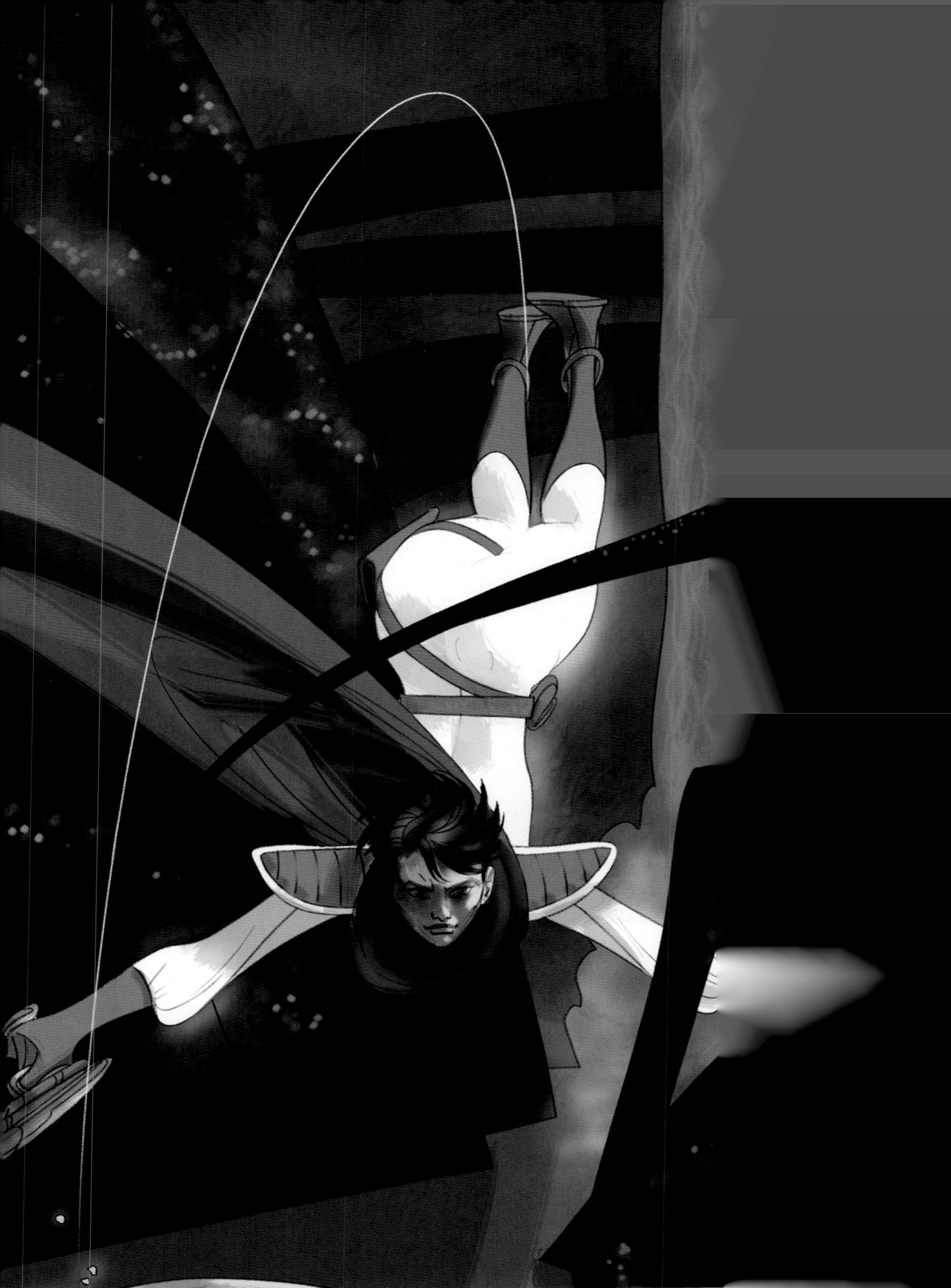

JESSE HAMM

Jesse's immaculate draftsmanship and strong eye for graphic design have won him so
that his comics work is sadly hard to come by. He did find the time to produce the grap
through DC's Minx line and a story for the special Hurricane Sandy–inspired issue of *Hav*

RON RANDALL'S
TREKKER™
OMNIBUS
"A labor of love by a master craftsman—and it shows on every page."
—Kurt Busiek (Astro City, Marvels)
FOREWORD BY
GAIL SIMONE

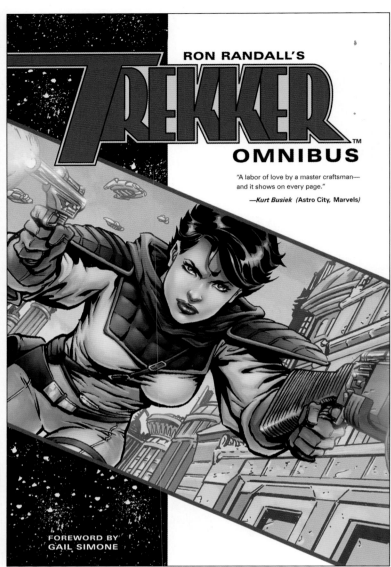